an encyclopedia for inquiring young minds

KINGFISHER

First published 2007 by Kingfisher
an imprint of Macmillan Children's Books
a division of Macmillan Publishers Limited
20 New Wharf Road, London N1 9RR
Basingstoke and Oxford
Associated companies around the world
www.panmacmillan.com

First published by Kingfisher Publications Plc 2007
This edition published 2008 for Index Books Ltd
10 9 8 7 6 5 4 3 2
2TR/0708/MPA/SCHOY(SCHOY)/128MA/C

ISBN 978 0 7534 1412 5

A CIP catalogue record for this book is available from the British Library.

AUTHORS:
Deborah Chancellor (Our Earth and My body chapters)
Deborah Murrell (Dinosaurs, Machines, People and places, and Space chapters)
Philip Steele (Animals and People through time chapters)
Barbara Taylor (Plants and Science chapters)

Printed in China

NOTE TO READERS
The website addresses listed in this book are correct at the time of going to print. However, due to the ever-changing nature of the internet, website addresses and content can change. Websites can contain links that are unsuitable for children. The publisher cannot be held responsible for changes in website addresses or content, or for information obtained through third-party websites. We strongly advise that internet searches should be supervised by an adult.

Contents

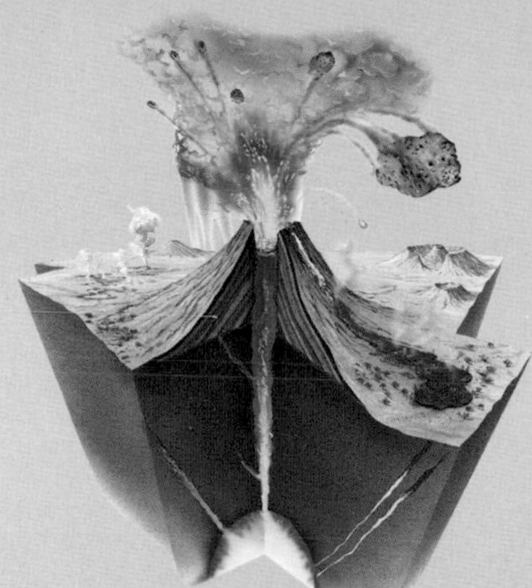

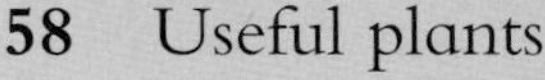

Dinosaurs

People and places

People through time

My body

Science

Space

Machines

Using this book

As well as lots of information, this book has many special ideas in it to help you enjoy it more. There are facts to astound, stories for the imagination, vocabulary notepads to expand your word sense, difficult questions with fascinating answers, and great activities and games. Enjoy exploring!

► Fact box

Look out for the exclamation mark on these boxes. Each fact box contains amazing facts about the subject matter that is being described. This fact box is from the chapter called 'People and places'. You will find it on page 133.

The Kwakiutl people
This tribe, like many native Indian tribes, lived in America long before Europeans arrived. Many carved tall totem poles like this one to tell the story of their tribe. They celebrated by dancing and wearing masks.

The Tinman
In the story 'The Wizard of Oz', the Tinman is sad because he is made of metal and has no heart. He goes in search of one, along with a scarecrow who needs a brain, a lion that needs courage and a girl called Dorothy who needs to find her way home.

◄ Story box

There are some wonderful stories, fairy-tales and myths in this book. Look out for the open book symbol. This story box is from the chapter called 'My body'. You will find it on page 208.

VOCABULARY

microphone
An electronic instrument that is used to pick up sound waves to be broadcast.

factory
A building, or group of buildings, in which objects are produced in large numbers.

◄ Vocabulary notepad

There are sometimes difficult words used in the text that need further explaining, so there is a notepad specially for this task. This vocabulary notepad is from the chapter called 'Machines'. You will find it on page 306.

► Question circle

Everyone has questions they are dying to ask. You will find circles with questions and their answers in every chapter. This question circle is from the chapter called 'Dinosaurs'. You will find it on page 104.

WHERE ARE FOSSILS FOUND?
Fossils are usually found where sun, rain or wind wear away the surrounding rock and expose them to view.

► Can you find?

These features will test what you can spot and name in the pictures. This planet-shaped Can you find? is from 'Space'. You will find it on page 273.

CAN YOU FIND?
1. a comet
2. an asteroid
3. a crater
4. two astronomers
5. the Moon

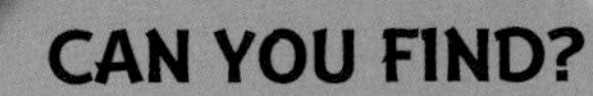

► Creative corner

The splodge of paint says it all! This is where you can let your creative self run wild. The book is packed with great things to make and do. This creative corner is from 'Animals'. You will find it on page 81.

CREATIVE CORNER

Winter food for wild birds

Take half a coconut shell or an empty plastic pot. Then ask an adult to melt some lard in a pan. Mix in seeds, unsalted nuts, porridge oats, cereal, bacon rind or cheese. Pour this mixture into the upturned shell or pot and leave to set. Turn the pot upside down and hang up outside, well away from cats.

▲ You will need

Plain and coloured paper, card, glue, string, elastic bands, scissors, pencils, an eraser, modelling clay, crayons, paints, paint brushes, marker pens, cardboard tubes, drinking straws, plastic pots and bottles, wool, sticky tape, compost, balloons, wooden rods, paper clips and fasteners.

▼ At the bottom of every right-hand page in the book you will find one or two useful websites. These have been carefully chosen to add to the information on the page.

Our Earth

As far as we know, Earth is the only planet in the universe with exactly the right conditions for life – and there is an amazing variety of life on the planet. The Earth has spectacular landscapes, ranging from icy mountains to lush rainforests to rolling sand dunes.

Our planet

The Earth is a planet of incredible extremes – from very hot and dry to cold, wet or windy. The Earth is home to millions of different species, living in a huge variety of habitats. A large habitat is called a biome. The Earth's main biomes are the desert, grassland, forest, rainforest, tundra and ocean.

HOW OLD IS THE EARTH?
Scientists believe that the Earth is about 4.5 billion years old, and that it was formed from material left behind after the birth of the Sun.

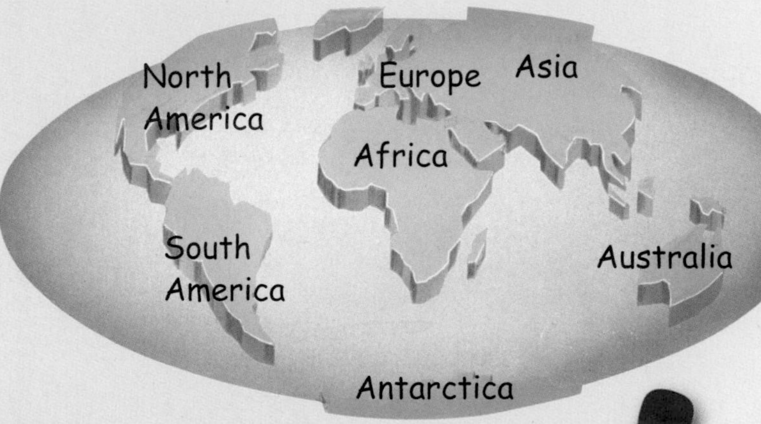

◀ There are seven large areas of land, called continents – North America, South America, Europe, Africa, Asia, Australia and Antarctica.

Day and night
The Sun lights up one half of the Earth, while the other half is dark. When it is daytime in one half of the world, it is night in the other half. The Earth is always spinning, and it takes 24 hours to make a complete spin. There is a period of night followed by a period of day.

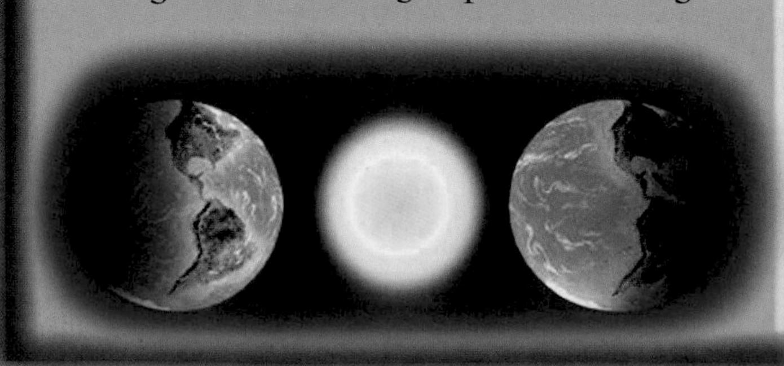

▲ The Earth is a planet in space and is shaped like a ball. The Earth looks blue when seen from space because over two-thirds of it is covered with sea water.

▶ The Equator is an imaginary line that runs around the middle of Earth. Places near the Equator have a tropical climate (below). Places further away are cooler, with a temperate climate (right).

VOCABULARY

temperate
A varied climate with four separate seasons each year.

tundra
Frozen and treeless land in countries near the North Pole.

◀ Africa has large areas of grassland, also known as savannah, that are home to some amazing wildlife. Giraffes are well adapted to the savannah and are able to feed on leafy treetops.

▶ The pattern of weather in a place over a long period of time is called the climate. The Earth has a variety of climates, from the frozen Arctic and Antarctic, to the blistering deserts of Africa and Asia.

▲ Like this jaguar in South America, over half of the world's plant and animal species live in rainforests.

Life on Earth

The Earth is bursting with life. Over millions of years, animals and plants have slowly adapted to survive in the parts of the world where they live. This process of change is called evolution. The surrounding area of a living thing is called a habitat. There are many habitats on Earth.

Fear of fire

In an African myth, Kaang, the Lord of all life, created the world. He let the people and animals live together on the surface of the Earth. But then the people lit fires, which frightened the animals away. After that, people and animals lived apart.

◀ Rainforests (coloured red on this map) are found in tropical areas of the world, near the Equator.

Just right for life

Scientists think life began in the oceans about 3.5 billion years ago. Some sea creatures evolved, moving to live on dry land. But many species stayed in the oceans. Some kinds of marine animals, such as jellyfish, have swum in the oceans for millions of years.

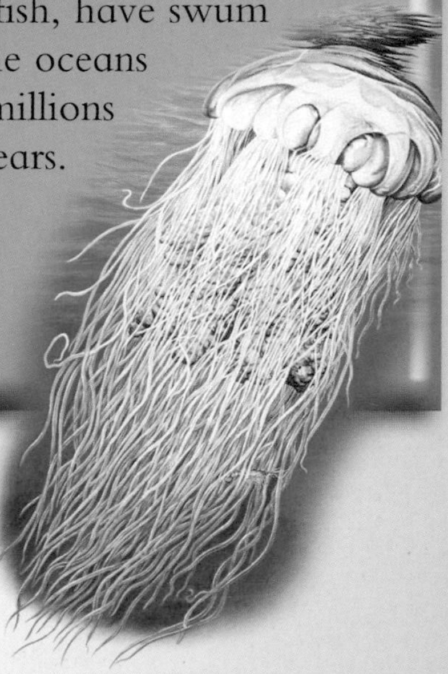

▲ Hot deserts are extremely dry habitats where not many creatures live. Camels are desert animals that are well adapted to the harsh climate. They can survive on very little food or water for as long as seven days.

▼ Ponds are a small habitat that are home to a particular group of plants and animals, such as toads. These living things depend on each other in a community called an ecosystem.

DO PEOPLE LIVE IN ANTARCTICA?

The only people who live in Antarctica are scientists, and they do not live there all the time. It is the world's coldest and windiest place.

Beneath the surface

The ground under your feet is part of the Earth's crust – a layer of solid rock that is 6 to 70 kilometres thick. Under the Earth's crust is a layer of hot rock called the mantle. Beneath that is the outer core, a layer of liquid rock. At the centre is an iron and nickel ball, called the inner core.

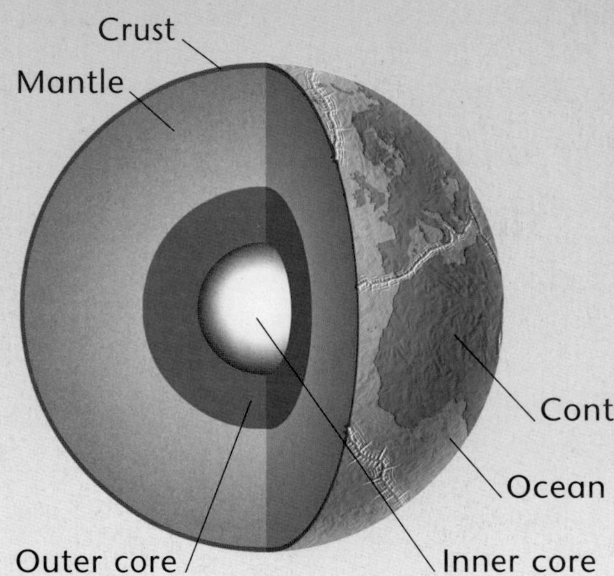

▲ The Earth's crust is thin under oceans and thick under mountains. The inner core is very hot, with temperatures of up to 5,000°C.

► Fossil fuels, such as coal, oil and gas, are buried in the Earth's crust. They are drilled out for us to use by oil rigs on land and at sea.

▼ Soil lies at the surface of the Earth's crust. It is important for plant growth, and provides shelter for animals and insects.

Treasure Island
In this story, a boy called Jim Hawkins goes on a voyage to find some buried treasure. A one-legged pirate called Long John Silver joins the search. After many adventures, they find the lost treasure hidden in a cave.

Emerald in rock

Rough emerald

Cut emerald

▲ Minerals are hard, natural substances found in rock in the Earth's crust. Rare minerals, such as emeralds, are called gems. They are cut and polished, then made into jewellery.

CAN YOU FIND?
1. bumblebee
2. ladybird
3. ant
4. butterfly
5. wren
6. earthworm

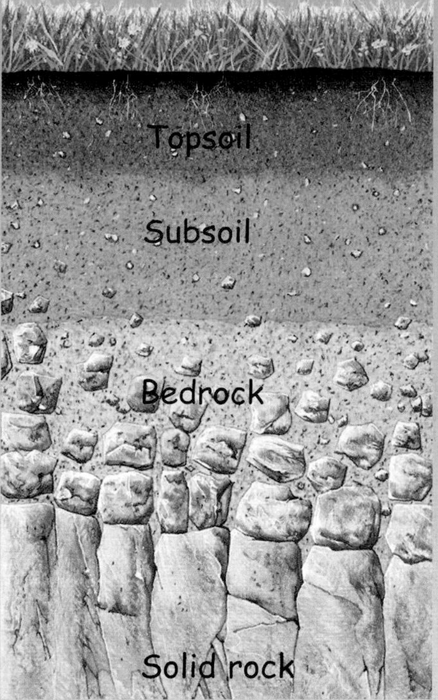

▲ The top layer of soil is the topsoil. Under this layer is subsoil, then small rocks, called bedrock, that lie on solid rock.

CREATIVE CORNER

Colourful soil

Collect some sandy, peaty and chalky soil. Mix a little of each with water, and smear each sample on white card. Compare the colours. You will see that different types of soil actually have different colours.

INTERNET LINKS: www.geography4kids.com • www.soil-net.com/cms_test/

Volcanoes

The Earth is a restless planet. Beneath the crust lies a layer of liquid rock called magma. This red-hot rock escapes through weak spots in the crust, bursting out of volcanoes both on the land and under the sea. There are about 700 active volcanoes.

WHERE IS EARTH'S LARGEST VOLCANO?
The massive Mauna Loa volcano is in Hawaii. Most of the volcano is actually under the Pacific ocean.

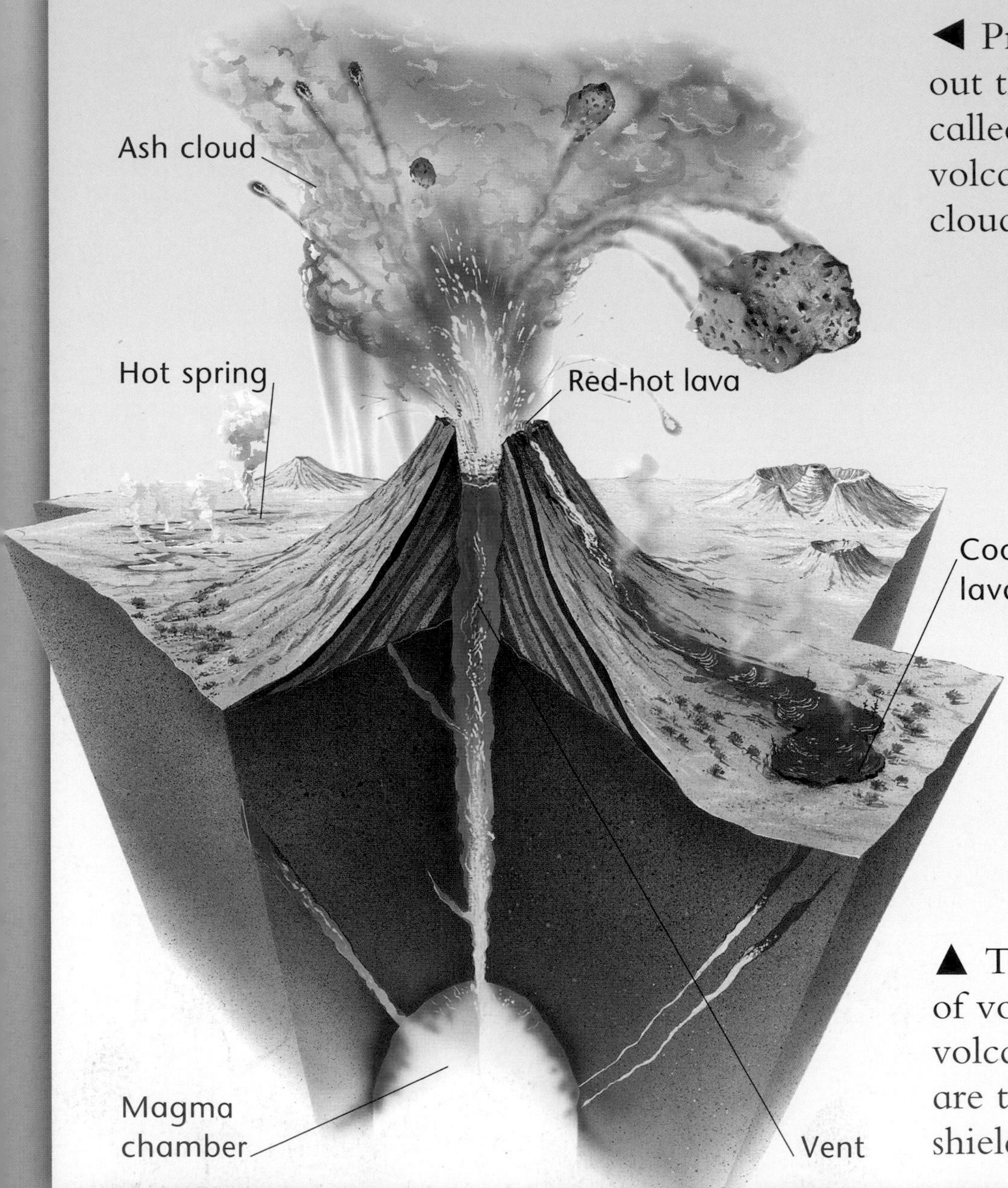

Ash cloud
Hot spring
Red-hot lava
Cooling lava
Magma chamber
Vent

◄ Pressure builds and forces out the magma through holes, called vents. The erupting volcano sends up lava and clouds of thick, dusty ash.

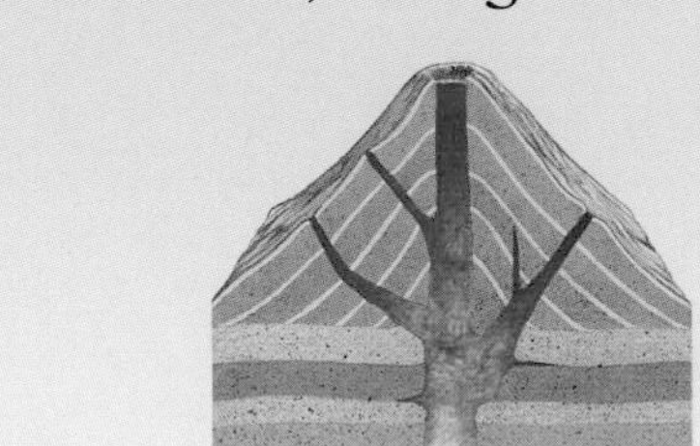

Composite volcano

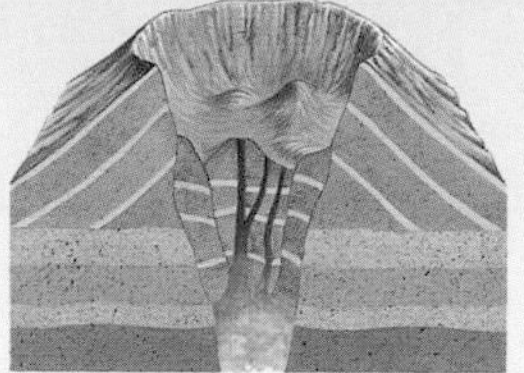

Caldera volcano

Shield volcano

▲ The most common type of volcano is the composite volcano. Caldera volcanoes are the most explosive, and shield volcanoes can be huge.

Earthquakes

The Earth's crust is a loose jigsaw of plates, which slide over the hot rock in the Earth's mantle. Earthquakes happen when the edges of these plates collide, pushing against or away from each other.

▲ Earthquakes may cause buildings to collapse. In countries where earthquakes happen, people practise what to do in an emergency.

▲ A crack in the Earth's crust is called a fault line. When two plates collide along a fault line, shock waves are sent out through the surrounding rock, making the ground shake.

▲ Undersea earthquakes can create giant waves called tsunamis. Tsunamis travel at speed for many kilometres. When they finally crash onto the shore, they can cause terrible damage.

Seismograph

An earthquake's vibrations are recorded by an instrument called a seismograph. A very sensitive machine measures the overall strength of an earthquake. The power of an earthquake is described with the Richter scale, numbered from 0 to 10.

The first Chinese seismograph

Mountains and caves

Mountains are made when two plates under the Earth's crust push together, forcing up huge folds of rock. Mountains get taller over millions of years, but ice, wind and weather wear them down, too, in a process called erosion. Rocky caves are found in mountains and underground.

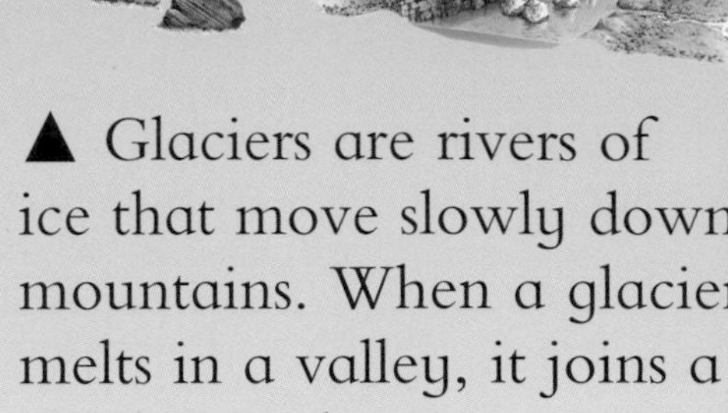

▲ Glaciers are rivers of ice that move slowly down mountains. When a glacier melts in a valley, it joins a river or makes a new one.

◀ If a mountain has jagged peaks to climb, it is still quite 'young'. The weather has not had time to smooth down the sharp rock.

Pied Piper
In a German folk tale, rats follow the Pied Piper's music out of the town of Hamelin. They are followed by the town's children, and all are led to live inside a mountain.

▼ The tallest mountain in each continent is shown below. The world's tallest mountain is Everest.

Everest (Asia) 8,850m
Aconcagau (South America) 6,942m
McKinley (North America) 6,194m
Kilimanjaro (Africa) 5,895m
Elbrus (Europe) 5,642m
Vinson Massif (Antarctica) 4,892m
Kosciusko (Australia) 2,228m

Stalagtites and stalagmites

Stalagtites grow down from the roof of a cave, and stalagmites grow up from the floor. The world's biggest stalagmite is 70 metres tall! There are different kinds of stalagmites and stalagtites.

► Dripping water in a cave contains a mineral called calcite. This hardens to form stalagmites and stalagtites. The process is very slow – 500 years to grow just 2.5 centimetres.

HOW BIG IS THE LARGEST CAVE?

The world's biggest cave is about 700 metres long, 300 metres wide and 70 metres high. It is in Sarawak, in Malaysia.

Rivers and lakes

A river's journey starts high above sea level, moving quickly downhill. As it nears the coast, it splits into streams then flows into the sea. Rivers and lakes give us drinking water, but they contain only one per cent of the world's fresh water. The rest is frozen at the poles or trapped underground.

Reservoir

Dam

▲ Dams are built across rivers to create lakes or reservoirs. Water from dams is used for drinking, and also to generate a power called hydroelectricity.

▼ The Sun's heat turns water in oceans, rivers and lakes into water vapour, which rises into the sky to form clouds. Water then falls back to the ground as rain. Rainwater collects in rivers, which flow into the sea. Then the water cycle starts all over again.

WHY WERE CITIES BUILT NEXT TO RIVERS?
In the past, boats were very important. Cities were built near rivers, so that they were easy to reach by boat and could trade easily.

Clouds form

Rain falls

Water evaporates

Rivers flow into the sea

▲ Lakes are big pools of fresh water surrounded by land. Lakes are an important habitat around the world for many living things, including flamingoes.

▲ When a river flows over a cliff or rocky ledge, there is a waterfall. Some waterfalls, such as Niagara Falls in North America, are very spectacular.

Queen Isis and the Nile

The ancient Egyptians believed the world was made by a god called Ra. Ra crowned his son Osiris king, and his daughter Isis queen. When Osiris died, Isis was so heartbroken that her tears flooded the River Nile.

▲ A kayak is a small boat with a two-bladed paddle. Steering a kayak through a fast-flowing river is called white-water kayaking, and is a popular water sport.

CREATIVE CORNER

Evaporation experiment

Put a bowl of water outside on a hot, sunny day. Mark the water level. Check the level again that evening. It is lower, because the sun has evaporated some of the water.

Oceans

The vast oceans cover well over half the Earth, providing a home for more living things than any other habitat. At the bottom of the sea, the ocean floor is a varied and fascinating landscape. Some underwater mountains and canyons are taller and deeper than anything on dry land.

◀ Oceans are shallow near the coast, but further out there are deep trenches that cut into the ocean floor. Underwater mountain ranges rise up from the depths. Some are thousands of kilometres long.

CAN YOU FIND?

1. oil rig
2. underwater island
3. tanker
4. ocean ridge
5. ocean trench
6. submarine

▲ There are five main oceans – the Pacific, Atlantic, Indian, Southern and Arctic. The Pacific is the biggest, and the Arctic is the smallest.

Rocky cliff in a bay

Cave is formed

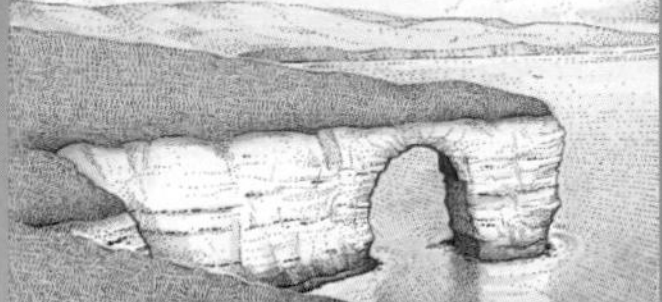

Cave becomes an arch

Stack is left behind

▲ Sea meets land at the coast. Waves constantly crash against coastal rock, and over time this wears away the rock, changing its shape. This is called erosion.

▶ Waves are made when the wind blows over the ocean. When a very strong wind blows for a long time, waves can rise as tall as 34 metres. Surfers make the most of big waves near the shore.

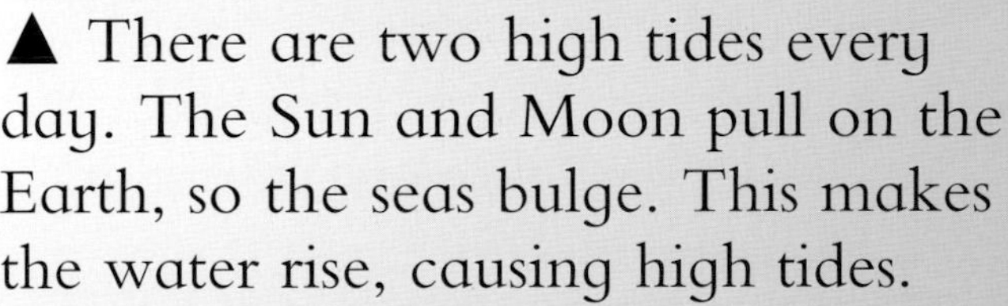

▲ There are two high tides every day. The Sun and Moon pull on the Earth, so the seas bulge. This makes the water rise, causing high tides.

◀ It is cold and dark on the ocean floor. In volcanic areas, jets of super-hot water burst out from under the Earth's crust. These are called black smokers.

CREATIVE CORNER

Make an underwater scene

Paint the inside of a shoebox blue. Draw and cut out pictures of sea creatures and hang them from the top of the box, using cotton and sticky tape. Cover the base with loose sand and small shells.

Air and wind

The Earth is surrounded by a blanket of gases, called the atmosphere. The atmosphere is very important because it protects us from the Sun's dangerous rays, and creates the right conditions for life. It also contains the water we drink and the air we breathe.

VOCABULARY

gas
A shapeless substance that fills a space.

current
Movement of a gas or liquid in a particular direction.

▼ The atmosphere has five layers. The troposphere, closest to Earth, is where the weather happens. The last layer is the exosphere, up to 900 kilometres above your head!

Exosphere (480—900km)

Thermosphere (80—480km)

Mesosphere (50—80km)

Stratosphere (11—50km)

Troposphere (0—11km)

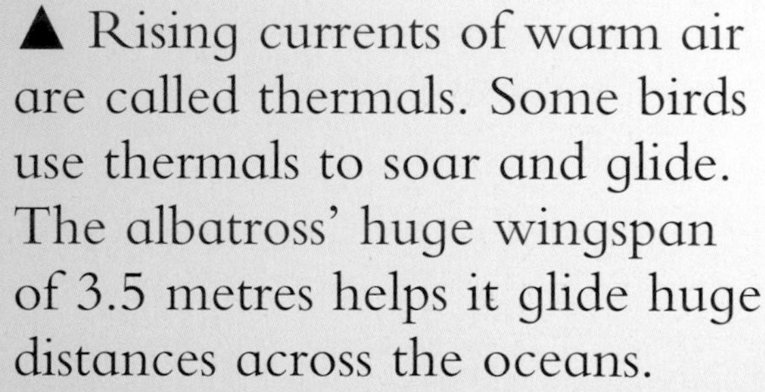

▲ Rising currents of warm air are called thermals. Some birds use thermals to soar and glide. The albatross' huge wingspan of 3.5 metres helps it glide huge distances across the oceans.

▲ Air is a mixture of gases, including oxygen. All plants breathe out oxygen. This is why tropical rainforests are so important to Earth, and must be saved from destruction.

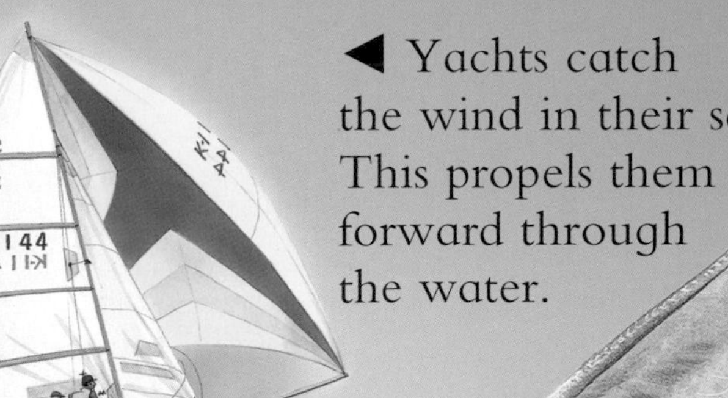

◀ Yachts catch the wind in their sails. This propels them forward through the water.

WHY DOES THE WIND BLOW?

When warm air rises, cold air rushes in to take its place. The cold air sinks, sweeping round as it reaches ground level.

Calm – Force 0

Breeze – Force 3

Wind – Force 6

Storm – Force 10

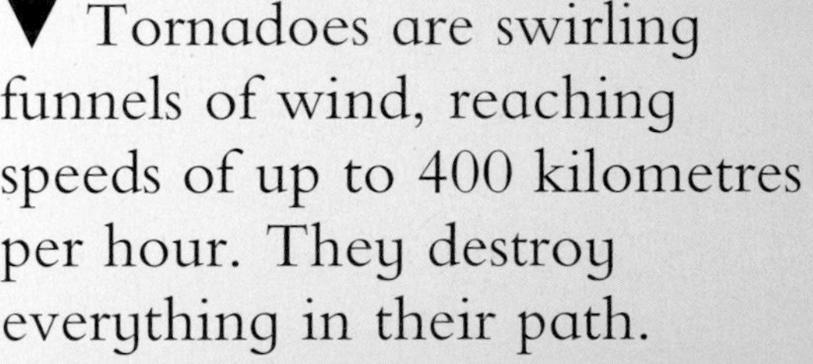

▼ Tornadoes are swirling funnels of wind, reaching speeds of up to 400 kilometres per hour. They destroy everything in their path.

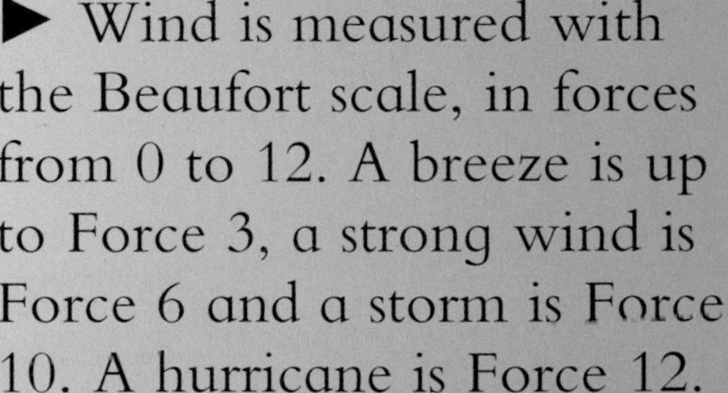

▶ Wind is measured with the Beaufort scale, in forces from 0 to 12. A breeze is up to Force 3, a strong wind is Force 6 and a storm is Force 10. A hurricane is Force 12.

CREATIVE CORNER

Make a windmill

The wind cannot be seen, but you can see it move things. Make a windmill by pinning the corners of four paper triangles together onto a wooden rod. Watch the wind turn the sails of your windmill.

INTERNET LINKS: http://kids.earth.nasa.gov/air.htm • www.geography4kids.com/files/atm_intro.html

Weather and climate

Weather is made in the troposphere, the part of the atmosphere that is closest to Earth. The air in the troposphere is always changing – it may be moving or still, wet or dry, hot or cold, or a mixture of these things. When air changes, so does the weather. The pattern of weather, or climate, varies around the world.

Freezing climate
Emperor penguins are one of the few species that can survive the freezing climate of Antarctica. The lowest temperature recorded there was minus 89°C – that is cold enough to shatter steel!

▲ Parts of the world that are close to the Equator have heavy rainfall. The rainy season in tropical countries can bring floods, especially in low-lying valleys and on plains.

► Clouds form at different heights in the sky. Their shapes can tell you what kind of weather is coming. Low stratus clouds may bring rain and high cirrus clouds may bring snow.

The Snow Queen
In Hans Christian Andersen's fairy tale, a boy called Kay is taken by the evil Snow Queen to her ice palace. Kay's sister Gerda travels across the world to rescue him. When Gerda finds Kay, her joyful tears melt his frozen heart, and they return home together.

Cirrus

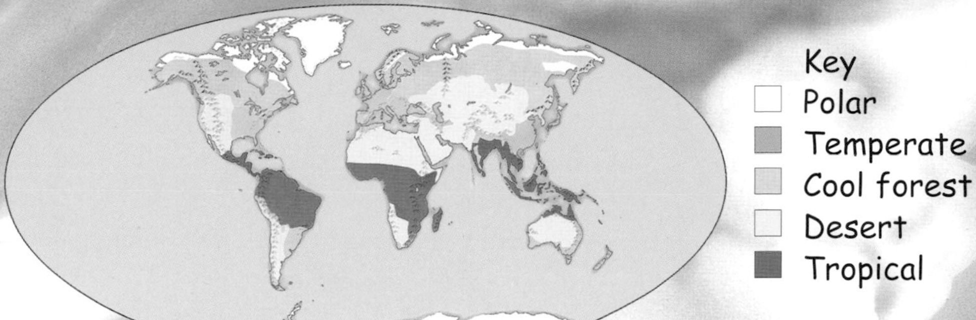

▲ This map shows the world's climates. The climate in a place is affected by how near it is to the Equator, how far it is from the sea and how high the land is.

Cumulus

Cumulonimbus

Stratus

The driest desert
Deserts are places where less than 20 centimetres of rain falls each year. The Atacama desert in Chile is the world's driest desert, because it rains there only a few times every century.

INTERNET LINKS: www.exploratorium.com/climate/index.html • www.bbc.co.uk/schools/whatisweather

Seasons

It takes a year for planet Earth to travel round the Sun. At different times of the year, one half of the world gets more sunlight than the other half. This means it is hotter in that half of the world, and colder in the other. The regular rise and fall in temperature around the world is the reason why the seasons change.

VOCABULARY

orbit
To travel around something in space, for example, a planet or star.

tropical
With a hot and humid climate that has a wet and a dry season.

◀ The middle of a hurricane is called the 'eye' of the storm.

▶ Hurricanes are powerful storms that reach wind speeds of up to 300 kilometres per hour. They are also known as typhoons and tropical cyclones.

Persephone and the seasons

In a Greek myth, King Hades took Persephone to the underworld to live. Zeus, King of the gods, said Persephone could return to the surface if she had not eaten anything in the underworld. She had eaten six seeds, so she has to stay for six months every year. During the six months she is away there is winter on Earth.

▲ The Earth tilts at an angle as it spins and orbits the Sun. It is summer in the half of the Earth that leans towards the Sun, and it is winter in the half that leans away from the Sun.

In spring, the weather warms up and plants begin to grow.

In summer, the sun shines and it is good to be outside.

WILL IT SNOW AT CHRISTMAS?

If you live in the northern half of the world, it may snow at Christmas. But in the south, Christmas is in summer, so it never snows there at Christmas.

In autumn, it cools down and leaves fall from the trees.

► The further north or south you are from the Equator, the further you are from the Sun's direct heat. The weather is more varied in this temperate climate, and there are four separate seasons: spring, summer, autumn and winter.

In winter, the weather is cold and the trees are bare.

INTERNET LINKS: www.bbc.co.uk/science/space/solarsystem/earth/solsticescience.shtml

Saving our planet

The Earth is an amazing planet, full of life and rich with natural resources. But sadly, we have not looked after our planet. Power stations, factories and vehicles send gases into the atmosphere, polluting the air. Our world is changing fast, and many species of animals and plants are in danger. We need to do everything we can to save our planet.

▲ Many animals, such as orang-utans, could soon become extinct because their habitats are being destroyed.

▼ Scientists believe that harmful gases in the atmosphere are trapping the Sun's heat, making the world warmer. This is known as climate change. All countries must work together to stop climate change happening.

Tiddalik the Frog

In an Australian folk tale, Tiddalik the frog drank all the water in the world. A wise wombat told the animals to make Tiddalik laugh. An eel danced, and Tiddalik burst out laughing. Water flowed over the Earth again.

▼ Bikes are fun to ride, and they do not pollute the air. Cycle your bike or walk on short journeys, instead of going by car.

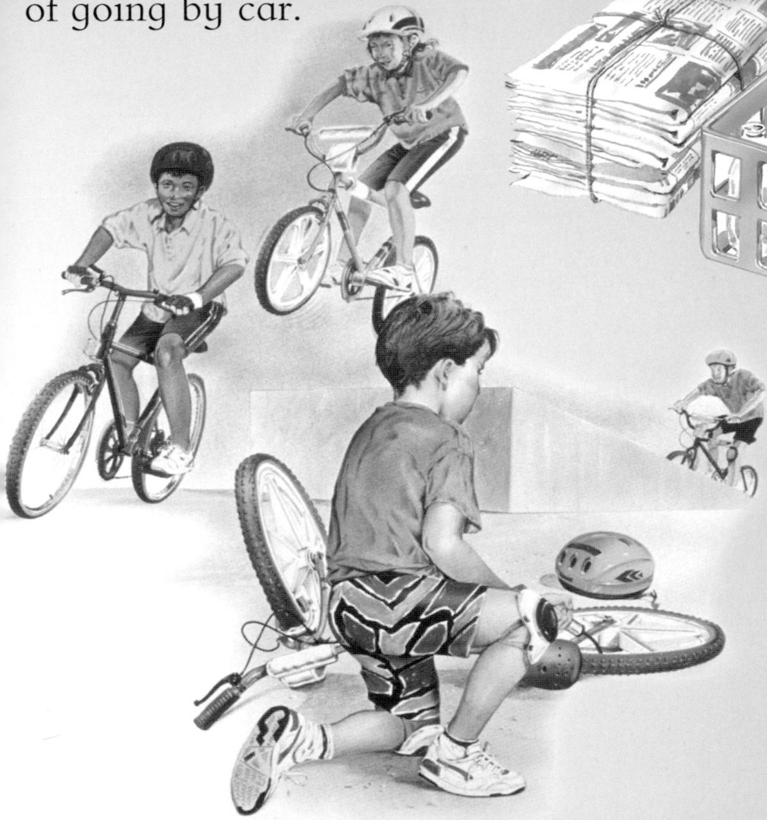

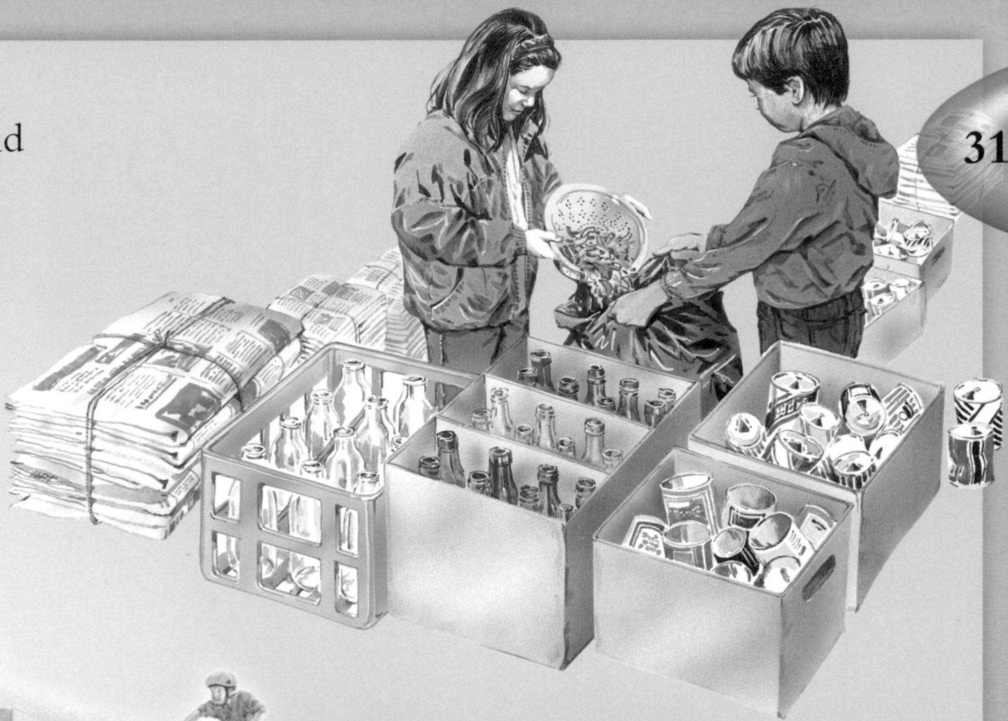

▲ Remember to sort your rubbish carefully before it is recycled. Glass, aluminium, paper and some plastics can be recycled. When a material is recycled, it is processed so it can be used again. This saves the Earth's precious resources.

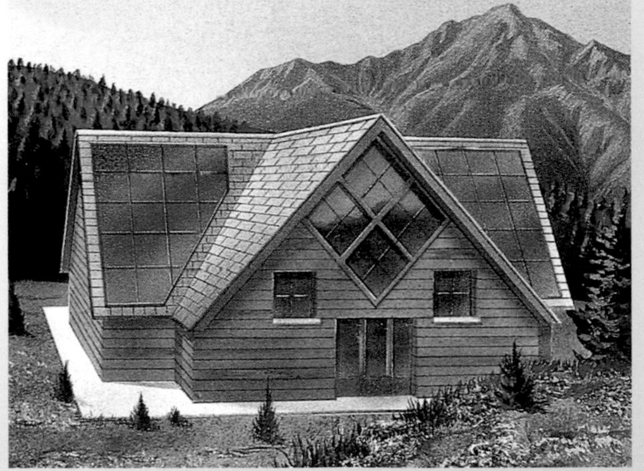

▲ Solar power uses the Sun's heat and light to make electricity. It is good for the environment because it is clean. Our energy mainly comes from fossil fuels, such as oil and coal, which create pollution.

CREATIVE CORNER

Make a junk model

Think about whether you can use something again before you throw it away. Boxes, cartons and packaging can be used to make excellent models. Try making a model of a robot from some of your old rubbish.

INTERNET LINKS: www.epa.gov/climatechange/kids • www.panda.org/

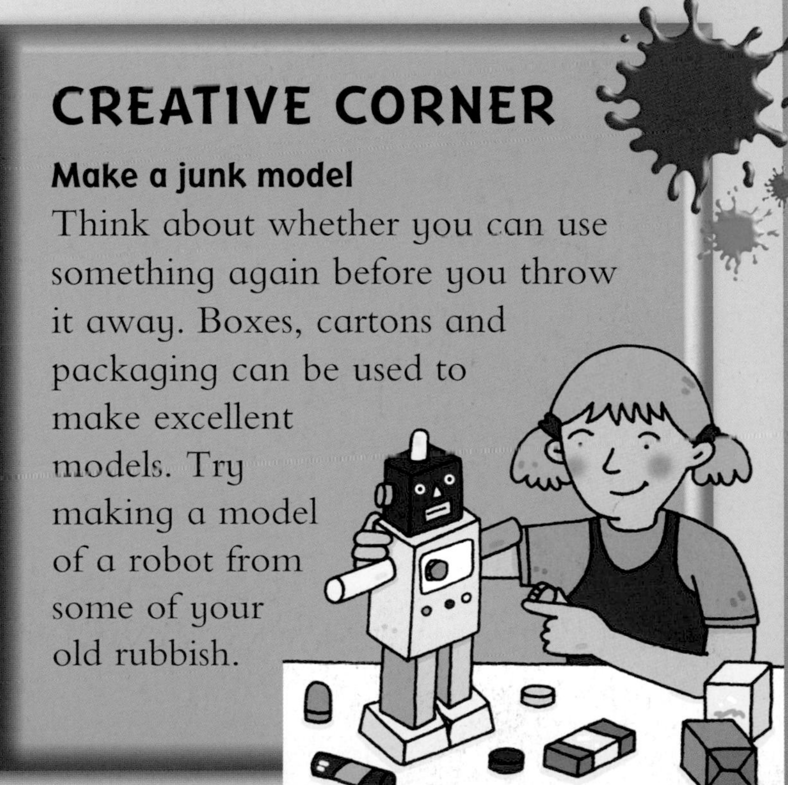

Now you know!

▲ Over two-thirds of planet Earth is covered with sea water. The large areas of land are called continents.

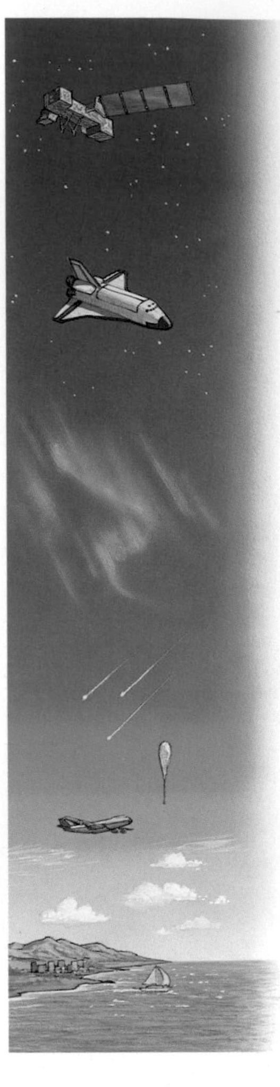

▲ Earth is protected by a blanket of gases, which is called the atmosphere. The air we breathe is in the atmosphere, and the weather is made up there, too.

▲ The environment of a living thing is called a habitat. There are many different habitats on Earth.

▲ Weather is made by changes and movements in the air. Climate is the pattern of weather that happens in a place over a long time.

▲ Many living things are in danger of dying out, and pollution is warming our climate. We must all keep the Earth clean and safe.

▲ Our Earth is a restless planet. Movements and pressures under the Earth's crust make volcanoes erupt and earthquakes happen.

► The water we drink comes from rivers, lakes and reservoirs. It is always being recycled, in a natural process called the water cycle.

Plants

From tiny tomato plants to gigantic trees, plants are vitally important to life on Earth because they make their own food. All animals have to eat plants, or animals that have eaten plants. As well as using plants for food, people also rely on them for clothing, medicine and fuel.

What are plants?

From tiny mosses to giant trees, plants are living things that make their own food. Animals cannot do this so they rely on plants to keep them alive. Like animals, plants breathe, reproduce and grow. Plants grow all through their lives.

Flower animals
Some animals look like plants. This sea anemone looks like a flower, but it is in fact an animal. It catches fish and other small creatures in its stinging tentacles.

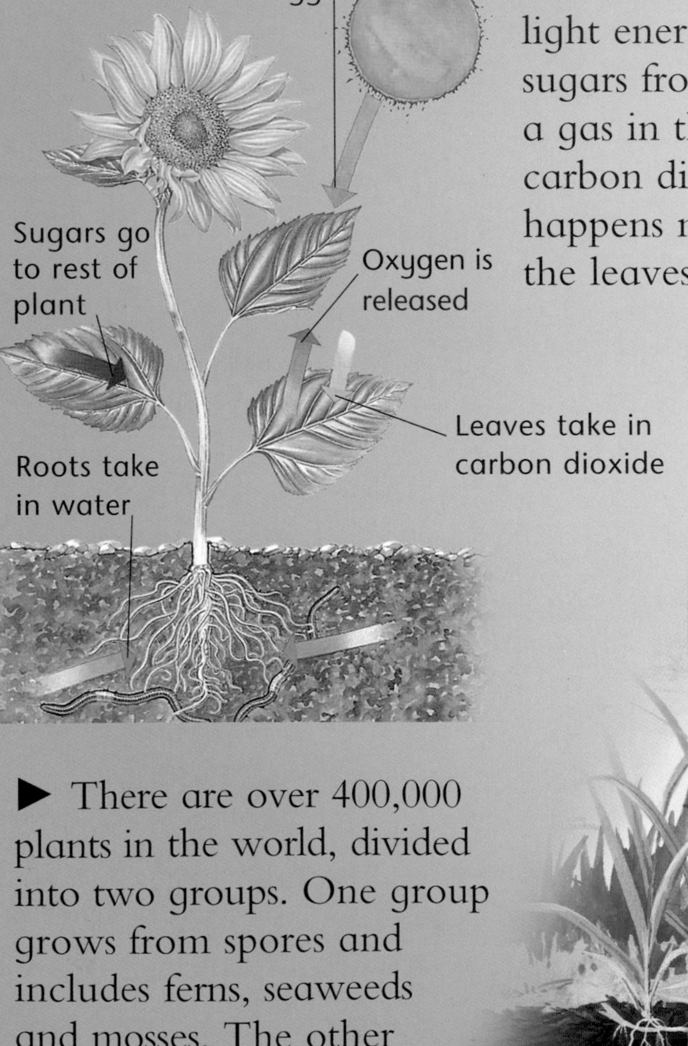

◀ Plants use the sun's light energy to make sugars from water and a gas in the air called carbon dioxide. This happens mainly in the leaves of a plant.

▶ There are over 400,000 plants in the world, divided into two groups. One group grows from spores and includes ferns, seaweeds and mosses. The other grows from the seeds made in flowers or cones.

▲ Inside a plant's stem are rows of pipes that carry food and water around the plant. Water travels up the plant from the roots to the leaves. Food travels both up and down the plant.

WHAT ARE FUNGI?

Fungi, such as these mushrooms and toadstools, are living things that are neither plants nor animals. But, like some plants, they grow from spores.

Inside a tree trunk you will find growth rings – one for each year of the tree's life.

Seedless plants

Plants such as seaweeds, mosses and ferns do not have flowers and so cannot make seeds. Instead, they produce new plants by releasing small spores. For spores to develop, these plants need water, so they grow in damp places or in water.

▼ Most moss plants grow low to the ground in cushions, clumps, tufts or flat mats. They have thin stems, simple leaves and no proper roots.

VOCABULARY

cell
A microscopic unit from which all living things are made.

spore
A tiny package of cells used in reproduction, which is the making of new plants.

▲ Liverworts belong to the same group of plants as mosses. They often grow on the soil in flowerpots.

Lichens are algae and fungi living together

1. Spores form in sacs

2. Fern releases spores

3. New fern plant grows

▲ Ferns produce spores in brown sacs under their leaves. A large fern may produce several hundred million spores in a year.

Amazing algae

Algae have no roots, leaves or flowers. But seaweeds, such as this kelp with a sea-lion swimming through it, have leaf-like fronds. They also have stalks called stipes and root-like 'holdfasts' that cling to the bottom. Most algae live in water.

► Millions of years ago, some horsetails grew as tall as trees. Today, they are small plants about as tall as poppies.

CREATIVE CORNER

Dinosaur world

Make a fern world for toy dinosaurs in a seed tray. Grow carrot tops in a little water in saucers. Then, when they grow, plant them in a layer of potting compost in the tray. You could also add garden mosses, or ferns from a garden centre.

Fungi

Fungi are not plants because they cannot make their own food. They absorb their food from other living things or dead remains. Fungi have no roots, stems or leaves. We only notice them when they produce mushrooms or toadstools for spreading the spores that grow into new fungi.

VOCABULARY

hyphae
The feeding threads of a fungus.

mycelium
A clump of woven hyphae, often seen as a mat of threads.

microscopic
Something so small that it can only be seen under a microscope.

1.Spores grow threads called hyphae

2.Threads weave to make a mycelium

3.Mushroom grows bigger

4.Spores fall from gills under cap

◀ Mushrooms grow from a clump of woven threads called a mycelium. The threads pack together to make mushrooms. These push up above the ground.

Fairy rings

Some fungi, such as the fairy ring mushroom, grow in a circle. They often appear overnight. This made people think that the mushrooms were magic circles where fairies danced. Fairy rings grow from an underground mycelium of threads that grows in a circle.

◀ Fungi can survive in caves because they do not need light to make food. They live on animal droppings and dead animals.

▲ Fungi are important in the natural world because they convert dead material into a form that other living things can use. This is natural recycling.

WHICH FUNGI HELP DOCTORS?

Some fungi produce chemicals called antibiotics, which help fight diseases. The most famous is a mould called Penicillium, used in the production of the drug penicillin.

▶ Microscopic fungi called yeasts are used to make wine and beer. The bubbles of carbon dioxide gas that they produce make bread rise.

CREATIVE CORNER

Spore prints

Cut the top off a mushroom, lay it on a piece of paper, and then cover it with a bowl. Leave it for 24 hours and then take a look. The spores will have formed a print of the mushroom on the paper.

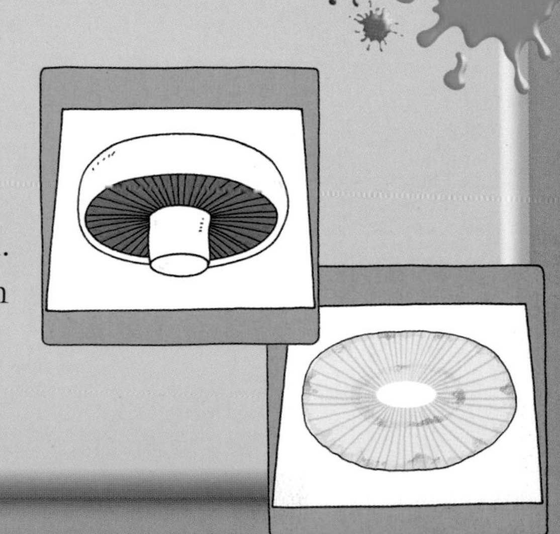

Seed plants

Many plants grow from seeds, which are made inside cones or flowers. Inside a seed is a baby plant. A hard, waterproof coat called a testa protects it. The seed takes in moisture, the case splits open, and roots and shoots sprout. When the seed has grown leaves, it can start to make its own food and grow.

VOCABULARY

pollen
A yellow dust made by cones and flowers. This has to join with an egg so that seeds can develop.

▲ When a bean seed starts to grow, the roots appear first. Next, a green shoot begins to grow upwards, towards the light. When it is above ground, the shoot grows green leaves.

▼ Seeds grow in the middle of flowers. These develop into fruits and nuts, such as the conker of the horse chestnut tree. The seeds of plants with cones are tucked inside the scales of the female cones, such as those in the cones of the larch tree.

Larch branch with cone

Horse chestnut leaf and flowers

Conker

► A greenhouse lets in light through the glass so that plants can grow. It keeps out the wind and traps heat, making plants grow faster.

Once above ground, the shoot grows leaves

Fantastic fruit

The world's biggest fruit comes from the Coco-de-mer, a palm tree that grows on the Seychelles Islands in the Indian Ocean. The fruit weighs up to 20 kilograms and takes five to ten years to ripen. Inside are only two or three seeds.

► When the seeds develop in a poppy, the petals fall off. The middle of the flower swells into a 'pepper pot' with holes around the top. The tiny black seeds are shaken out of the holes by the wind.

Poppy flowers are folded up inside buds.

Bees bring yellow pollen dust from other poppy flowers.

Seeds develop and are shaken out by the wind.

CREATIVE CORNER

Cress people

After eating a boiled egg, keep the eggshell. Gently scrape the inside clean, wash it and then put some wet cotton wool or paper in the bottom. Sprinkle in your cress seeds. Paint a face on the eggshell and wait for the cress 'hair' to grow!

Plants with cones

Most of the plants that produce their seeds in cones are trees called conifers. Many of the cones are woody but some, such as juniper cones, look like berries. Most conifers are evergreen, which means they have leaves all year round.

The largest trees
The redwood tree family from North America includes the world's biggest trees. They can grow over 80 metres high and measure up to 30 metres around the base of the trunk. The thick, red, spongy bark of redwoods helps them to survive the heat of forest fires.

► Conifer leaves may be flat and narrow, or look like needles or scales. If conifer bark is damaged, a sticky stuff called resin usually oozes out to protect and seal the wound.

▼ The seeds inside cones provide a useful source of food for animals. The 'crossed' bill of the crossbill is ideal for opening the scales of pine cones to reach the seeds.

Silver fir

Cedar of Lebanon

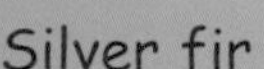

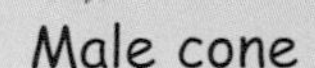

Male cone Female cone Ripe female cone

▲ Each conifer produces male and female cones. The male cones make pollen and the female cones produce seeds. In warm weather, the ripe female cones open and the winged seeds float away on the wind.

VOCABULARY

cone

A tight cluster of modified leaves. The seeds inside a cone may take up to three years to ripen.

▲ Yew trees are part of the conifer family, but do not produce true cones. Their seeds develop inside red, fleshy cups, called arils.

Ginkgo

Ancient plants

Ginkgo trees and cycads are grouped with conifers because they produce seeds but do not have flowers. Cycads have cones, but ginkgo seeds grow in fleshy fruits. Both plants have been growing on Earth for hundreds of millions of years. Their ancestors were alive when dinosaurs roamed the Earth.

Cycad

Stone pine

Coastal redwood

Italian cypress Phoenician juniper Norway spruce

Flowering plants

The job of a flower is to make seeds. Before seeds can develop, pollen (a yellow dust that contains male sex cells) has to join with female egg cells. Most flowers rely on the wind or animals to bring pollen from another flower of the same kind.

HOW LONG DO PLANTS TAKE TO FLOWER?

Most plants flower every year, or every two years. The slowest flowering plant is *Puya raimondii*, which takes 150 years to flower, then dies.

Stigma catches pollen from other flowers

Filament

Anthers (yellow sacs of pollen)

Style leads from stigma down to ovary

Petal

Ovary with egg cells

Sepal

▲ Usually, a flower has an outer ring consisting of sepals, with a ring of petals inside it. Within the petals is a ring of male parts (anthers and filaments). The female parts (ovary, stigma and style) are in the flower's centre.

▼ There are two main groups of flowering plants. Monocots have narrow leaves, flower parts in threes and seeds that sprout one leaf. Dicots have flower parts in fours or fives. The seeds sprout two leaves.

Buttercup

Corn marigold

Clover

Wind power

Some flowers, such as these hazel catkins, use the wind to carry their pollen from flower to flower. Wind pollinated flowers are small and dull-coloured. They do not have to attract insects to carry the pollen.

► Can you see the yellow pollen dust on this bee? When the bee visits another foxglove, some of the pollen sticks to the female parts of the flower. This transfer of pollen is called pollination.

Bird's-eye primrose

Nettle-leaved bellflower

Crocus

Daisy

Sea holly

St John's wort

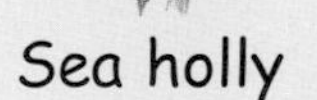

▲ Some plants have one flower on the end of a long stem. Other flowers, such as primroses, are grouped together in flowerheads.

Poppy

Knapweed

CREATIVE CORNER

Flower pressing

Lay a sheet of paper on thick cardboard. Position the flowers so they do not touch. Put a second piece of paper on top, and then some heavy books. Leave the flowers for two weeks until they are dry. Lift the flowers out and use them to make cards.

How seeds spread

Plants spread their seeds in four main ways. Some seeds are blown away by the wind or washed away by water. Other plants throw out their own seeds, although they do not travel very far. Many plants use animals to help them spread their seeds.

▲ Squirting cucumbers burst open and fling out their seeds. The seeds may travel several metres before they fall to the ground.

▼ When birds eat fruit, the seeds they swallow pass through their bodies. They come out in their droppings, which are deposited away from the plant that made the seeds.

VOCABULARY

fruit
Part of a plant that grows from the flower and contains the seed or seeds.

nut
A hard, dry fruit with one seed inside. Many trees grow nuts.

► Some seeds stick to the coats of animals, such as this maned wolf, when they brush against the plants. The seeds may be carried a long way before they fall off.

▲ Dandelion flowers produce lots of seeds, each with a fluffy parachute on top. The parachutes catch the wind and the seeds float away.

► Seeds from fleshy fruits are often spread by animals that eat them. The fruits may have bright colours or a shiny surface to attract the animals. The tough seed walls protect the seeds when they are eaten.

CREATIVE CORNER

Make helicopter seeds

Some seeds, such as lime, spin when they fall. Make your own 'helicopter' seed by cutting the shape below out of thin card. Cut along the dotted lines. Stick some modelling clay on the bottom to give weight. Fold the blades up at point A and down at point B. Then throw the seed up in the air and watch it spin to the ground.

WHY DO ANIMALS BURY NUTS?

Animals such as squirrels and jays bury nuts as a store of food for the winter. They often store more than they need. The spare nuts may then grow into new plants.

Broadleaved trees

Broadleaved trees have broad, flat leaves and flowers that develop into seeds enclosed in a fruit. Many broadleaved trees, such as oak and apple, are deciduous. This means they lose their leaves in the autumn or in a dry season. Others, such as holly trees, are evergreen. They have leaves all year round.

Roots
Some trees, such as the fig (right), have very long roots to reach water hidden deep underground. Rainforest trees (below) take up nutrients from the soil's surface with only shallow roots.

▼ Older, tougher roots are used mainly for anchoring the tree, while younger, thinner roots take in water and minerals from the soil.

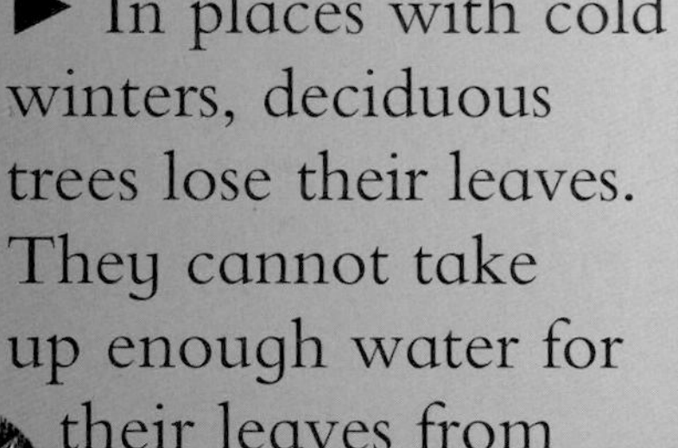

► In places with cold winters, deciduous trees lose their leaves. They cannot take up enough water for their leaves from the frozen soil.

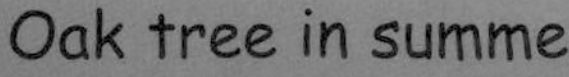

Oak tree in summer

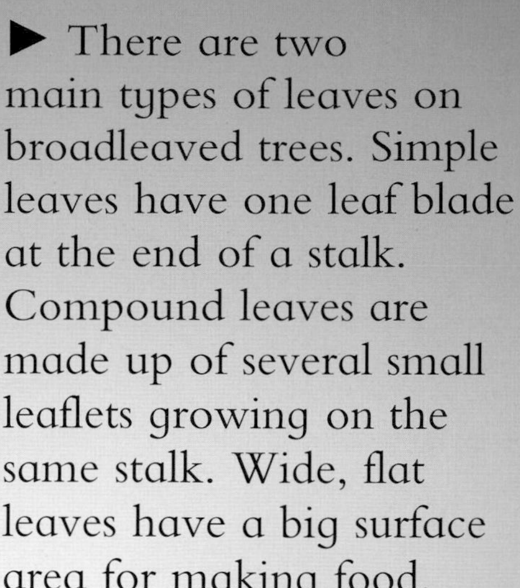

► There are two main types of leaves on broadleaved trees. Simple leaves have one leaf blade at the end of a stalk. Compound leaves are made up of several small leaflets growing on the same stalk. Wide, flat leaves have a big surface area for making food.

► Every year, a tree grows a new ring of wood under the outer layer of the bark. When a tree is cut down, you can tell the age of the tree by counting the rings inside its trunk.

Oak tree in winter

CREATIVE CORNER

Leaf pictures

Collect your favourite leaves. Press them (see Flower pressing on p.45) and let them dry naturally. Now you can glue the leaves on paper in a pattern to make pictures. Try making pictures of different trees.

Rainforest plants

Rainforests grow around the middle of the world (the Equator), where it is hot and wet all year round. Plants grow well in this environment. Rainforests are home to at least half of all plant species in the world. As there are no seasons, rainforest trees are evergreen.

Layers of life

Rainforests grow in several layers. Most life is found in the top layer, called the canopy, which receives the most rain and sun. Between the canopy and the forest floor is an understorey. This contains smaller trees, climbing plants and large-leaved shrubs that can grow in the shade. The forest floor is dark and covered with a carpet of leaves.

▲ Some plants grow on the branches of rainforest trees, where they are nearer to the sunlight. These plants are called epiphytes and most of them do not harm the trees on which they perch.

► The towering rainforest trees are 30 to 50 metres tall. Their leafy tops form a green roof to the forest. Climbing plants twist around their trunks and their roots help to hold the soil together.

Tarzan of the apes

The author Edgar Rice Burroughs created a character called Tarzan, who was raised by apes in the depths of the African jungle. Tarzan became the king of his ape tribe and had many adventures swinging through the trees.

Rainforest plants have thick leaves with pointed tips that help the rain drip off easily.

► Epiphytes called tank plants have a watertight cup of waxy leaves that holds many litres of water. Animals, such as frogs, use these tree-top pools as nurseries.

CREATIVE CORNER

Make a bottle garden

Put a layer of gravel in a large, open-necked bottle and add compost. Now put in some plants. Add moss and sticks to make it look like the forest floor. Pour in a cupful of water before putting on the cap. You will not have to water your garden again.

Water plants

Many plants grow in the fresh water of ponds and rivers, and in the salty water of the sea. Water plants are surrounded by nutrients, but may find it hard to get enough light or oxygen. Some water plants float freely, while others are rooted in the mud or fixed to rocks.

▲ In the fresh water of ponds and lakes, there are many water plants, including lilies, reeds and willow trees. Insects and animals need water plants to give them food or shelter, and to make oxygen.

WHICH PLANTS FLOAT ON WATER?

Duckweeds often cover the water's surface. Their leaves float on the water, absorbing light and making food. Their roots hang in the water, taking in nutrients.

▼ The very smallest plants of all are types of algae, which you can only see through a microscope. They float in lakes and oceans, and are called phytoplankton.

▲ Mangrove trees live in swamps where there is little oxygen in the mud. Special roots grow above the mud and take in oxygen from the air.

VOCABULARY

seaweed
Any plant or plants growing in the salty water of the sea.

mangrove
A tropical tree that grows in marshes or near the sea.

◀ The giant water lily from the rivers of the Amazon rainforest grows huge leaves that are strong enough to take the weight of a small child.

◀ Green seaweeds live near the surface of the sea, while red and brown seaweeds live at greater depths.

Desert plants

Plants find it difficult to survive the lack of water in a desert. Desert plants have deep or wide-spreading roots to collect as much water as possible. They may also store water in swollen stems or underground roots.

▲ Pebble plants are made of two fleshy leaves, which are full of water. They look like stones so that animals do not eat them.

▼ Deserts are very hot places, so many of the animals that live there come out only at night. During the day, the tiny elf owl hides inside the giant cactus, where it is cooler. It comes out to hunt when it is dark.

CAN YOU FIND?

1. elf owl
2. Gila woodpecker
3. saguaro cactus
4. rattlesnake
5. kit fox
6. roadrunner chasing a lizard

► Date palms grow well in desert oases, which are natural springs of water in a dry desert. The water in the oases may come from distant mountains and flow underground through the rocks until it comes to the surface in the desert.

▲ Some plants survive long periods as seeds buried in the desert sands. When it rains, they quickly flower and produce seeds. When a cactus flowers, water escapes from the petals, so they flower for only a few days a year.

Cactus lunch

The land iguana (a large lizard) lives in desert-like parts of the Galapagos Islands, in the Pacific ocean. It feeds mainly on the prickly pear cactus, breaking off the cactus spines before swallowing the juicy stems. The spines of a cactus are really its leaves. They do not lose water as easily as a wide, flat leaf.

Meat-eating plants

Some plants trap insects and other small animals. This meat provides these plants with the extra goodness they need to survive in poor soil. Plant traps include leaves full of water, sticky leaves, or spiny leaves that snap shut like an animal's jaws.

HOW MANY MEAT-EATING PLANTS ARE THERE?
Over 600 different kinds have been identified so far. There are many more waiting to be discovered.

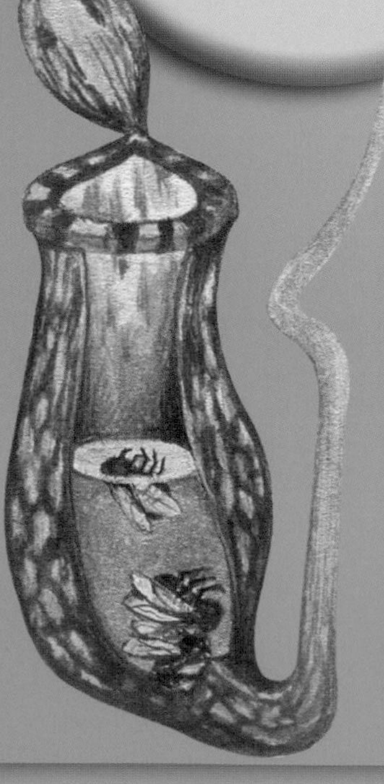

◀ After trapping insects, this pitcher plant slowly dissolves their bodies to make a soupy meal. The pitcher plant then soaks up the meal through its leaves.

▲ Insects land on the leaves of Venus fly traps to eat the sweet nectar they produce. If they brush against sensitive trigger hairs on the inside of each leaf, the trap snaps shut. It closes in an amazing one-third of a second!

A habitat for meat-eating plants

Meat-eating plants live worldwide, from cold peat bogs and flooded grasslands to hot, tropical rainforests. Peat bogs, like this one, form over thousands of years as lakes are gradually filled in with mud and plants.

▼ The leaves of sundew plants are covered with special hairs that have drops of 'glue' on their ends. Insects are attracted to the shiny drops, but they become stuck fast when they land.

CREATIVE CORNER

Dangerous gardening

Buy some meat-eating plants at a garden centre. Ask how they should be cared for. Put them in your bedroom or kitchen to catch flies and other insects.

Useful plants

From food and clothing to fuel and medicine, plants are very useful to people. For example, the wood from trees is used for building, and the stems of the rattan palm are shaped to make cane furniture, baskets and ropes.

The first people
A traditional native American legend tells how the first people were black and scaly, and lived underground. A priest called Yanauluha taught them how to grow plants, make medicine and live on the surface of the Earth.

► Spices are made from the flowers, fruits, stems, roots and seeds of plants. Some spices are very hot, while others are sweeter.

▼ Fruits and vegetables are an important part of a healthy diet. Eating five items of fruits and vegetables each day will keep your body working well.

Leek Onion Potatoes
Cauliflower Cabbage Carrot

Plants for fuel

Some plants can be made into a type of fuel, which can be used instead of petrol to power car engines. Petrol is made from oil, which will run out in the future. Plant fuel will not run out. The problem is that it takes a lot of land to grow the plants, so forests are cut down to make space.

Rosy periwinkle, a treatment for leukaemia

Aloe juice, a treatment for burns

Foxglove, a treatment for heart disease

▲ Before modern medicines were invented, people only used plants to treat illnesses and diseases. Many of the modern remedies still use plant products.

▼ Apples and other fruits may be picked by hand before going to the shops to be sold. Other plants, such as the fluffy cotton used to make clothes, may be harvested using big machines.

CREATIVE CORNER

Grow a herb garden

Choose seeds of herbs that you like to eat. Sew them thinly in plant pots indoors, pressing them firmly into the compost. Water from beneath. When the plantlets are 5cm high, transplant them to a large pot or window-box outside.

Unusual plants

The plant world is amazing. It includes the biggest and oldest living things, plants that glow in the dark, and seeds that sprout after thousands of years. The most amazing fact is that animals and people would not be able to live in a world without plants.

▼ Bamboo is the fastest growing plant. It can grow 90 centimetres in a day. Sometimes, creaking can be heard as the plant grows upwards.

◀ The largest living things are the giant redwood trees of North America. The biggest is over 80 metres tall and over 2,000 years old.

Two-leaf wonder

The Welwitschia mirabilis plant grows only two leaves, which are 2 to 8 metres long and tear into thinner strips with age. Dew collects under the leaves, helping the plant to survive in the Namib Desert of Africa. The plant lives for 400 to 1,500 years.

◀ The biggest flower belongs to the rafflesia plant of southeast Asia. The flower is up to one metre across and smells of rotting meat.

Plants in danger

At least one out of every eight plant species is in danger of dying out, or becoming extinct. People are the main cause of plant extinctions. Habitat destruction, chemical poisoning and climate change are threatening the survival of many plants.

▲ The biggest danger to plants is the destruction of their habitat, such as cutting down forests for timber and draining wetlands to build houses.

▲ Bee orchid plants are threatened by people turning grassland habitats into farmland. In doing this, they dig up plants and damage young shoots by trampling on them.

Saving plants

To save the world's rare plants, scientists need to find out which plants are endangered. They must plan ways to protect and manage habitats. Rare plants can also be grown in botanical gardens or preserved in seed banks. Some plants can be re-introduced into the wild.

INTERNET LINKS: http://library.thinkquest.org/27257/rafflesia.html • www.bgci.org/conservation

Plants at home

All sorts of plants can be grown in pots, window-boxes, hanging baskets and gardens. Plants are grown from seeds, but they can also be grown from pieces of older plants, such as cuttings, bulbs or stems that sprout new plants. To grow well, plants need light, air, water and warmth. However, different plants need different growing conditions.

▲ Ladybirds are good for the garden because they eat the greenfly that suck the sap from plants.

◄ Woody shrubs and trees can be grown from cuttings taken in the autumn. Some shrubs root more easily if the cutting has a sliver of wood from the main stem.

▼ Wild plants like these attract wildlife, such as butterflies and birds. Climbing plants provide shelter for snails, and birds may nest among the leaves.

Jack and the beanstalk
In an English tale, Jack swaps a cow for some magic beans, which grow into a huge beanstalk. Jack steals gold coins, a hen that lays golden eggs and a harp from a giant at the top of the beanstalk. The giant chases Jack, but Jack chops down the beanstalk and the giant falls to his death.

▲ Hanging baskets are good places to grow trailing plants. The baskets need to be watered frequently as they dry out quickly.

◀ Bulbs consist of an underground stem and a bud, which is surrounded by leaves that are full of stored food. Flowers such as hyacinths and daffodils grow in spring using food stored in the bulb.

▲ You can grow wild plants or herbs from seed, or flowers from bulbs, in a window-box or pots for a patio. The containers need to have drainage holes in the bottom.

CREATIVE CORNER

Growing plants from cuttings

Take cuttings from plants in the summer months. Cut off the tips of side shoots or young stems without flowers. Gently pull off the lower leaves and plant the cuttings in soil or peat-free compost. When the cuttings grow roots, they will be able to develop into new plants.

Now you know!

▲ Plants use the energy in sunlight to make their own food from water and carbon dioxide. Animals and fungi cannot do this.

▲ Some plants, such as mosses and ferns, reproduce using spores instead of seeds. Spores are smaller and simpler.

▲ A lot of plants produce their seeds in flowers. Some plants produce their seeds in cones.

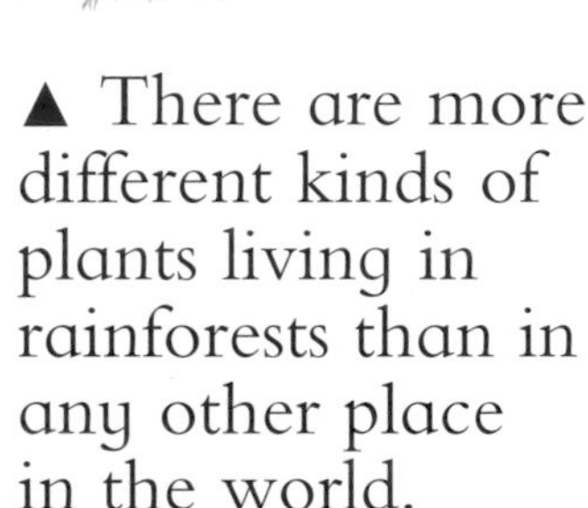

▲ There are more different kinds of plants living in rainforests than in any other place in the world.

▲ When a tree is cut down, you can tell its age by counting the rings inside the trunk.

▲ Plants spread their seeds using the wind, water or animals. Some plants throw out their own seeds, but they do not go very far.

▲ People use plants for all sorts of purposes, including building houses, flavouring food, treating illnesses and making cars go.

► A few plants trap insects for extra food. They trap the animals using sticky leaves, spiny leaves, or leaves full of water.

Animals

Animals are living beings. They have developed in different forms which can survive on almost every part of the planet, on land, in the sea or in the air. They include everything from the tiniest creepy crawly to the largest whale, flying beetles and squeaking bats, colourful parrots, monkeys, apes – and humans, too.

What is an animal?

There are about 10 million different animal types, or species, living on Earth today. Animals are life forms made up of tiny units called cells. Animals can take in life-giving oxygen from air or water. They can move from one place to another. They can take food into their bodies and digest it.

CAN YOU FIND?

1. flying animals
2. the biggest eye
3. the longest neck
4. water animals
5. the biggest animal
6. the fastest animal

▼ Animals can live in all sorts of places. Some can swim in water or fly in the air, while others live on land. Animals with backbones are called vertebrates. Boneless animals are called invertebrates.

The first animals

A very old story from Sierra Leone in Africa tells how God made spare skins for humans, so that they could survive death. God ordered Dog to take these skins to the humans, but on the way Dog fell asleep and Snake stole all the skins. That is why snakes can now change their skins while humans die when they get old – and why many people do not like snakes.

Extinct animals

Animals have developed, or evolved, over millions of years. Some species have died out or become extinct. The dodo was a turkey-sized pigeon that lived on islands in the Indian Ocean. It was hunted for food and became extinct in about 1680.

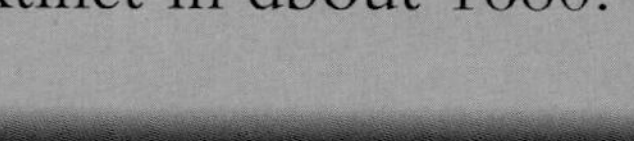

Albatross

Blue whale

Giant squid

Crocodile

Cheetah

Soft bodies, hard shells

Molluscs are invertebrates with soft bodies. Some have hard shells. Molluscs include slugs, snails, all sorts of shellfish, squids and octopuses. Crustaceans are armour-plated invertebrates. They include crabs, lobsters and woodlice.

WHEN DO SNAILS SHUT UP?
In cold winters, snails may seal up their shells with a chalky substance and wait for spring and warmer weather to come.

VOCABULARY

invertebrate
An animal that does not have a backbone or spinal column.

crustacean
An animal that lives mostly in water, and has a hard shell and jointed limbs.

▼ Many molluscs and crustaceans live on seashores and in rockpools, alongside other sea creatures including starfish.

Crab

Octopus

Starfish

▲ Woodlice like to live in damp, dark places. They may often be found under rotting logs or stones in the garden. They have seven pairs of legs.

▲ Snails are found on land, in ponds and in the sea. They carry shells on their backs and can draw back inside the shells if they are threatened. Most slugs have no shell outside their bodies.

Lobster

The hermit crab

The hermit crab is a crustacean. Instead of having its own body armour, it squeezes into the empty shell of a mollusc. This hermit crab has found its new home in the shell of a whelk.

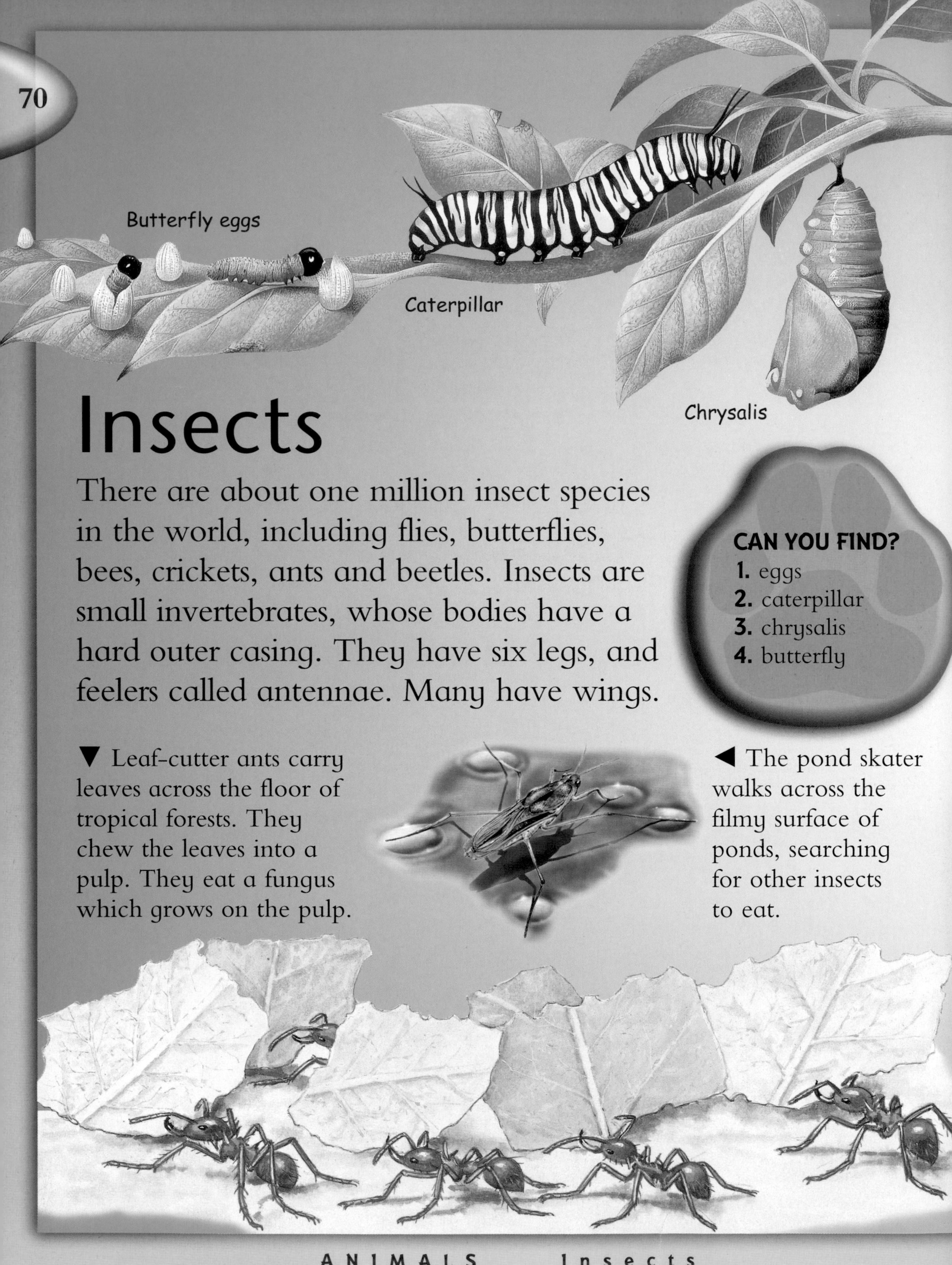

Insects

There are about one million insect species in the world, including flies, butterflies, bees, crickets, ants and beetles. Insects are small invertebrates, whose bodies have a hard outer casing. They have six legs, and feelers called antennae. Many have wings.

CAN YOU FIND?
1. eggs
2. caterpillar
3. chrysalis
4. butterfly

▼ Leaf-cutter ants carry leaves across the floor of tropical forests. They chew the leaves into a pulp. They eat a fungus which grows on the pulp.

◀ The pond skater walks across the filmy surface of ponds, searching for other insects to eat.

▲ The monarch butterfly lays eggs on the milkweed plant. The caterpillar hatches out and eats the leaves. It turns into a chrysalis, which then changes into a butterfly.

All change

Some wasps chew tiny bits of wood and mix it with saliva to make a beautiful paper nest. The queen wasp lays her eggs in the nest. The wasps defend the nest fiercely and can deliver a very painful sting.

CREATIVE CORNER

Making butterfly prints

Fold 4 sheets of A5 card in half, then draw a butterfly outline. Cut out both sides of the fold as shown. Colour in wing patterns and body shapes. Make a mobile with three plastic drinking straws and cotton thread. Tie on the butterflies and hang from the ceiling.

Spiders

Spiders belong to a group of eight-legged invertebrates called arachnids. Spiders may be tiny, or big and hairy. Millions of spiders may be found in just one grassy field. Spiders can produce silk that they use to swing through the air, protect their eggs or capture the insects that they eat.

► This European garden spider has caught a fly in its strong, sticky, silken web. Spiders eat a huge number of insects.

Black widow spider, USA

Wandering spider, Brazil

▲ Spiders have fangs for killing their prey. Most spiders are harmless to humans, but these two are deadly.

CREATIVE CORNER

Spider's web

Twist 3 pipe-cleaners to make the 6 'spokes' of the spider's web. Then tie one end of a piece of thread to the upright spoke, near the centre. Move in an outwards spiral, looping the thread around each spoke. When the web is complete, cut and tie. Draw, colour and cut out a spider on card and stick it at the centre of the web.

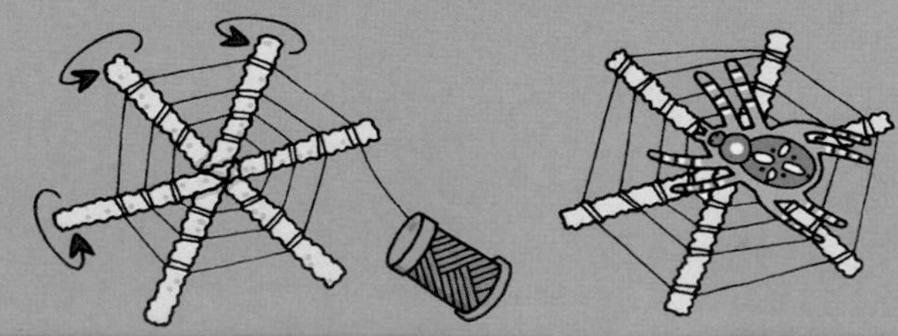

Scorpions

Scorpions are arachnids that live in hot countries, and are often found in deserts. They have big pincers, and an arching tail with a venomous sting. They eat mostly insects and spiders.

▼ A scorpion carries her young on her back. After about 12 days, they are ready to look after themselves.

WHY DO SCORPIONS DANCE?

Before scorpions mate, they perform a courtship dance. During this, they wave their pincers and tails in the air.

The tale of Arachne

The ancient Greeks told a tale about a proud woman called Arachne. When she challenged the goddess Athena to a weaving contest, the goddess became very angry. She turned Arachne and her descendants into spiders.

► If a scorpion is threatened, it can inject a nasty venom into the animal that threatens it. It does this through the curved spine at the end of its tail.

Fish

Fish are animals that swim in rivers, lakes and oceans. They have bodies covered in scales. Some species may be tiny, while others are giants up to 15 metres long. Many fish eat insects or water creatures, including other fish. Some feed on plankton, which are tiny creatures and plants that drift in the ocean.

HOW MANY FISH ARE THERE?
About 27,700 species of fish live in the oceans, and about 2,300 species live in streams, rivers and lakes.

Fish bodies
Fish are vertebrates. They use their tails and fins to help them swim and keep their balance in the water. Most fish take in the oxygen they need by passing water through gills behind their heads.

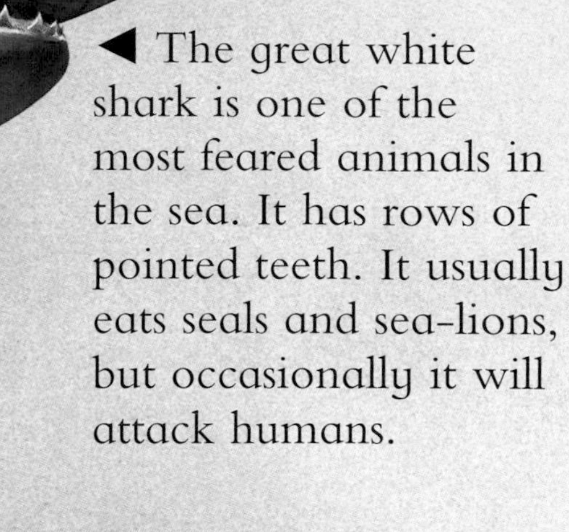

◀ The great white shark is one of the most feared animals in the sea. It has rows of pointed teeth. It usually eats seals and sea-lions, but occasionally it will attack humans.

◀ Corals are small creatures that live in warm oceans. As they die, their chalky remains build up into banks, called coral reefs. All sorts of fish make their homes in reefs.

A fish that saved the world

Hindus tell how at the dawn of this age a man called Manu saved a tiny fish he found in the river. The fish, Matsya, grew bigger and bigger, for it was really the god Vishnu. Manu first put Matsya in a bowl, then in a tank, then in a lake, and finally in the sea. Matsya warned Manu that a great flood was on the way. He told Manu to build a boat and fill it with the seeds of all living things. The boat was towed to a high mountain, where it survived the great flood.

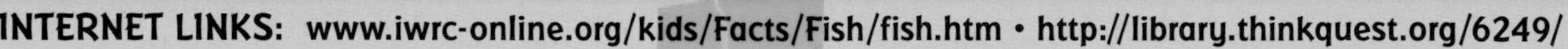

INTERNET LINKS: www.iwrc-online.org/kids/Facts/Fish/fish.htm • http://library.thinkquest.org/6249/

Amphibians

Amphibians are animals that live partly in the water and partly on land. They include frogs, toads, newts and salamanders. Most species lay their eggs in water. The young breathe under water through gills, but they may later develop lungs to breathe air.

Axolotl
This amphibian lives only in two lakes in Mexico. Its feathery gills extend outside its body. Axolotls generally stay in this stage of development, without ever growing into land animals.

◀ Male midwife toads carry strings of eggs around their back legs. After three weeks they enter the water, where the eggs hatch.

The frog prince
The way in which frogs change their shape inspired many fairy-tales. One tells of a princess who is helped by an ugly frog. She does not realize that he is really a handsome prince who has been turned into a frog by a wicked fairy. The spell is only broken when she kisses him.

▼ The common frog of Europe and Asia lives in marshes and other damp areas. It lays its eggs or spawn in ponds.

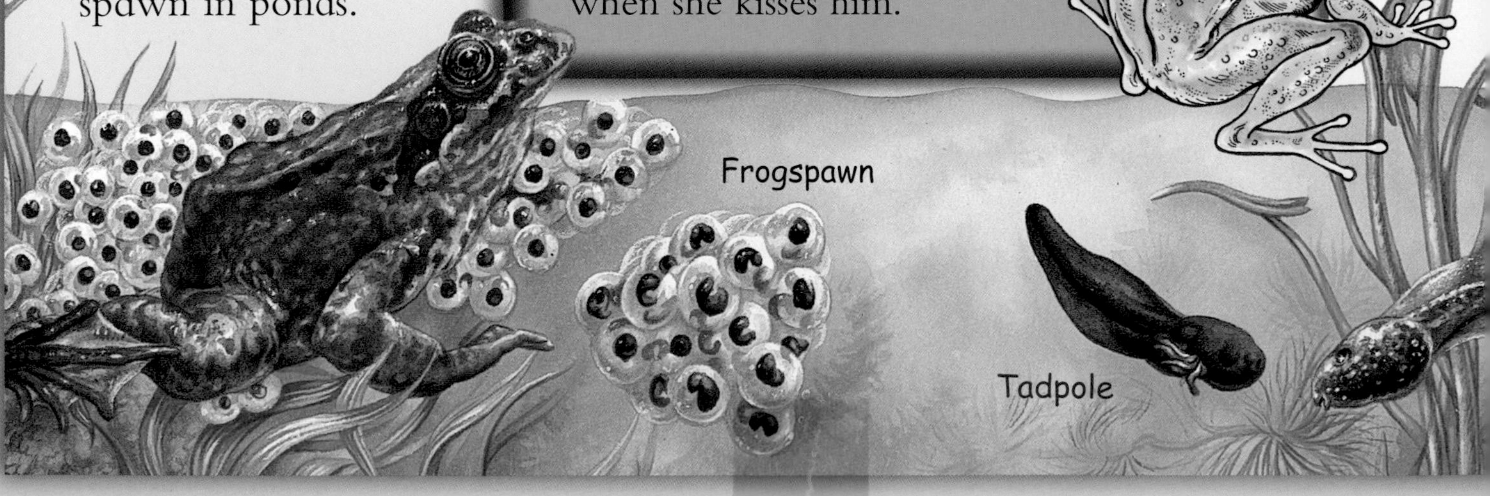

Frogspawn

Tadpole

▲ Newts and salamanders have long bodies and keep their tails as adults. They eat small creatures such as worms and slugs.

CREATIVE CORNER

Swim like a frog

The rear legs of frogs are really powerful. Can you swim frog-style? Next time you go swimming, have a competition to see who can go the longest distance with just three froggy leg-kicks.

▲ Treefrogs live in rainforests. They have disc-shaped suckers on their toes, which help them climb up trees to hunt insects. They return to ponds to lay their eggs.

Reptiles

Reptiles include snakes, lizards, alligators and crocodiles, tortoises, turtles and terrapins. They are egg-laying vertebrates whose bodies are protected by scales or horny plates. Reptiles are cold-blooded creatures, unable to create their own body warmth. That is why they bask, lying in warm sunshine to raise their temperature. Snakes and some lizards have no legs.

WHY DO SNAKES' TONGUES FLICKER?
Snakes have forked tongues with a special sensor that helps them 'taste' the air and pick up the scent of their prey.

▲ The giant tortoises that live on the Galapagos Islands can grow up to 1.5 metres long and weigh over 135 kilograms. They eat grass, leaves and the fruit of the cactus.

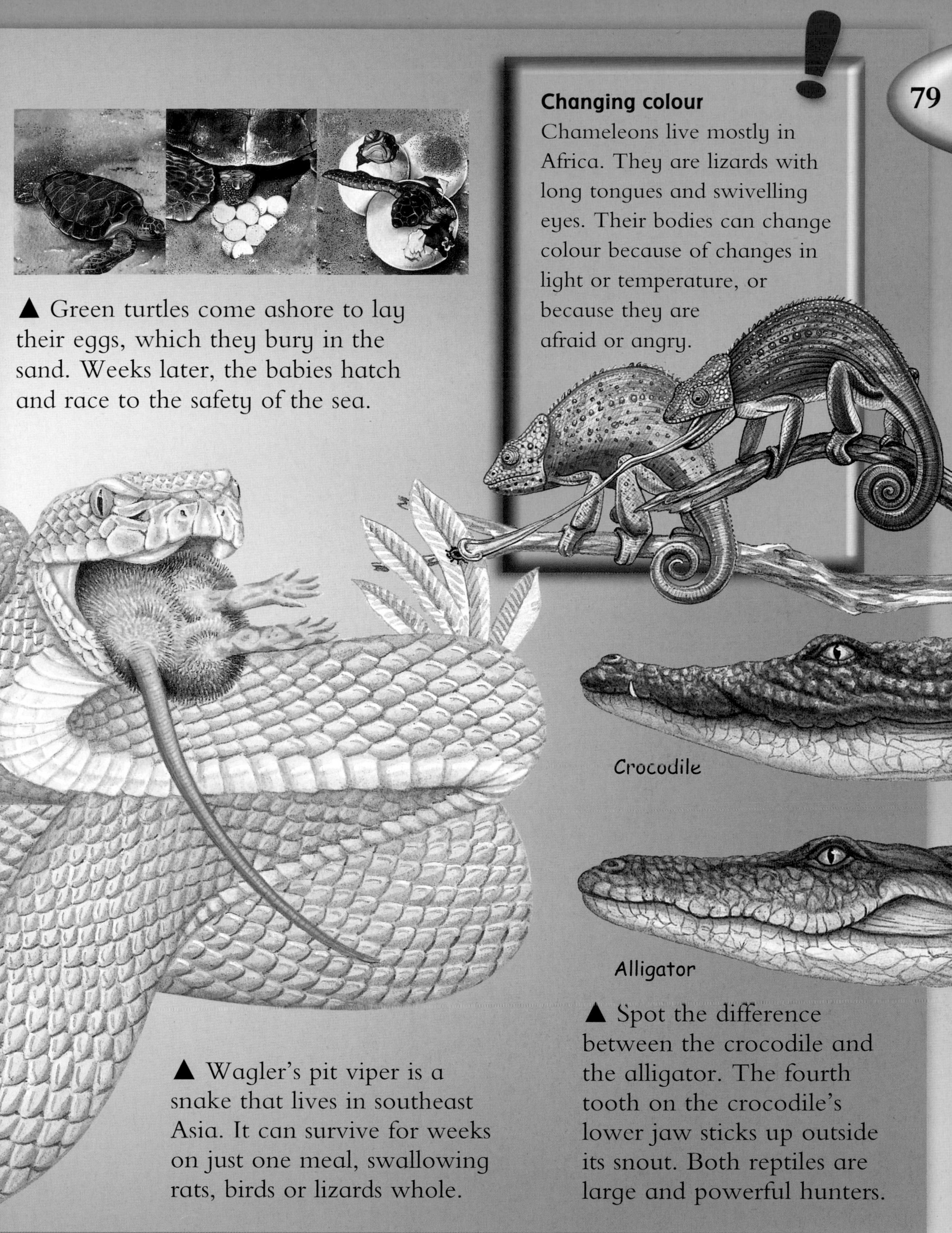

▲ Green turtles come ashore to lay their eggs, which they bury in the sand. Weeks later, the babies hatch and race to the safety of the sea.

Changing colour

Chameleons live mostly in Africa. They are lizards with long tongues and swivelling eyes. Their bodies can change colour because of changes in light or temperature, or because they are afraid or angry.

▲ Wagler's pit viper is a snake that lives in southeast Asia. It can survive for weeks on just one meal, swallowing rats, birds or lizards whole.

▲ Spot the difference between the crocodile and the alligator. The fourth tooth on the crocodile's lower jaw sticks up outside its snout. Both reptiles are large and powerful hunters.

◀ Swallows spend winter in the far south, but each summer they fly to North America, northern Europe and Asia to breed. Long animal journeys are called migrations.

Birds

Birds are found almost everywhere in the world, from tropical forests to the icy coasts of Antarctica. Birds are egg-laying vertebrates, whose bodies are covered in feathers. Most birds are able to fly, but some are flightless.

The falcon god
Ancient peoples revered birds because they could fly. Birds were sometimes thought to be spirits or the messengers of the gods. In ancient Egypt, the god Horus was the protector of the pharaoh, the Egyptian king. Horus was often pictured with the head of a falcon, which is a bird of prey.

WHY DO BIRDS HAVE FEATHERS?

Feathers keep birds warm and also make it possible for them to fly. Under the outer feathers are small, fluffy ones, called 'down'.

► Seabirds, such as gannets, eat fish and shellfish. They can paddle, swim or dive as well as fly. Many seabirds nest on the ledges of steep cliffs, in large groups called colonies.

► These birds are all flightless. They walk or run, but cannot use their wings. Ostriches live in Africa, emus in Australia, rheas in South America and kiwis in New Zealand.

A frightened ›bit runs as a golden ›gle closes in for the kill. ›is bird of prey has a hooked ›ak and very sharp talons.

CREATIVE CORNER

Winter food for wild birds

Take half a coconut shell or an empty plastic pot. Then ask an adult to melt some lard in a pan. Mix in seeds, unsalted nuts, porridge oats, cereal, bacon rind or cheese. Pour this mixture into the upturned shell or pot and leave to set. Turn the pot upside down and hang up outside, well away from cats.

What is a mammal?

Cats, dogs, elephants, monkeys, rabbits, whales and humans are all mammals. Mammals are warm-blooded vertebrates that breathe air. They feed their babies on mothers' milk. Mammals are the most intelligent animals on Earth.

▲ Mice can have babies several times a year. They are gnawing mammals, or rodents, and live in most parts of the world.

▲ A baby African elephant can be 1 metre tall and weigh up to 90 kilograms. An adult may grow to 3.2 metres and weigh 5 tonnes.

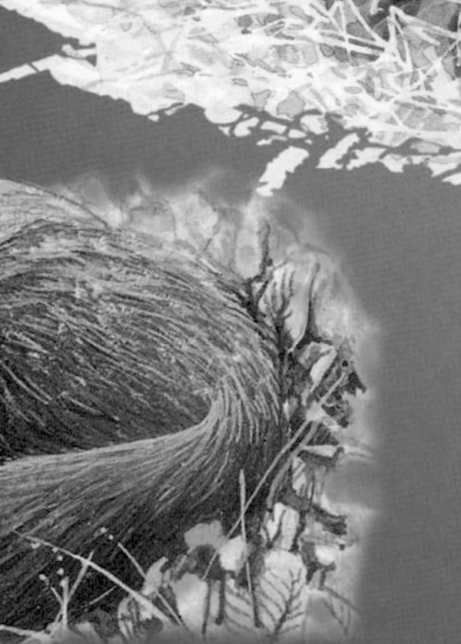

◀ The platypus is an unusual mammal because it lays eggs. It lives on Australian river banks. It has claws and webbed feet, and a bill shaped like a duck's.

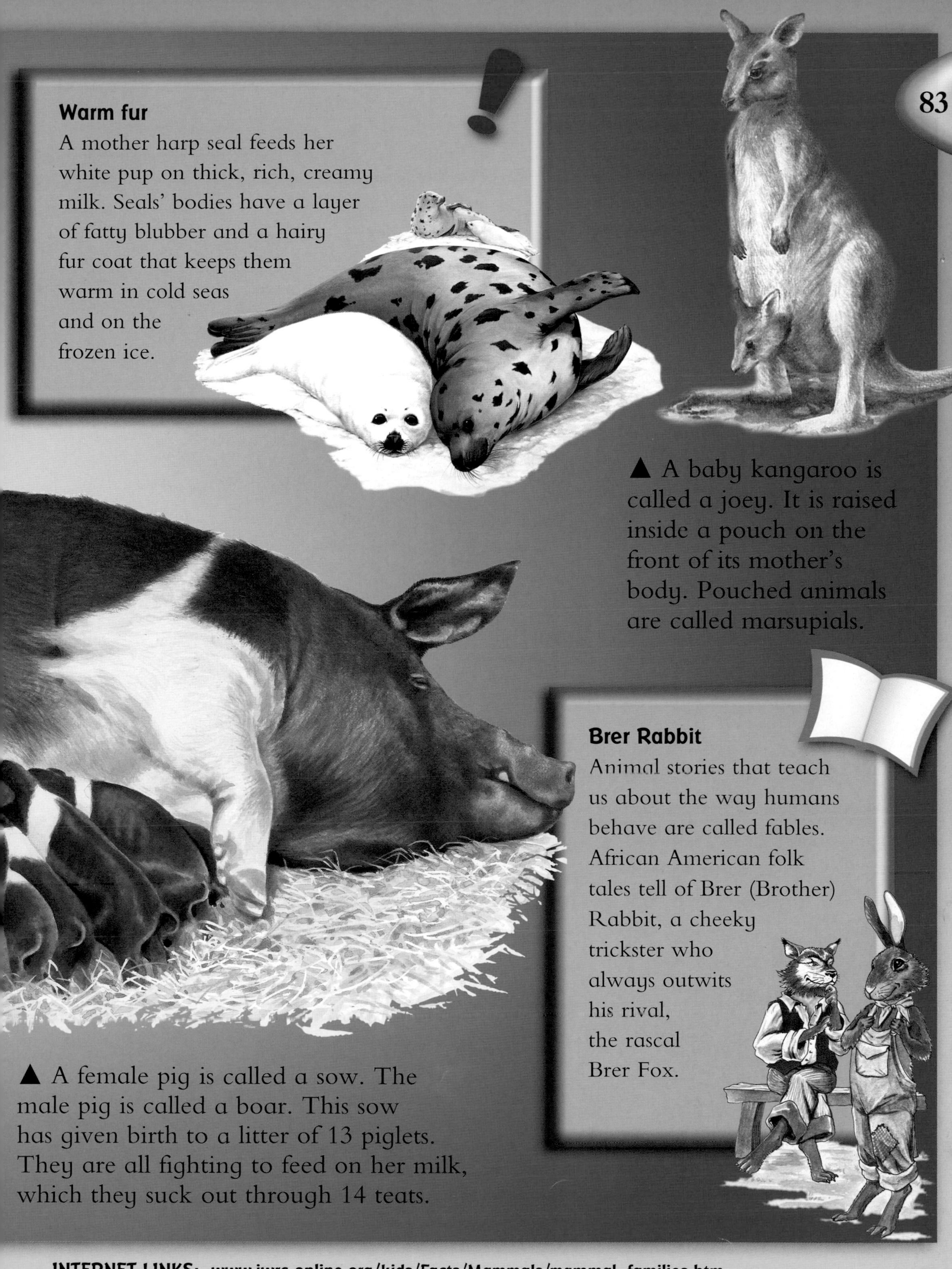

Warm fur

A mother harp seal feeds her white pup on thick, rich, creamy milk. Seals' bodies have a layer of fatty blubber and a hairy fur coat that keeps them warm in cold seas and on the frozen ice.

▲ A baby kangaroo is called a joey. It is raised inside a pouch on the front of its mother's body. Pouched animals are called marsupials.

Brer Rabbit

Animal stories that teach us about the way humans behave are called fables. African American folk tales tell of Brer (Brother) Rabbit, a cheeky trickster who always outwits his rival, the rascal Brer Fox.

▲ A female pig is called a sow. The male pig is called a boar. This sow has given birth to a litter of 13 piglets. They are all fighting to feed on her milk, which they suck out through 14 teats.

Meat-eating mammals

Mammals that eat meat, including big cats, wild dogs, bears and seals, are called carnivores. Some carnivores hunt and kill live prey, such as fish, birds, deer or rabbits. Others feed mostly off dead animals, or carrion.

▲ A giant anteater in South America uses its claws to break up a termites' nest. It has a long, sticky tongue for eating the insects.

▲ The American black bear catches salmon, birds, mice and other small mammals, and insects. It also likes to feed on berries and nuts.

WHAT IS A FOOD CHAIN?

Animals eat other animals or plants to stay alive. A fox eats a bird. A bird eats a snail. A snail eats a leaf. This sequence is called a food chain.

▲ Shrews are insect-eaters. They are tiny creatures with pointed noses. To stay alive, they must eat their own weight in food each day.

▼ Lionesses chase a small antelope on the grassy plains of Africa. Lions are powerful and fierce hunters. They live in groups called prides.

How the leopard got its spots

In the *Just-So Stories*, written in 1902, an English writer called Rudyard Kipling tells the funny story about how the African animals got their stripes and spots. He claims the five-spot patterns on a leopard's coat are the marks of fingerprints from the hand of a hunter.

Hyenas

Packs of hyenas live in Africa and Asia. They can hunt for themselves, but mostly live on dead animals, or carrion. They scavenge the scraps and bones when lions or other creatures make a kill.

Plant-eating mammals

Animals that can digest plants such as grass or leaves are called herbivores. They include mammals such as horses, cows, goats, deer, antelope and camels. Animals that get all their energy from plants need to graze most of the time.

▼ The African elephant eats grasses, leaves, fruit and branches. It uses its trunk for smelling, carrying food or water to its mouth, spraying water and lifting objects.

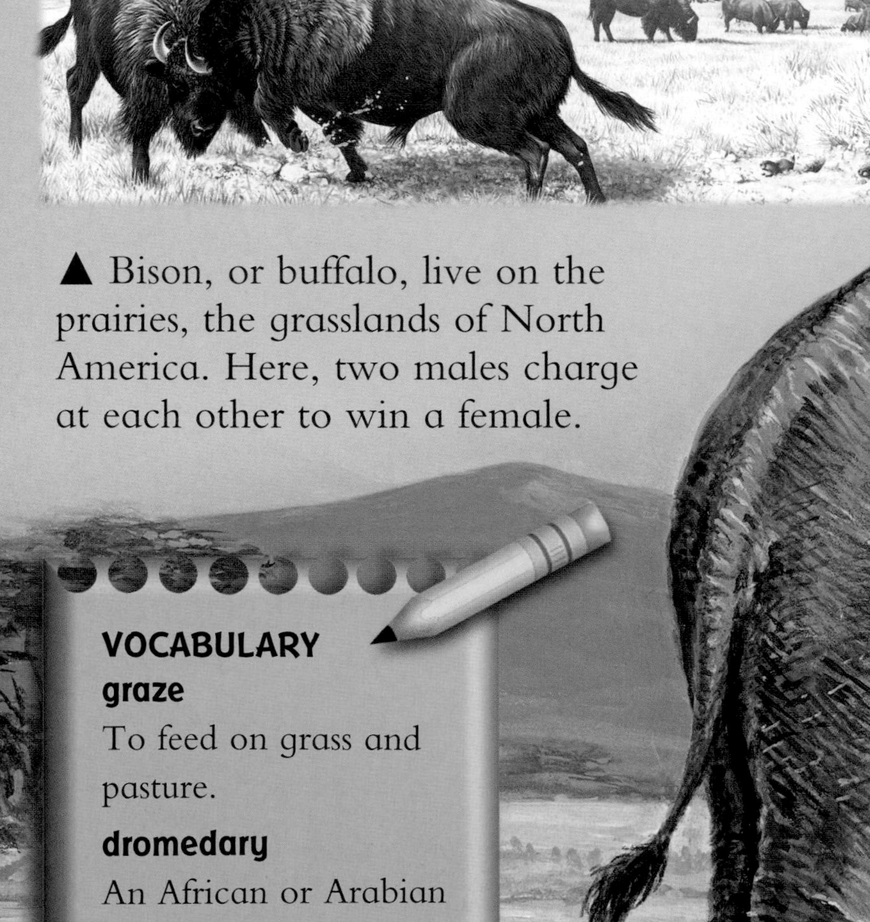

▲ Bison, or buffalo, live on the prairies, the grasslands of North America. Here, two males charge at each other to win a female.

VOCABULARY

graze
To feed on grass and pasture.

dromedary
An African or Arabian camel that has a single hump. The rare Bactrian camel from Asia has two humps.

▶ The giraffe eats various twigs and leaves. Its long neck allows it to feed on high branches that smaller animals cannot reach. Its mouth is protected from sharp thorns.

▶ The Arabian camel, or dromedary, lives in hot deserts, eating any leaves or bushes it can find. It can travel for long distances without water. Its hump is a store of fat that it converts into food.

CREATIVE CORNER

Nature detective

Look out for signs of different animals feeding in parks and the countryside. Acorns, nuts and pine cones may have been gnawed by squirrels. Bark may have been stripped from trees by deer. Short grass may have been grazed by cattle, sheep or rabbits.

WHY DO ELEPHANTS HAVE TUSKS?

Tusks are special teeth. They can be used for digging, tearing bark from trees or for attacking an enemy.

INTERNET LINKS: www.kidsplanet.org/factsheets/elephant.html • http://kidstu.fatcow.com/links/giraffelinks.htm

Marsupials

Marsupials are a group of animals found in Australia and the Americas. They include kangaroos, Tasmanian devils, wallabies, bandicoots, koalas, wombats, Australian possums and American opossums. When a marsupial baby is still tiny, it climbs into its mother's pouch and grows there.

▲ There are more than 60 species of possum living in Australia and the islands of New Guinea and Sulawesi. These marsupials are tree creatures which come out at night.

WHO PLAYS POSSUM?

'Playing possum' means pretending to be dead. Opossums in North America go limp when in danger, so that attackers leave them alone.

▼ Koalas are marsupials that look like small bears. After a koala leaves the pouch it may be carried on its mother's back. Koalas feed on eucalyptus leaves.

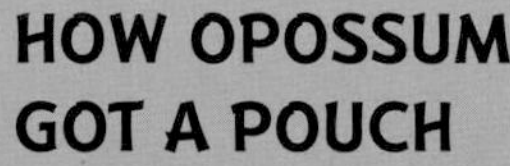

HOW OPOSSUM GOT A POUCH

An old native American tale tells how Big Bat kidnapped Opossum's babies. Terrapin rescued them and made a special pouch for Opossum to keep her babies in so that nobody could ever steal them again.

Bats

There are more than 1,000 species of bats in the world. Bats are flying mammals that come out to feed at dusk. Most bats eat insects, but some eat fruit, nectar or fish. A few suck blood from birds or cattle. By day bats roost in caves, trees or buildings.

▲ Some large fruit-eating bats are called flying foxes. Only a few of this species survive. They live on Rodrigues Island in the Indian Ocean.

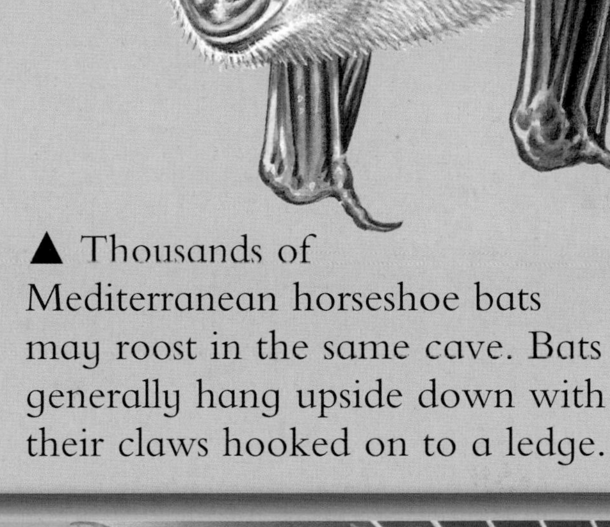

▲ Thousands of Mediterranean horseshoe bats may roost in the same cave. Bats generally hang upside down with their claws hooked on to a ledge.

How bats find their prey

Bats give out a high-pitched sound as they fly. If the sound meets another object such as a moth, an echo bounces back to the bat. This helps them find prey in the dark.

Sea mammals

The world's oceans are full of fish and other tasty sea creatures. Many mammals have taken to living in or around the sea in order to catch them. They include seals, sealions, walruses, whales, dolphins and porpoises, manatees and polar bears.

▼ Walruses live in the far northern waters of the world. They are big, heavy mammals. Walruses have tusks that are up to a metre long. They use the tusks to scrape clams to eat from the ocean floor.

Jonah and the whale
During a storm at sea, Jonah was thrown overboard and swallowed by a whale. He lived inside the whale for three days before being spat out onto dry land.

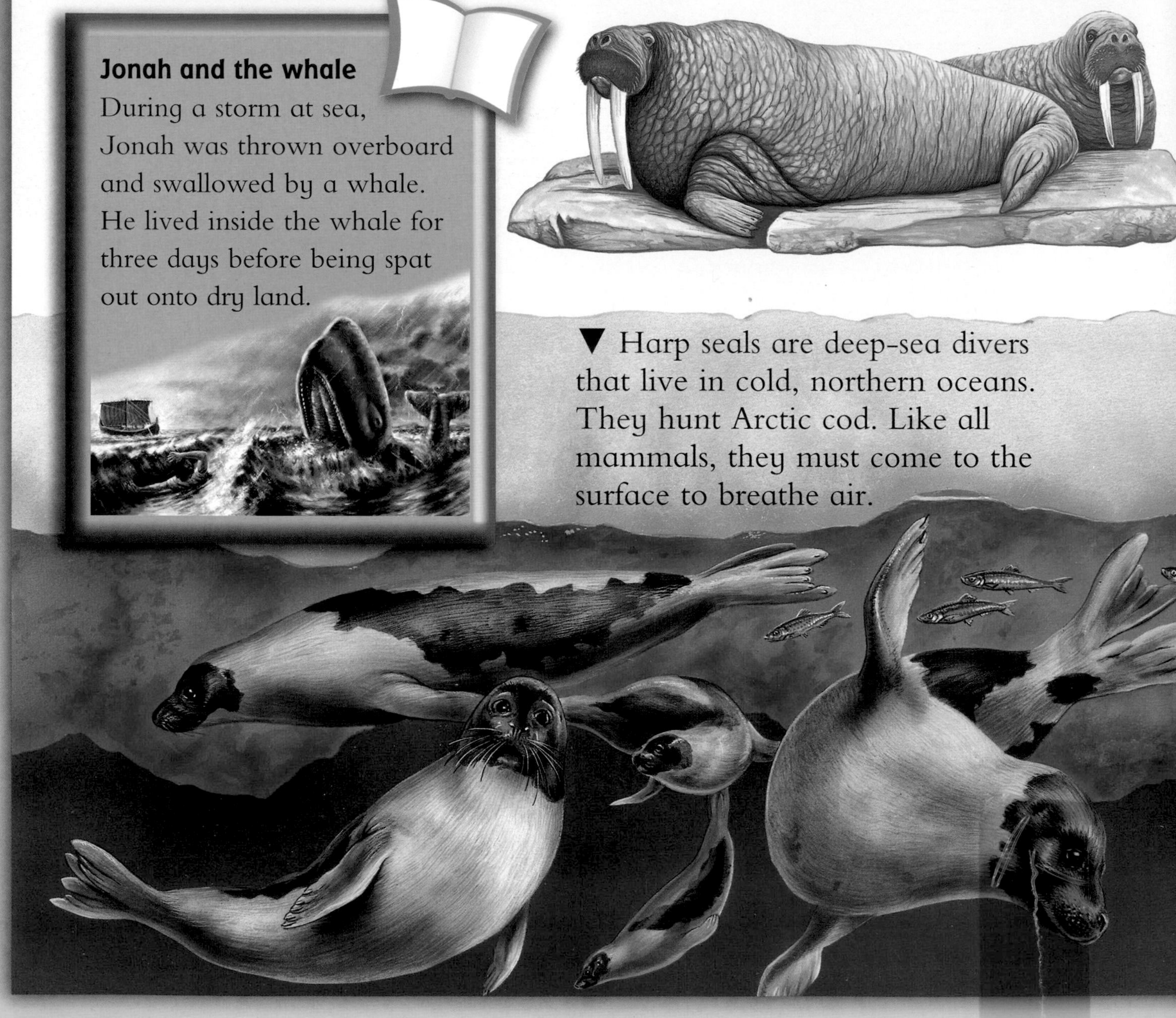

▼ Harp seals are deep-sea divers that live in cold, northern oceans. They hunt Arctic cod. Like all mammals, they must come to the surface to breathe air.

CAN YOU FIND?

1. tusks
2. teeth
3. flippers
4. tails
5. mammals with blubber

▲ Polar bears live in the Arctic. They cross the ice to hunt seals, fish and birds. They are very strong swimmers.

► Whales and ocean dolphins such as the killer whale look like huge fish, but they are mammals. Some whales filter tiny creatures from the ocean as they swim along. Others have sharp teeth for attacking fish or seals.

Apes and monkeys

Monkeys and apes are the closest relatives of human beings. We all belong to an intelligent group of mammals called primates. Apes have no tails and sometimes walk upright. Monkeys usually live in trees, and can swing through the branches using their long arms and tails.

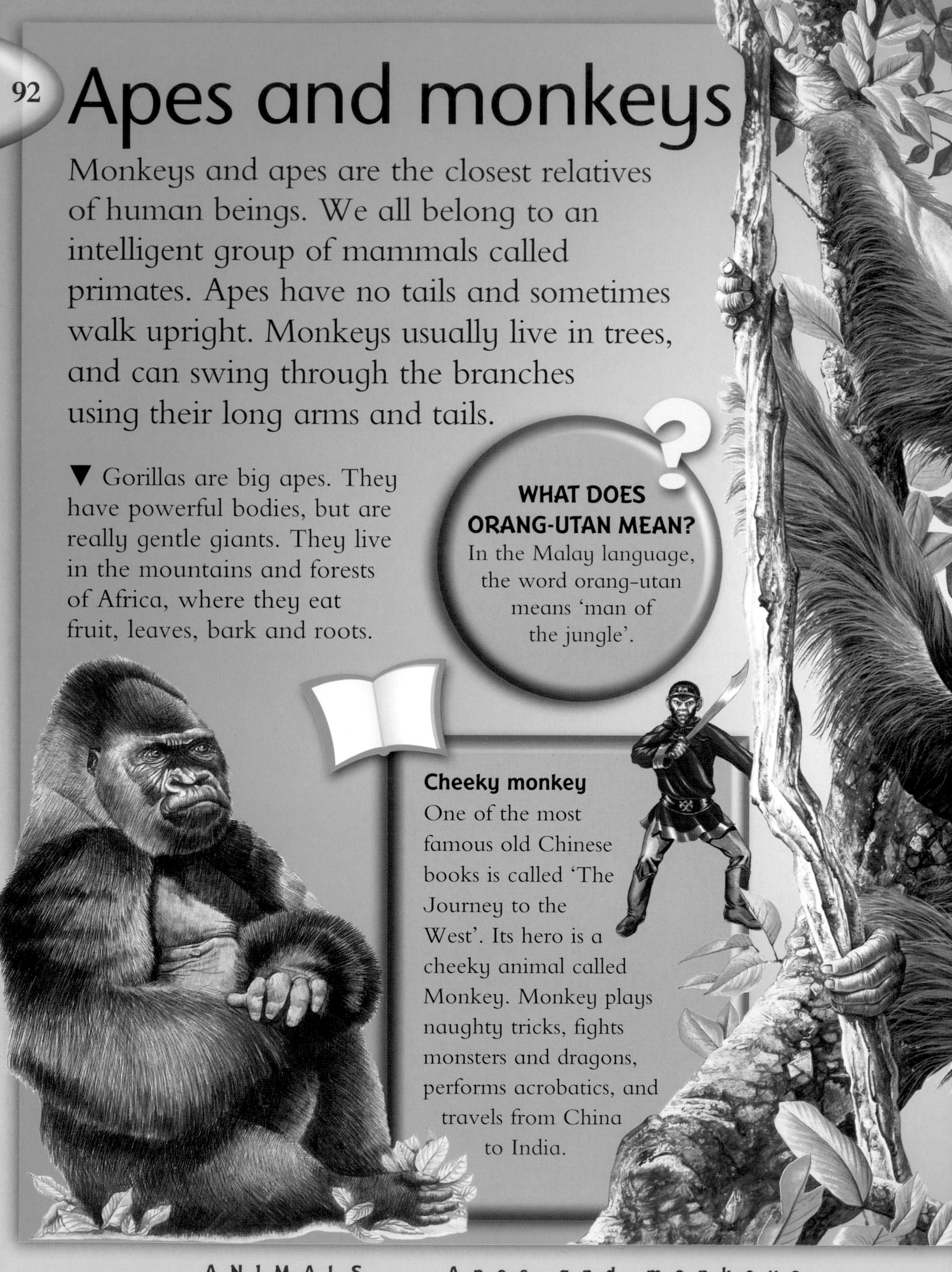

▼ Gorillas are big apes. They have powerful bodies, but are really gentle giants. They live in the mountains and forests of Africa, where they eat fruit, leaves, bark and roots.

WHAT DOES ORANG-UTAN MEAN?
In the Malay language, the word orang-utan means 'man of the jungle'.

Cheeky monkey
One of the most famous old Chinese books is called 'The Journey to the West'. Its hero is a cheeky animal called Monkey. Monkey plays naughty tricks, fights monsters and dragons, performs acrobatics, and travels from China to India.

▼ Orang-utans are apes that live in southeast Asia. They build nests in the tree tops and eat fruit, birds' eggs and honeycombs. Sadly, many of their forests are being cut down.

▲ Nine species of howler monkey live in the rainforests of Central and South America. Their tails help them cling to branches. Howlers are large monkeys and can roar very loudly.

Using tools

A chimpanzee, watched by its baby, uses a stick to poke termites out of their mound. This clever ape has learned to use a tool in its search for food. Chimpanzees live in large groups in African forests.

Animals in danger

The world is filled with more and more people. They build new towns and roads. They cut down forests or drain swamps where animals live. Land, water and air are poisoned. Many animals find it hard to survive these changes. Some are even in danger of becoming extinct.

▲ Animals that have very little land to live on are at risk. The Komodo dragon is the world's biggest lizard. It lives on just a few tiny islands in Indonesia.

▲ Queen Alexandra's birdwing is the world's biggest butterfly. It is only found in one strip of forest in Papua New Guinea. Parts of this are being cut down.

Rhinos and unicorns

Five species of rhinoceros live in Asia and Africa. All are in danger of dying out because they are hunted for their horns. In the Middle Ages, the rhino's strange horn inspired all sorts of tales about unicorns.

VOCABULARY

conservation
Protecting animals and looking after where they live.

habitat
The type of land in which an animal naturally lives, such as forest or desert.

▶ The beautiful quetzal lives in Central America. For years, it was hunted for its feathers. Now, the forests where it lives are being cleared by poor farmers to grow crops.

◀ Bengal tigers live in India. They are protected animals, but hunters still kill them. They are also losing their habitat. There may be only about 4,500 left in the wild.

◀ The giant panda is very rare. It lives in the misty bamboo forests of China. These are being cut back as villages grow. The panda is an international symbol of animal conservation.

CREATIVE CORNER

Design a poster

Make a colourful poster to let people know about an animal or a habitat that is under threat. It might show a tiger or a panda, or perhaps animals from a local wood that is due to be cut down.

Now you know!

▲ Butterflies are insects. They have wings and six legs.

▲ Spiders have eight legs. Their bodies can produce silky thread to make webs.

▲ Swallows migrate each year. They fly thousands of kilometres from one continent to another.

▲ Frogs are amphibians. They spend their lives in water and on land.

▲ Most fish can breathe under water. They do this using gills, which are openings on the sides of their head.

▲ Snails are molluscs. They have soft bodies that are protected by the hard shells on their backs.

◄ A baby kangaroo is called a joey. When it is first born, it climbs up into its mother's pouch.

▲ Snakes are reptiles. They bask in the sun to get warm.

Dinosaurs

What were dinosaurs? When did they live? The prehistoric world is a fascinating subject. Experts are gradually putting together a good picture of what our world was like millions of years ago when dinosaurs roamed the Earth.

What are dinosaurs?

Dinosaurs were reptiles that lived on the Earth long before humans ever appeared. These reptiles dominated life on the land for more than 150 million years, before dying out about 65 million years ago. There were many different kinds of dinosaur. They lived at different periods of time and on every continent of the world.

◀ Like other fossils, those of dinosaurs are often found in cliffs or rock faces, where the surface of the rock has worn away to expose the layers below.

▲ When footprints or other marks left by dinosaurs are preserved as fossils, they are called trace fossils. These can tell us about dinosaur behaviour.

▲ 1. When a dinosaur died, its soft parts rotted away. Some dinosaur bones sank into mud and, over thousands of years, turned into rock.

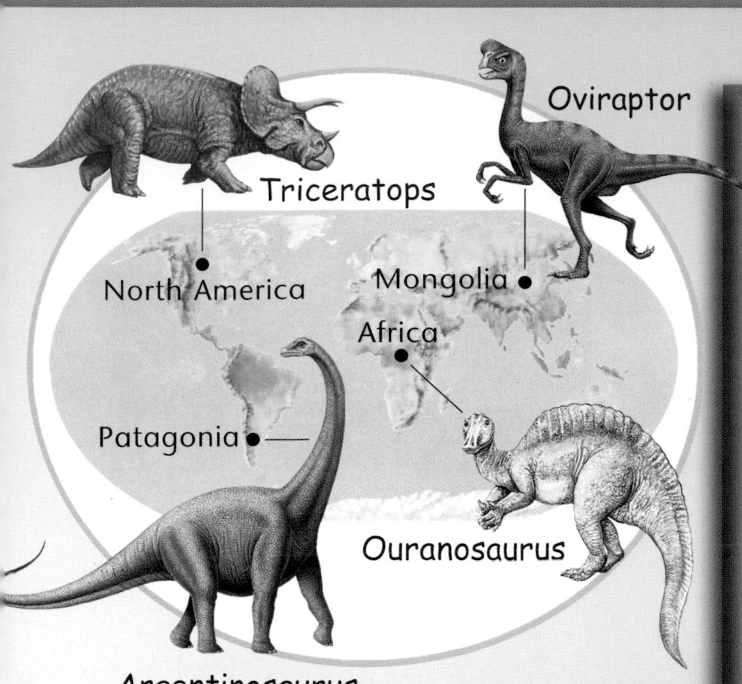

▲ Dinosaur fossils have been found all over the world. There have been recent large finds in the areas marked on the map. These mean that experts now know important information about the dinosaurs found there.

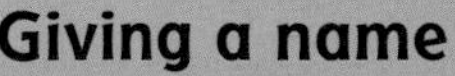

Giving a name

The word 'dinosaur' means 'terrible lizard'. It was first given to these ancient creatures in 1842 by an English palaeontologist, or fossil expert, called Richard Owen. He wanted the name to reflect the awesome size of many of the large dinosaurs.

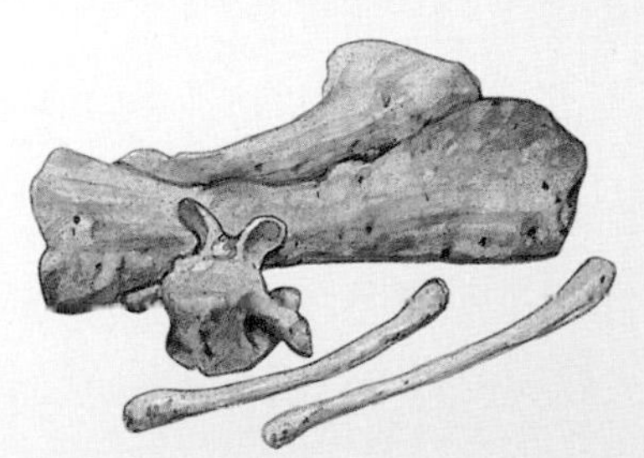

◀ Fossils are not usually complete skeletons. Sometimes only a few bones are found, and scientists have to guess what the rest of the animal might have looked like.

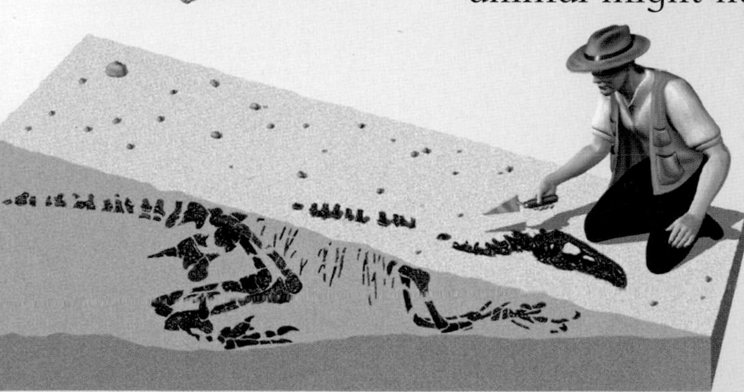

▲ 2. Millions of years later, scientists find the fossil skeleton. They carefully dig it out from the ground and try to work out what the animal looked like when it was alive.

▲ In order to show people what dinosaurs looked like, many museums reconstruct entire skeletons. The leg bones of this plant-eater give an idea of how massive the entire animal would have been.

Dinosaur timeline

The time when the dinosaurs lived is called the Mesozoic Era. It was the period between two major events in which many animals became extinct, or died out. During the Mesozoic Era, Earth was very warm, which helped new animal types to develop.

Be there dragons?
Dragons feature in the folklore of many countries, often as symbols of power. They were probably made up by early people to explain the large fossil bones of dinosaurs they found.

Dinosaur timeline

Triassic ▲ 
245 million years ago

Jurassic ▲ 
208 million years ago

Cretaceous ▲
144 million years ago

Triassic

▼ The early dinosaurs in the Triassic were small. However, in the Late Triassic there were some large plant-eaters, such as Plateosaurus.

Early dinosaurs
Coelophysis was a small dinosaur with hollow bones. It was a quick-moving hunter and meat-eater that lived in the Late Triassic. It is one of the earliest known dinosaurs.

Jurassic

▼ In the Late Jurassic, Allosaurus was the largest meat-eating dinosaur in North America. The first birds and modern mammals also developed during this period.

Insect-eaters

Compsognathus (above) was a small chicken-sized dinosaur that lived in Europe in the late Jurassic. It probably ate insects and small lizards.

Cretaceous

▼ New groups of dinosaurs appeared in the Cretaceous. Struthiomimus ('ostrich mimic') had long legs for running away.

Ready for attack

Tyrannosaurs lived at this time and many plant-eaters had to defend themselves from attack. Ankylosaurs (below) could not run easily, so relied on a well-armoured body, with its bony plates or spikes.

Types of dinosaur

Some 300 kinds of dinosaur lived in many different parts of the world, from 230 million years ago until they died out 65 million years ago. Dinosaurs were reptiles and they were all shapes and sizes. Today's reptiles include lizards, snakes, crocodiles and tortoises. Like most other reptiles, dinosaurs lived on land and laid eggs.

► Some dinosaurs were as tall as houses, while some were as small as chickens. The carnivores (meat-eaters) among them would either hunt their prey or eat dead animals that they found. Other dinosaurs were herbivores (plant-eaters), that browsed on trees and other plants.

Apatosaurus (plant-eater)

Spinosaurus (meat-eater)

Styracosaurus (plant-eater)

Panoplosaurus (plant-eater)

Oviraptor (meat-eater)

Stygimoloc (plant-eat

CAN YOU FIND?

1. scales
2. spines
3. horns
4. tail
5. jaws
6. teeth

VOCABULARY

reptile
A cold-blooded, scaly, four-legged animal that lays its eggs on land.

skeleton
The framework of bones that holds up the body of an animal.

Saurischian Tyrannosaurus skeleton

Ornithischian Stegosaurus skeleton

▲ Scientists divide dinosaurs into two main groups. The ornithischians, 'bird-hipped dinosaurs' (above) have hips similar to modern-day birds. The saurischians, 'lizard-hipped dinosaurs' (top) have hips similar to modern-day lizards.

Modern-day dinosaurs?
The thorny devil lizard lives in Australia today. It has cone-shaped spines all over its body to protect it from predators. There are similar spines on some of the dinosaurs on this page.

Finding fossils

When the fossil of a dinosaur is found, a team of experts and scientists get together. They excavate it, or dig it out of the ground, very carefully. The fossilized parts of a skeleton are taken away for scientists to examine.

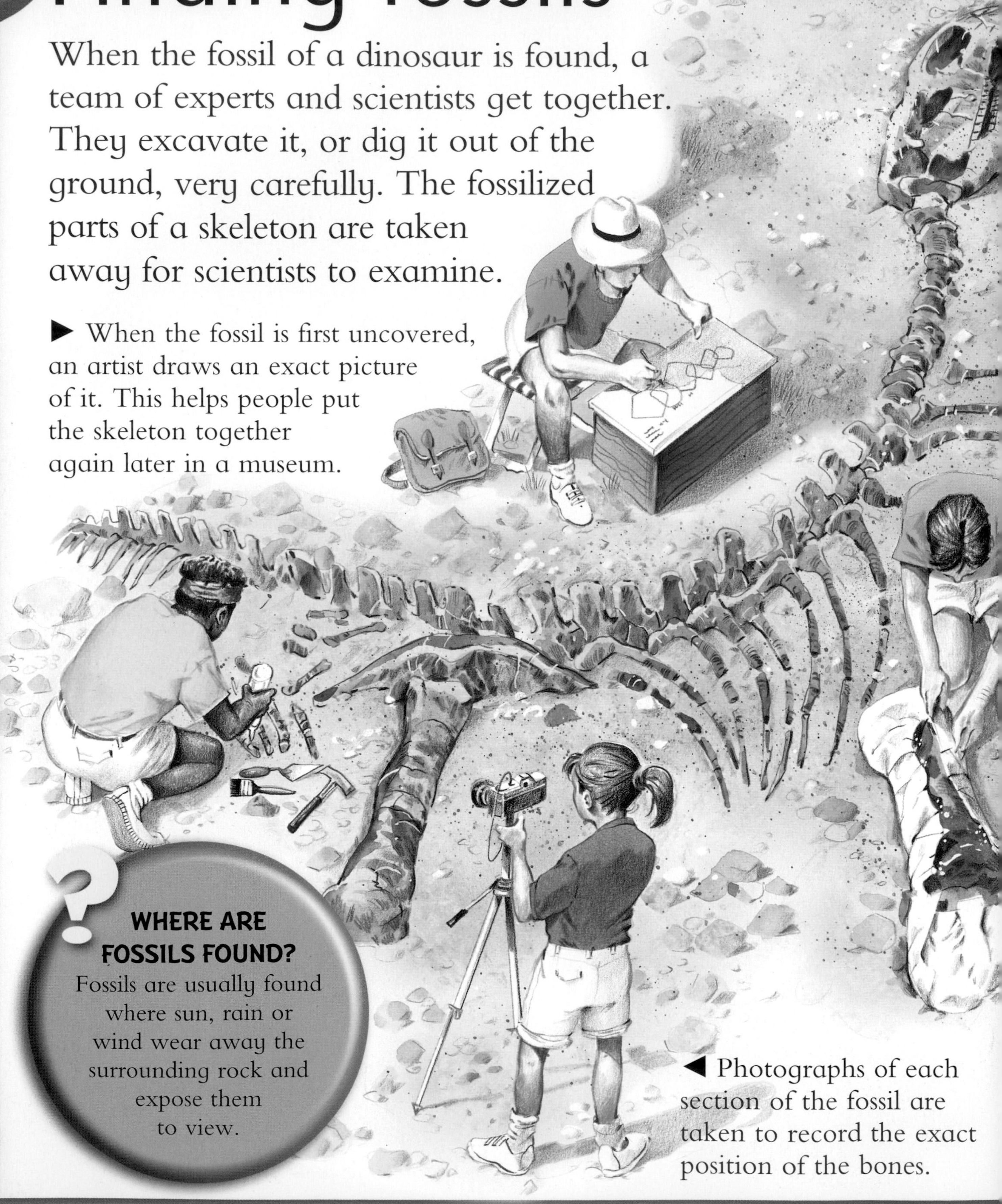

► When the fossil is first uncovered, an artist draws an exact picture of it. This helps people put the skeleton together again later in a museum.

? **WHERE ARE FOSSILS FOUND?**
Fossils are usually found where sun, rain or wind wear away the surrounding rock and expose them to view.

◄ Photographs of each section of the fossil are taken to record the exact position of the bones.

◀ Fossils are very delicate. The surrounding soil must be removed carefully so as not to damage them. This person is using a soft brush to gently sweep the soil away from the bones.

◀ Once the bones are removed from the ground, they are wrapped very carefully in plaster of Paris, to protect them while they are loaded into a truck and transported, usually over very bumpy ground.

CAN YOU FIND?

1. a camera
2. tail bones
3. a hammer
4. skull bones
5. the spine
6. an artist

CREATIVE CORNER

Make a fossil of a twig

Press a twig into a small piece of modelling clay. Brush a little oil onto the clay, then mix some plaster of Paris and pour it into the shape of the twig. When the plaster is dry, gently remove the clay from your fossil twig.

INTERNET LINKS: www.bbc.co.uk/sn/prehistoric_life/dinosaurs/making_fossils/

Meat-eating dinosaurs

The meat-eating dinosaurs, the carnosaurs, were ferocious. They used their sharp teeth and claws to catch their prey. Some, such as Avimimus, were fast runners and chased after their prey. Others, such as Allosaurus, probably hunted by hiding until a prey animal came past.

◄ Tyrannosaurus had thick, curved teeth. We know that its prey included the horned dinosaur, Triceratops, because the saw-like edges at the back and front left distinctive marks on the bones.

A meaty diet

When a dinosaur, or other animal, is described as a carnivore, it simply means that it ate the flesh of other animals. Some carnivorous dinosaurs hunted and killed prey for themselves. Some fed on prey killed by other predators, or animals that had died a natural death. Many dinosaurs survived on whatever was available. They ate other dinosaurs, fish, and the eggs of birds or other dinosaurs.

► The tyrannosaurs, or 'tyrant lizards', were among the largest meat-eaters. This one is attacking a Corythosaurus, or 'helmet lizard'.

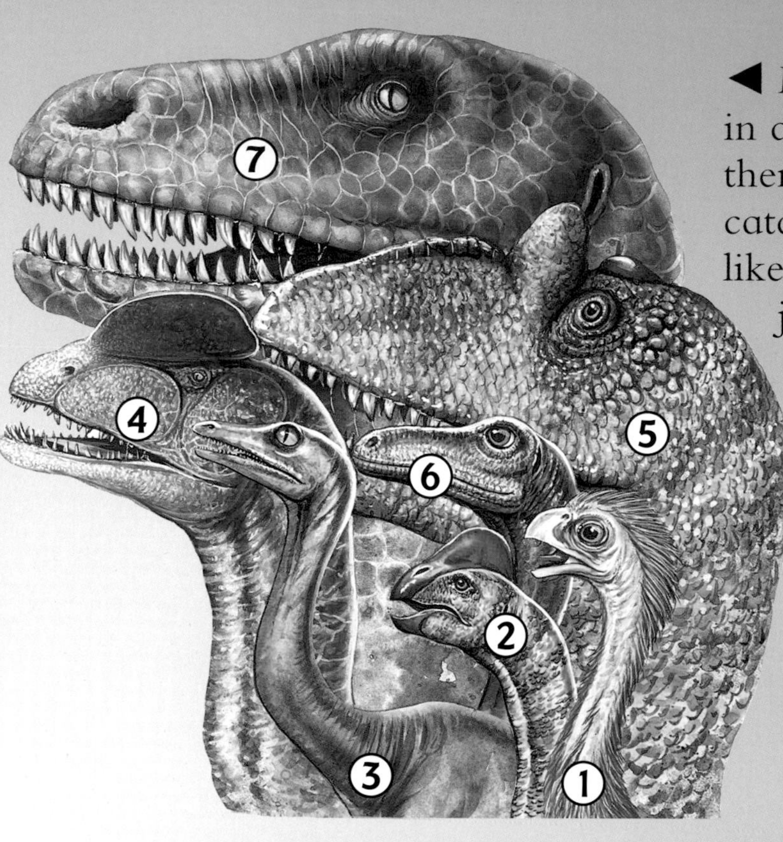

◀ Meat-eating dinosaurs came in all shapes and sizes. Each of them was specially adapted for catching and eating prey. Most, like carnivores today, had strong jaws, sharp teeth and claws.

1. Avimimus 2. Oviraptor 3. Struthiomimus
4. Dilophosaurus 5. Allosaurus
6. Troodon 7. Tyrannosaurus

VOCABULARY

prey
An animal that other, often larger, animals hunt and eat.

predator
An animal that hunts and eats other animals as prey.

WHAT WERE HORNS FOR?

Horns may have helped protect plant-eaters, like this Triceratops (below), from predators.

CREATIVE CORNER

Make a carnosaur tooth

Shape a carnosaur tooth out of bakeable modelling clay, using the tooth on p.106 as a model. Ask an adult to bake the clay for you. Then paint it to look just like a real carnosaur tooth!

Dinosaur weapons

Many dinosaurs were equipped with natural weapons – their teeth, horns and claws. Some used these to attack other animals when hunting for food or fighting for territory. Some used them purely to defend themselves or their young. Many dinosaurs relied on them for both attack and defence.

HOW DID THEY HUNT?

There is evidence that some dinosaurs, such as Deinonychus, hunted in packs. Others, such as Tyrannosaurus, may have hunted alone.

► Some dinosaurs, like these Oviraptors, ate the eggs of other dinosaurs, when they could find them. Long claws were useful for hooking them out of nests.

CAN YOU FIND?
1. thumb claw
2. sickle-shaped claws
3. long snout
4. egg stealer
5. prey
6. predator

▲ Allosaurus was one of the most successful predators. Its sharp, pointed teeth and strong jaws were perfectly suited for tearing meat and crushing bones.

◀ Deinonychus probably hunted in packs. Its name means 'terrible claw', and it had ferocious claws on both front and rear limbs, including a huge, sickle-like claw on its second toe.

▶ Baryonyx may have used its large thumb claws to hook fish out of the water to catch in its long snout.

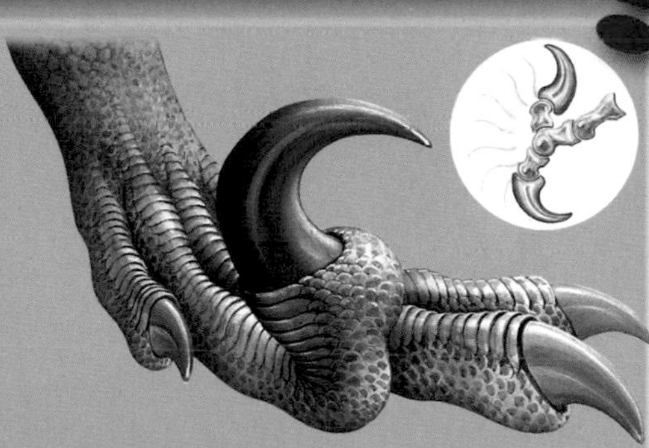

Deadly claws

The claws on Deinonychus' second toes were upward-turned and curved. They were weapons of pure destruction. Experts are not sure whether it would have used them for stabbing or slashing prey.

CREATIVE CORNER

Make a moving dinosaur jaw

Cut two long strips of card and snip tooth shapes. Now punch holes in both ends of the strips. Push a pencil through, bending the card. Wind elastic bands around the pencil to keep the card in place.

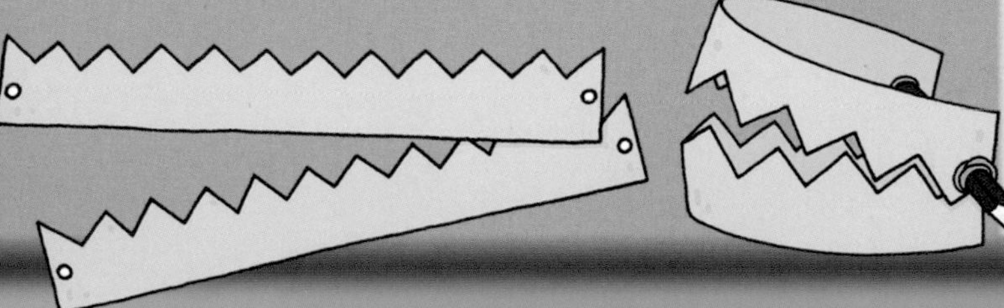

Fiercest of all

The tyrannosaurs were the fiercest of all the predators. They were also among the largest known meat-eating land animals of all time. Some scientists believe that smaller tyrannosaurs could run and catch plant-eaters larger than themselves.

► Tyrannosaurus Rex stood over 8 metres tall. It ate dead dinosaurs that it found, and followed herds of plant-eaters, attacking any old, sick or young animals that became separated from the rest.

WHAT DID THEY LOOK LIKE?
We do not know what colour dinosaurs were, but experts usually assume that they blended into their natural habitat.

Basking lizard
Modern reptiles, such as this lizard, are cold-blooded. They need to bask in the sun to get warm. For a long time, scientists believed dinosaurs were cold-blooded. Now they think that some were warm-blooded – able to generate their own heat, like modern birds and mammals.

► The family of tyrannosaurs belonged to a group of dinosaurs called theropods. Theropods walked on two feet and had three toes on each foot.

► Little is known about dinosaur skin, as it is not usually preserved. This fossil of a Carnotaurus shows that it had scaly skin, so it is possible that Tyrannosaurus also had scales like this.

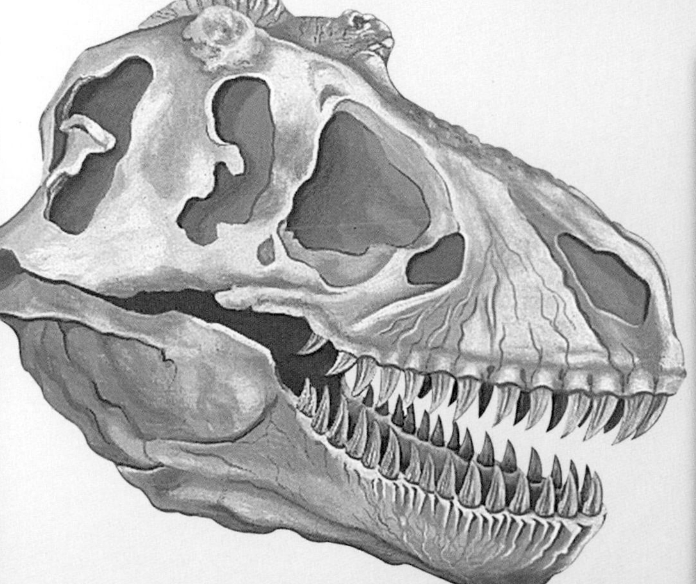

▲ A Tyrannosaurus' skull was half as long as its body. It must have had very strong neck muscles to support its weight. The teeth were curved and very sharp. It used them to tear chunks of meat off to eat.

CREATIVE CORNER

Dinosaur hunting game

Each player has two counters. The first player moves one of his counters to the empty central spot. Taking turns, the players continue to move one counter at a time to an empty spot, until one player can no longer move.

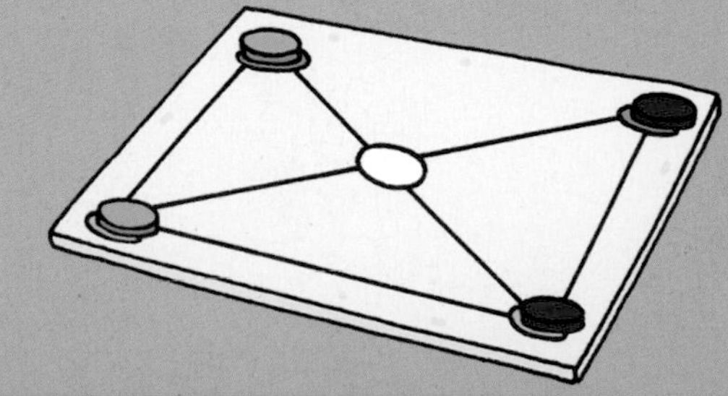

Plant-eating dinosaurs

The herbivores, or plant-eating, dinosaurs, were often much larger than the carnivores, or meat-eating, dinosaurs. However, they were usually slower, which meant that the meat-eaters could hunt them. Many plant-eaters had long necks so they could reach up to the leaves on tall plants and trees.

WHY DID THEY EAT PLANTS?
Plants get energy from the sun, and store it. Plant-eating dinosaurs ate the plants to give themselves energy.

▼ The largest dinosaurs were the plant-eaters. If it stood on its hind legs, this Barosaurus could lift its enormous head up as high as 15 metres in the air to feed off the tops of the trees.

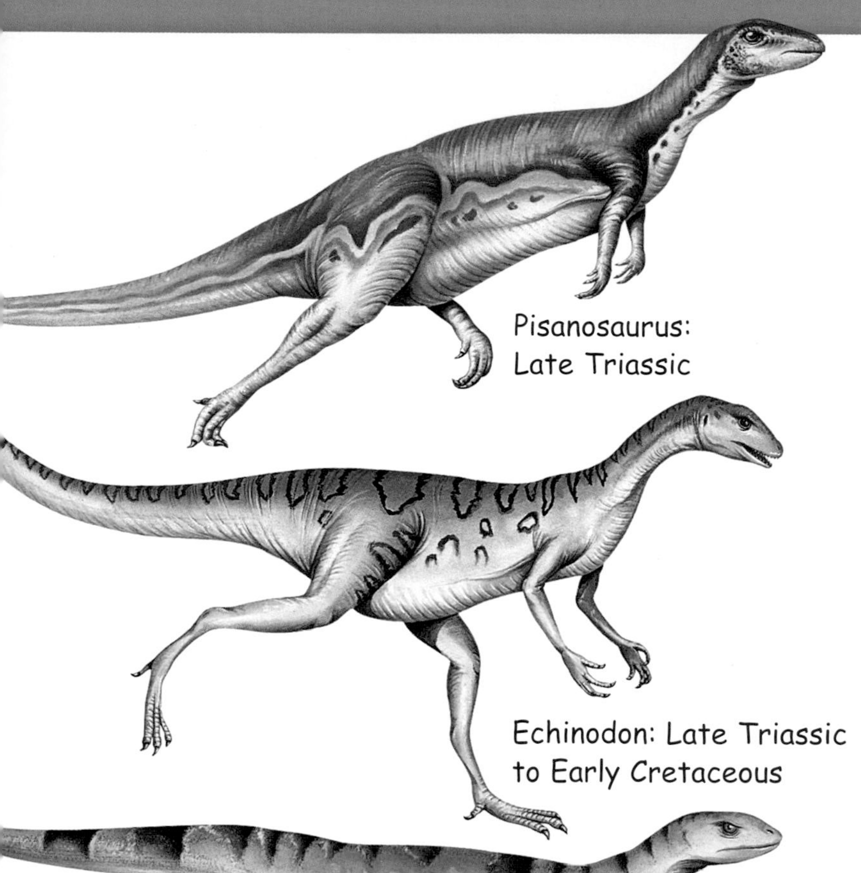

Lesothosaurus:
Late Triassic to
Early Jurassic

▲ There were many different species in the family of ornithischians, or bird-hipped dinosaurs. They were all herbivores.

VOCABULARY

species
A group of animals that can breed with one another, but not with other species.

ginkgo
A medium-sized tree that developed about 270 million years ago.

▲ Edmontosaurus was a large, plant-eating dinosaur that lived during the Late Cretaceous. It was about 13 metres long. Its skull (above) shows that it had many small teeth, for grinding up plant food.

Plants the dinosaurs ate

When dinosaurs lived on Earth, the plants were very different from today's. Early plants were ferns (like this horsetail), ginkgos and conifers. Flowering plants and seeds did not develop until the Cretaceous period.

Dinosaur giants

Among the first plant-eating dinosaurs, and the first land animals tall enough to feed on trees, were the prosauropods, such as Plateosaurus. Prosauropods lived all over the world, and there were more of them than any other large land animal. They were replaced by the sauropods, the true giants of the dinosaur world.

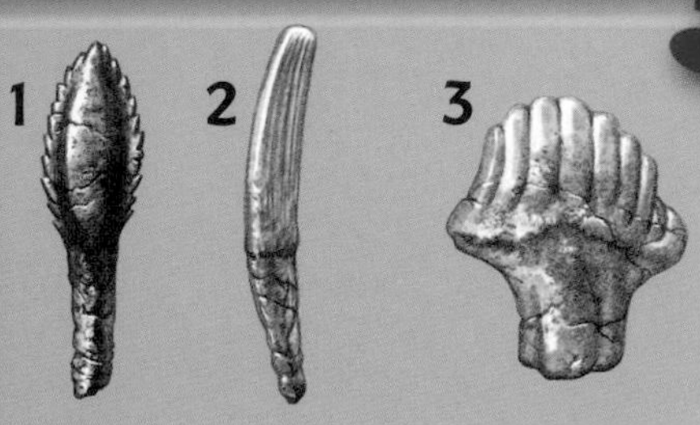

Dinosaur teeth
Plateosaurus' sharp, leaf-like teeth (1), and Diplodocus' pencil-shaped teeth (2) would have been good for stripping plants. Stegosaurus' blunt, ridged teeth (3) could nip off leaves and probably chew them too.

▼ Seismosaurus was a diplodocid. This family of dinosaurs had incredibly long necks and tails. A Seismosaurus reached up to 11 metres tall.

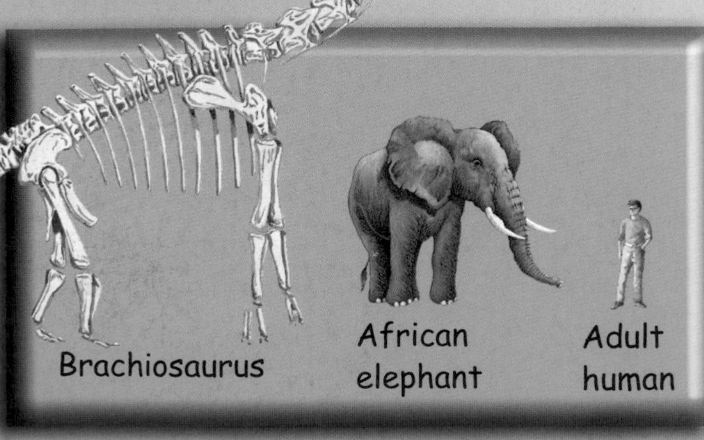

▲ Supersaurus may have been up to 35 metres in length. The name means 'super lizard' and the dinosaur was probably the largest of the diplodocid family.

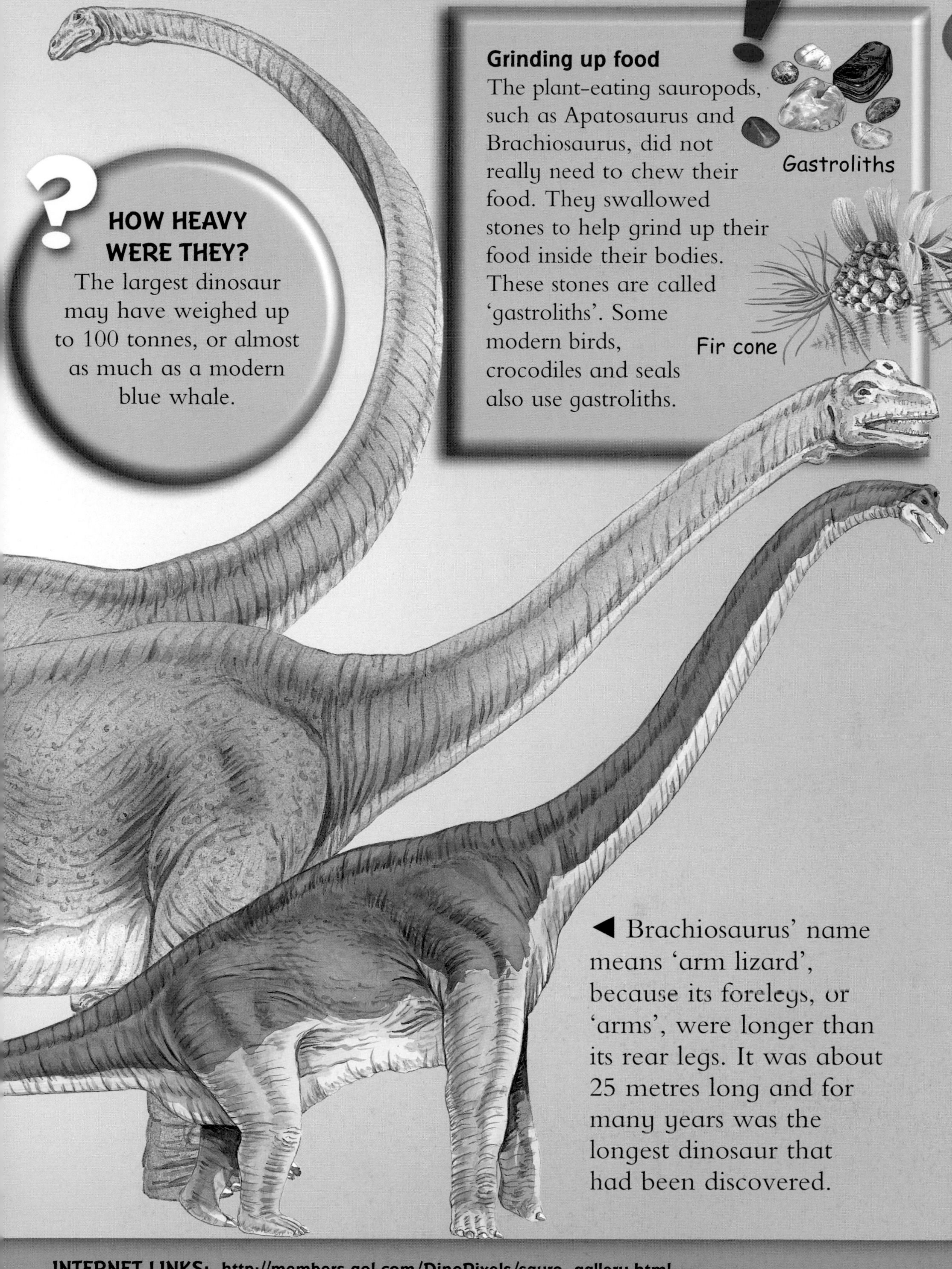

HOW HEAVY WERE THEY?

The largest dinosaur may have weighed up to 100 tonnes, or almost as much as a modern blue whale.

Grinding up food

The plant-eating sauropods, such as Apatosaurus and Brachiosaurus, did not really need to chew their food. They swallowed stones to help grind up their food inside their bodies. These stones are called 'gastroliths'. Some modern birds, crocodiles and seals also use gastroliths.

Gastroliths

Fir cone

◀ Brachiosaurus' name means 'arm lizard', because its forelegs, or 'arms', were longer than its rear legs. It was about 25 metres long and for many years was the longest dinosaur that had been discovered.

Self-defence

Like modern animals, dinosaurs had to defend themselves. Many of them were preyed on by meat-eating dinosaurs. The adults needed to protect their young from attack, and males would sometimes have fought over territory or females.

▲ Pachycephalosaurs had thickened bones on the top of their skulls. They probably fought each other by butting heads.

VOCABULARY

hide
The pelt or skin of one of the larger animals.

territory
An area in which an animal lives and may protect from others of its kind.

Bony plate on back

Spike on tail

► The bony plates on Stegosaurus' back look tough, but they were made of thin bone and probably did not protect the animal well. However, Stegosaurus had a very thick hide, and a ferociously spiked tail that it could swing at an attacker.

Protective tails

Ankylosaurus (1) had a lump of thickened bone on the end of its tail, like a club. Stegosaurus' (2) bony spikes were covered in horn. Some experts believe that Diplodocus (3) used its long, whip-like tail in self-defence.

► The name Triceratops means 'three-horned face'. The plant-eater may have used its horns in self-defence, but experts now believe that it used them mainly in display, much like modern reindeer.

CREATIVE CORNER

Matching animals

Some of today's animals have defensive weapons that are similar to those of dinosaurs. See if you can find and copy pictures of modern animals with similar means of defence, such as horns, tusks or scales.

Dinosaur babies

Dinosaurs reproduced by laying eggs. These protected the young dinosaur inside, and provided it with food while it grew. It is difficult to say whether dinosaurs were caring parents, but there is evidence that some looked after their eggs and young.

◀ Oviraptors laid their eggs and then covered them with sand. By sitting on top, the parent's body warmth would have kept the eggs warm at night.

Egg stealer?

The first Oviraptor discovered was sitting on top of a nest of eggs. The scientists thought it had been killed trying to steal another dinosaur's eggs – its name means 'egg thief'. In fact, it had probably died trying to protect its own eggs, not stealing those of other dinosaurs!

VOCABULARY

reproduce
To produce babies, or young animals.

embryo
The form of a partly grown baby animal, like those found in eggs before they are hatched.

WHAT SHAPE WERE THE EGGS?

Dinosaur eggs were either round or oval, rather like a football or rugby ball. They also had hard, brittle shells.

◀ Maiasaura's name means 'good mother lizard'. Many Maiasaura nests have been found with the remains of adults, young, embryos and broken eggshells. This suggests that the adults looked after their eggs and young.

▲ Fossilized footprints suggest that Apatosaurus travelled in herds. The young were kept in the centre of the group for protection against predators.

▲ Some dinosaurs made nests like the fossilized one shown here, found in China. Others laid their eggs in a row, as if they laid them while they were walking along.

Reptiles of the seas

The word 'dinosaur' is sometimes wrongly used for other prehistoric creatures, such as pterosaurs, and various kinds of marine, or sea-living, reptiles. These animals were related to dinosaurs, but evolved as separate groups.

▲ Archelon's name means 'ancient turtle'. The largest turtle that ever lived, it was 4 metres long and 5 metres wide from flipper to flipper.

► Plesiosaurs were a large group of marine reptiles. There were two kinds of plesiosaur. One kind, such as Elasmosaurus, had long necks and large bodies. The other, such as Kronosaurus, had short necks, large heads and strong jaws.

Kronosaurus

The Loch Ness monster

In 1933, someone spotted what they thought was a large animal in Loch Ness, a lake in Scotland. The 'Loch Ness monster' is often said to look like a plesiosaur. But it is highly unlikely that an animal of this size would have gone unseen until the 20th century.

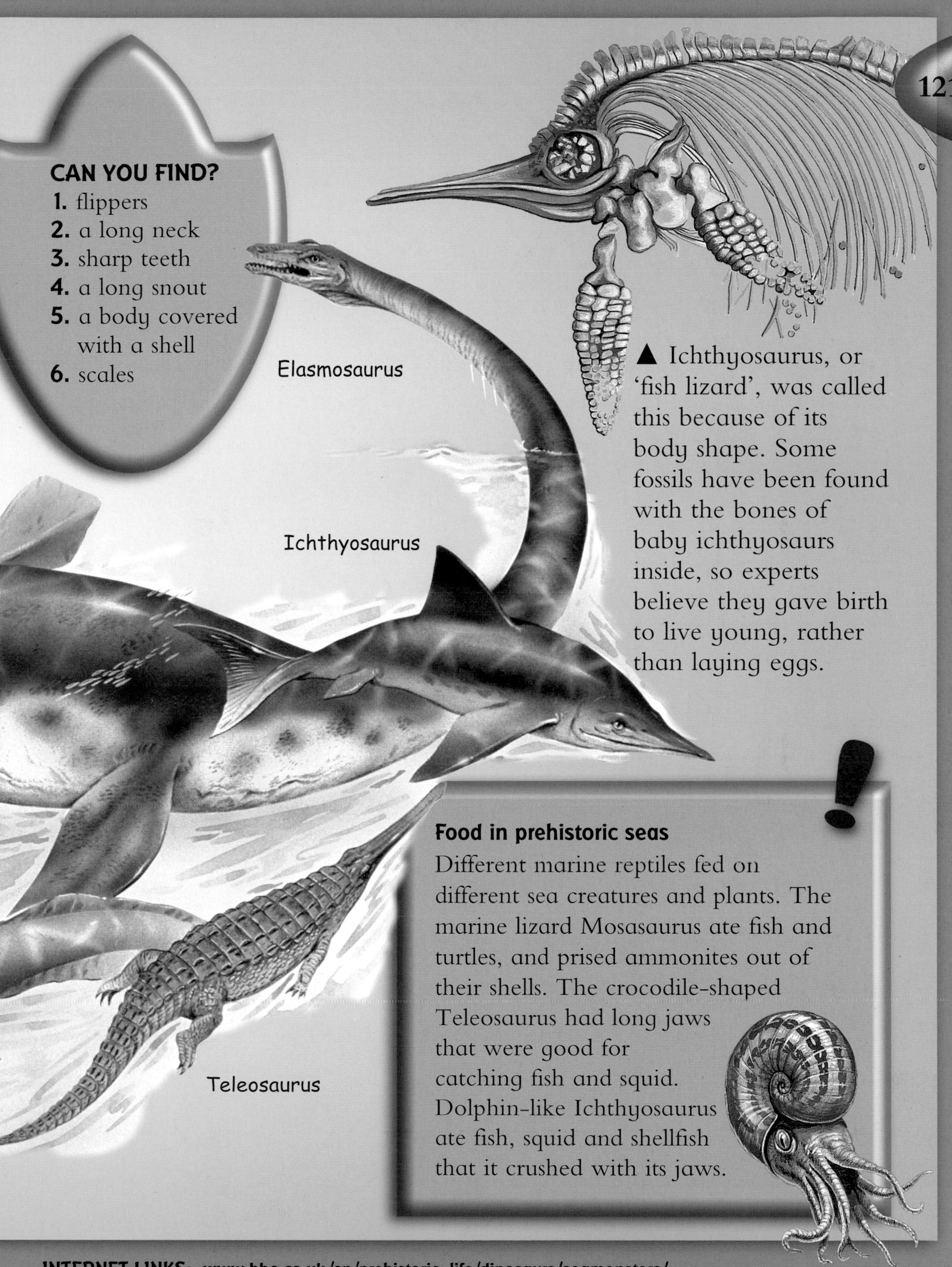

CAN YOU FIND?
1. flippers
2. a long neck
3. sharp teeth
4. a long snout
5. a body covered with a shell
6. scales

▲ Ichthyosaurus, or 'fish lizard', was called this because of its body shape. Some fossils have been found with the bones of baby ichthyosaurs inside, so experts believe they gave birth to live young, rather than laying eggs.

Food in prehistoric seas

Different marine reptiles fed on different sea creatures and plants. The marine lizard Mosasaurus ate fish and turtles, and prised ammonites out of their shells. The crocodile-shaped Teleosaurus had long jaws that were good for catching fish and squid. Dolphin-like Ichthyosaurus ate fish, squid and shellfish that it crushed with its jaws.

Reptiles of the air

The first pterosaurs, or flying reptiles, lived during the Triassic period. Their wings were made of skin that stretched from the fourth finger to the body and rear legs. Some may have had furry bodies. None of the early pterosaurs had a wingspan bigger than about 3 metres.

◀ A Pteranodon fossil was found with fish bones in the area of its throat. As a result, experts believe that at least part of its diet was fish. Unlike Rhamphorhynchus, it had a beak without teeth, like a modern bird.

Pterodaustro strained plankton from water through its bristle-like teeth.

◀ Pteranodon and Quetzalcoatlus were two pterosaurs that lived during the Late Cretaceous. They both ate fish and flew high in the sky, like modern-day albatrosses.

Dimorphodon used sharp teeth to eat insects, fish and reptiles.

▶ Different pterosaurs had different shaped bills, or beaks. The bill shape may have decided what they ate and how they found their food.

Dsungaripterus used the front of its bill to remove shellfish from rocks.

WERE THEY DINOSAURS?

People sometimes refer to pterosaurs as dinosaurs but, although they are probably related, they are not dinosaurs.

▼ Rhamphorhynchus was a pterosaur with a wingspan of nearly 2 metres. It lived during the Late Jurassic. It was a meat-eater, and the sharp teeth in its long jaws were very useful for snatching slippery fish.

CREATIVE CORNER

Pteranodon kite

Use drinking straws and sticky tape to make a diamond-shaped frame. Cut a piece of paper slightly larger than the diamond and draw a Pteranodon on it. Tape to the frames. Tie a long piece of string to the centre.

The first birds

Scientists are almost certain that our modern birds evolved from dinosaurs. It is believed that the ancestors of birds were the small theropods such as Compsognathus. Archaeopteryx is the oldest bird to have been discovered so far.

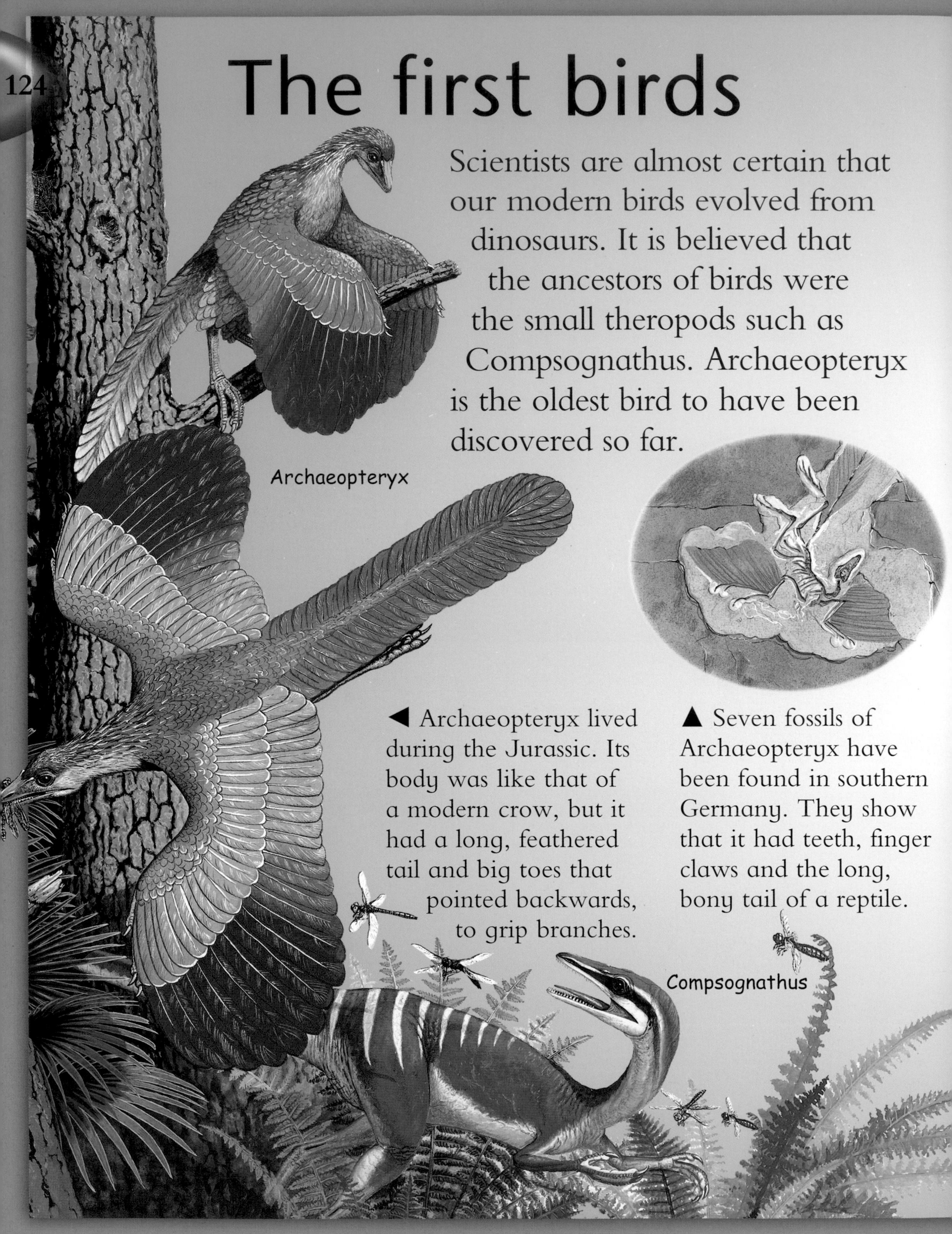

◀ Archaeopteryx lived during the Jurassic. Its body was like that of a modern crow, but it had a long, feathered tail and big toes that pointed backwards, to grip branches.

▲ Seven fossils of Archaeopteryx have been found in southern Germany. They show that it had teeth, finger claws and the long, bony tail of a reptile.

► Confuciusornis was a bird that was about the same size as Archaeopteryx, and lived in the early Cretaceous. It could perch like a modern bird. It ate plants and lived in large groups.

VOCABULARY

ancestor
A relative, from which an animal or person is descended.

theropod
Meat-eating dinosaurs with short front legs that ran or walked on their hind legs.

WHY DID THEY HAVE FEATHERS?

Feathers keep birds warm and dry. Feathers were probably more important for this than for flying for both birds and dinosaurs.

► Titanis was an enormous, flesh-eating, flightless bird that became extinct at least two million years ago. It was about 2.5 metres tall and had a huge, axe-like beak. It was part of a group of birds called the 'terror birds'.

◄ Caudipteryx was a flightless animal, about the size of a turkey, that lived in the Early Cretaceous. Scientists are not sure if it was a theropod dinosaur or a bird, although most think it was a dinosaur, but perhaps had ancestors that flew.

End of the dinosaurs

By the late Cretaceous, many kinds of dinosaurs and other animals had died out naturally. Then, about 65 million years ago, there was a mass extinction in which all the large land animals and many marine animals died out. Of the dinosaurs, only the theropods survived, in the form of birds.

► There is evidence that an asteroid hit the Earth. This would have caused dust clouds and blocked out the sun's light. Earth would have been cold and dark, and the plants and animals would have died.

Volcanic eruption
Some scientists think that the extinction was caused by volcanic eruptions. Many of them could have caused the same effects as an asteroid strike.

WHAT IS AN ASTEROID?

An asteroid is a rocky body, like a small planet, that drifts in space. There are thousands of asteroids in the Universe.

▲ Another theory is that mammals caused the end of the remaining dinosaurs by eating their eggs. Certainly the mammals were a very successful group of animals – after the extinction, the next age is known as the Age of Mammals.

Survivors

The extinction killed most, but not all, animals. Marine turtles swim in our seas today. Tuataras, which are related to both lizards and snakes, are members of a family that evolved at the time of the dinosaurs.

Green turtle

Tuatara

Now you know!

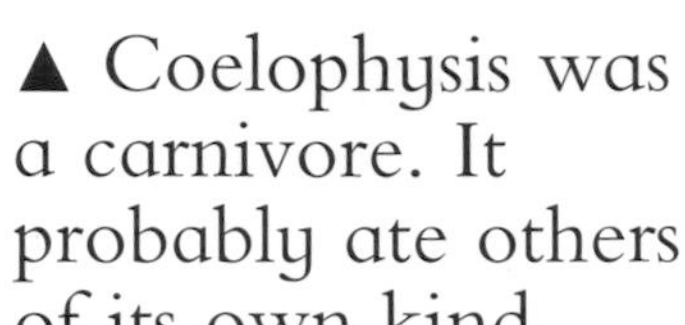

◀ Pterosaurs, the flying reptiles, were not dinosaurs. However, they were closely related.

▲ Coelophysis was a carnivore. It probably ate others of its own kind.

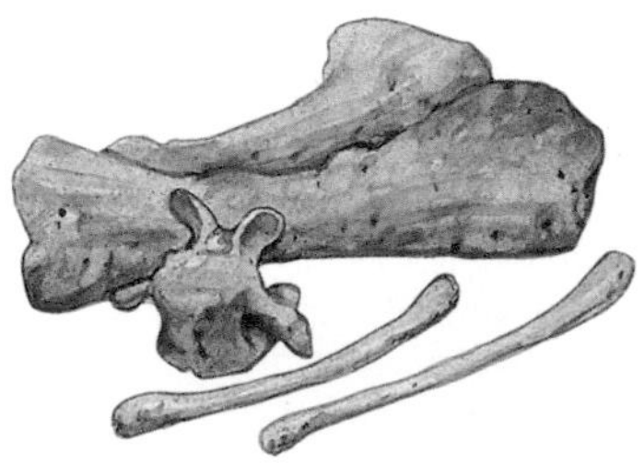

▲ Fossils are bones or other remains that are preserved in rock. They tell us about animals and plants that no longer exist.

▲ Many dinosaurs had scaly skin, spines or horns. They could have used them for attacking other animals, or defending themselves from attack.

▲ Modern birds are the descendants of some lizard-hipped dinosaurs. Archaeopteryx is the oldest bird found so far.

▼ Many dinosaurs ate only plants. In fact, most of the biggest dinosaurs were plant-eaters.

▲ Plant-eating dinosaurs had strong, blunt teeth for chewing. Meat-eaters often had large, pointed teeth for catching and killing prey.

▲ Dinosaurs died out about 65 million years ago, along with about half of all the animals on Earth. Scientists are still not quite sure why.

People and places

People have evolved, or developed, in different ways in order to cope with the landscape they live in, and the plants and animals available to them. Today, communication between people around the world is better than ever, and we are gradually growing to understand and celebrate our differences.

Our world

The world is mostly covered by sea, but there are seven main areas of land, which we call continents. People live on six of these: North America, South America, Europe, Africa, Asia and Australia.

Antarctica

Although some animals live on Antarctica, there are no native people. The only people there are visiting scientists or explorers.

North America

The continent North America includes Canada, the USA, and many other countries and islands. It is the third largest of the major land masses, after Asia and Africa. The world's largest island, Greenland, is part of North America.

▼ The Grand Canyon, in Arizona, USA, is a deep valley carved by the Colorado river over millions of years. It is 446 kilometres long and in places it is more than 1,800 metres deep.

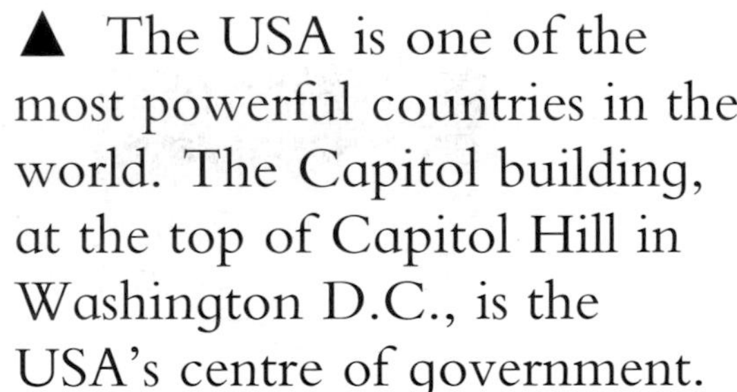

▲ The USA is one of the most powerful countries in the world. The Capitol building, at the top of Capitol Hill in Washington D.C., is the USA's centre of government.

▲ Thanksgiving is a holiday in the USA when people stop to appreciate the Earth and the food it provides. It is often celebrated with a special meal.

The Kwakiutl people
This tribe, like many native Indian tribes, lived in America long before Europeans arrived. Many carved tall totem poles like this one to tell the story of their tribe. They celebrated by dancing and wearing masks.

▲ Canada is famous for the Royal Canadian Mounted Police, its national police force. The serving officers are often referred to as the 'Mounties'.

◀ The Statue of Liberty, which stands in New York harbour, was a gift from France to the USA. It was given to celebrate the friendship between the two countries.

▲ Travelling by sleds pulled by huskies is the best way to move about in the most northern parts, where it is extremely cold.

CREATIVE CORNER

Make a cowboy doll
Cover an empty cardboard tube with brown paper. Draw, colour and cut out a head, arms and legs, and stick them onto the tube with glue. Now add clothes, a cowboy hat and bandana, and maybe even a guitar!

South America

South America is made up of 12 separate countries. This continent can be divided into three main types of landscape. There are the Andes mountains on the western coast, rainforest in the northeast and dry, grassy plains in the south.

Chocolate diet
Cocoa comes from the seeds of the cacao tree. It is used not only in chocolate bars and drinks, but also in savoury dishes. It has been an important product in the economy since ancient times, and may have first grown at the base of the Andes mountains.

► Angel Falls in Venezuela is named after an American, James Angel. At 979 metres, it is the highest waterfall in the world. It also drops uninterrupted for an amazing 807 metres.

◄ The jaguar is the largest big cat in South and Central America, and very rare in the wild. It is excellent at climbing trees and swimming, and often catches fish in the rivers.

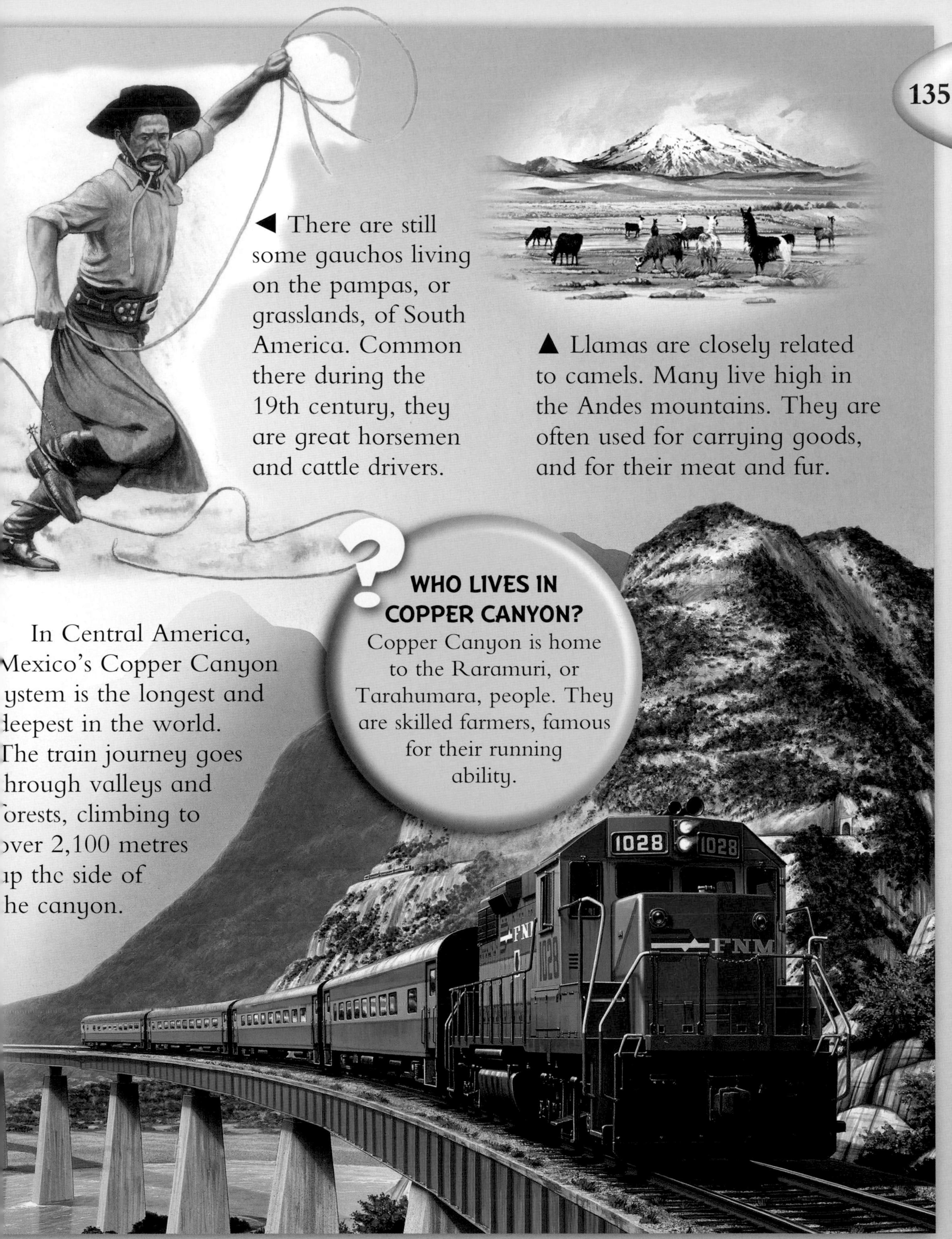

◀ There are still some gauchos living on the pampas, or grasslands, of South America. Common there during the 19th century, they are great horsemen and cattle drivers.

▲ Llamas are closely related to camels. Many live high in the Andes mountains. They are often used for carrying goods, and for their meat and fur.

WHO LIVES IN COPPER CANYON?
Copper Canyon is home to the Raramuri, or Tarahumara, people. They are skilled farmers, famous for their running ability.

In Central America, Mexico's Copper Canyon system is the longest and deepest in the world. The train journey goes through valleys and forests, climbing to over 2,100 metres up the side of the canyon.

Europe

Europe is the second smallest continent, and contains many small countries within its borders. It has a large coastal area, and many European nations have a long history of sailing and trading. European traditions and cultures have spread to many other parts of the world.

▲ The Mediterranean has a warm climate and beautiful beaches. Many people take their holidays there.

◀ Flamenco is an exciting form of dance that began in Andalusia, Spain. This country in southern Europe shares borders with Portugal and France.

Helping with the housework?
Kobolds are a kind of elf or sprite in German folklore. They are said to do domestic chores, but may play tricks on members of the household if they are not kept happy. The metal cobalt is named after them.

◀ There are several high mountain ranges in Europe, such as the Alps (shown here) and the Pyrenees. The valleys are often very fertile – suitable for growing many kinds of crops.

▶ Some of the more northern countries of Europe have snow from November to April. The people living in these areas ski as a practical way of getting around.

◀ There are many castles in Europe. They were usually built for rich and powerful rulers. This one was built in Bavaria, Germany, for Ludwig II.

▶ The Netherlands is famous for its windmills, built to grind corn and drain fields of water. The country is also known for growing beautiful tulips.

Fruits ready for picking

Wine-making is an important industry in parts of Europe, such as Germany, France and Italy. Grapes ripen in the warm sun and are ready to pick in autumn. Their juice is used for wine and vinegar.

INTERNET LINKS: www.yourchildlearns.com/europe_map.htm

Africa

Africa is an extraordinarily varied continent. There are more than 50 countries, and they are home to many different peoples and cultures. Africa's northern coast has rich, fertile land, but south of it is the harsh Sahara desert. Even further south, there are areas of rainforest.

Tribal customs
In traditional African cultures, masks are often used for dancing and other rituals. This bronze mask of a ram's head is from Benin, on the western coast of the continent.

► There are large, bustling cities built on or near the coast. Many ships trade far and wide from these ports. Tourist ships also visit.

◄ Traditional spice markets, or souks, with their bright colours and rich scents, are still popular today in northern Africa.

▲ The island of Mauritius, off Africa's eastern coast, is known for its natural beauty, warm seas and fishing.

▼ The official colour of the Masai people of Kenya and Tanzania is red. They always wear something in that colour.

CAN YOU FIND?
1. feather
2. a head-dress
3. a large collar
4. bangles
5. necklace

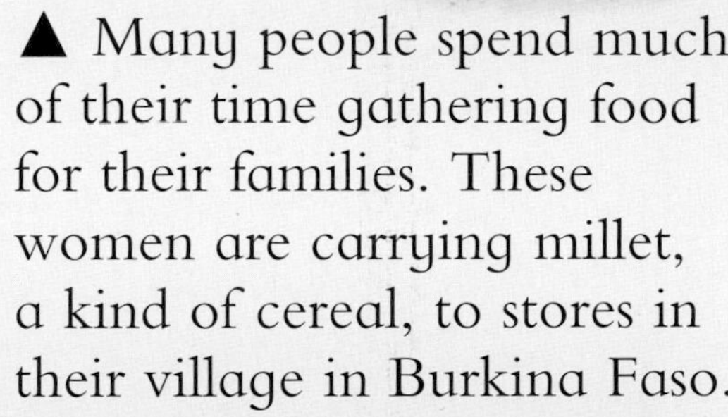

▲ Many people spend much of their time gathering food for their families. These women are carrying millet, a kind of cereal, to stores in their village in Burkina Faso.

▼ The nomadic tribes of Africa, who travel many kilometres at a time, use camels for transport in the desert.

CREATIVE CORNER

Make an African mask

Cut a mask shape from a piece of card, with holes for the eyes. Draw animal or human features on it and decorate it. You could add wool 'hair' and cardboard horns. Thread a string through holes to tie it onto your head.

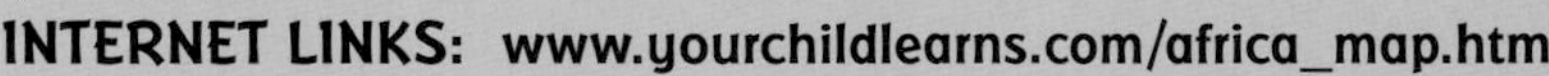

Asia

Asia is the largest continent, with about one-third of the world's total land area. It is home to about two-thirds of the world's people. In the north is a frozen area of ice. Much of the central area is desert, and in the south there are tropical beaches, islands and rainforests.

Climbing Everest
The highest mountain, Mount Everest, is in Asia. It is 8,850 metres high. The first people to climb to the top were Sir Edmund Hillary of New Zealand and Tenzing Norgay of Nepal, in 1953.

▲ People in Japan travel by train more than in any other country. The Shinkansen, or bullet train, travels at 300km/h. It goes even faster in tests!

Dragon trap
In the Japanese religion Shinto, Susanowo was god of sea and storms. He lured an eight-headed serpent to drink eight vats of rice wine. While it drank, he cut off all its heads and tails.

▶ India's famous Taj Mahal was built by Shah Jahan, a Mogul emperor of India, in memory of his wife, Mumtaz Mahal, who died in 1631.

▲ Most of the Russian Federation's land is in Asia, but its western tip, including the capital, Moscow, is usually said to be in Europe. Moscow's famous Red Square is bordered by the Kremlin, the government's main building, and St Basil's Cathedral.

▼ The Russian Federation plants millions of hectares of wheat, barley and grain for food. The country is also one of the world's top producers of oilseed, which is taken from sunflowers.

WHAT IS RICE?

Rice is a member of the family of grasses. Its grain (part of the seed) is an important food in many parts of the world, especially in Asia.

▼ The picture below shows Chinese people working in flooded fields. Paddy fields like this are a common sight in the rice-growing countries of southeast Asia.

INTERNET LINKS: www.yourchildlearns.com/asia_map.htm • www.historyforkids.org/learn/china/

Australia

Australia is the only country that is also a continent. Most Australians live on the eastern and southeastern coasts. The interior of the land is dry and harsh, though some aboriginal Australians, the country's original people, still live there.

▲ One of Australia's main exports is its wool, which shearers cut from sheep each year.

▲ Sydney is the oldest and largest city in Australia. Its opera house is often seen as a symbol of the country.

The Great Rainbow Snake

This is an important figure in aboriginal Australian tradition. It is said that the snake created the rivers, and can be seen in the sky as a rainbow.

▶ It is necessary to transport goods over very long distances in Australia. To keep costs down, companies use powerful trucks to pull several trailers at once. These are known as road trains.

▲ Some children in Australia live so far away from each other that they 'go to school' using the radio or the Internet.

▲ Birds of paradise are known for their beautiful feathers. These are often used in ceremonial head-dresses, like this one.

VOCABULARY

shearer
A person who cuts, or clips, the wool of a sheep or other animal.

aboriginal
One of the first inhabitants, or people, to live in a particular country.

▲ On Easter Island, in the Pacific ocean, there are more than 600 giant statues, carved over 1,000 years ago.

▲ In Rotorua, New Zealand (an island nation close to Australia), geysers, or spouts, of hot water and mud shoot up from lakes.

▶ New Zealand's first inhabitants were the Maori people. They came from Polynesian islands further north.

Languages

Being able to speak is one of the things that makes people different from other animals. Human language has taken thousands of years to develop. It allows us to share complicated ideas, and discuss subjects such as politics, philosophy and the arts.

Semaphore
This is a language used for communicating over long distances. The sender spells out words with flags. He moves them to a different position for each letter or number.

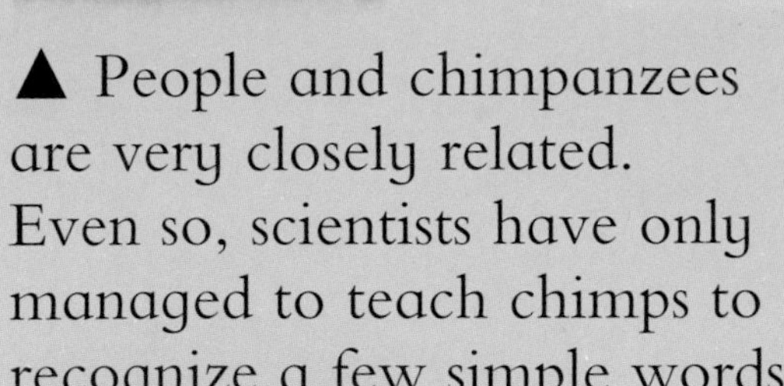

▲ People and chimpanzees are very closely related. Even so, scientists have only managed to teach chimps to recognize a few simple words.

CAN YOU FIND?

1. television
2. computer
3. books
4. telephone
5. newspaper

► Today, we have many different technologies that allow us to communicate. Most of them are word-based, but many of them also use other sounds and images.

▶ We also use our bodies to communicate our feelings. This is yet another 'language' that we use. Japanese people, for example, often bow to each other as a mark of respect.

▲ Different languages are written in different ways. This set of symbols, for example, is Chinese for 'Chinese people'.

IS LATIN DEAD?

Latin is a 'dead' language in that nobody speaks it in their day-to-day life. But it is still useful for reading old texts, which help us learn about past civilizations.

▲ Children learn to speak and read different languages at school. They may do this from books, or by using computers or tapes.

▶People who have difficulty hearing or speaking often use sign language. There are signs for common words.

CREATIVE CORNER

Make an international collage

Using books or the Internet, find out what the word 'hello' is in as many languages as you can. Make a collage of children, label each one with a language, and add a speech bubble showing the word in that language.

Homes

Early people took shelter in natural caves. Learning to build homes meant that later groups of humans could travel further, and live in places without natural shelter. The houses we build today depend on the materials available locally, as well as the kinds of weather we need to protect ourselves against.

VOCABULARY

nomads
People who have no permanent home, but travel to find food.

concrete
A building material made by mixing cement, pebbles or gravel, and water.

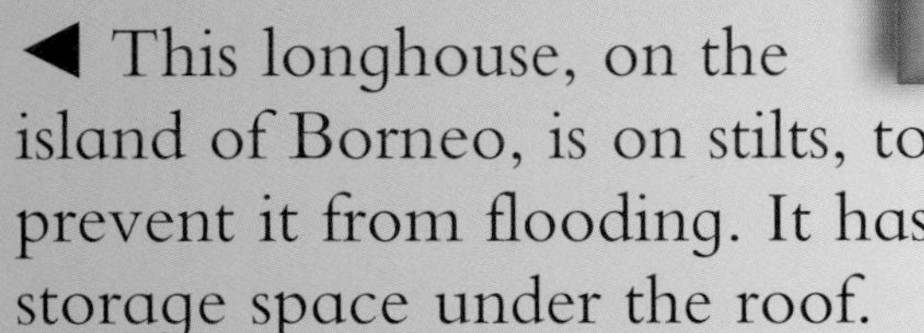
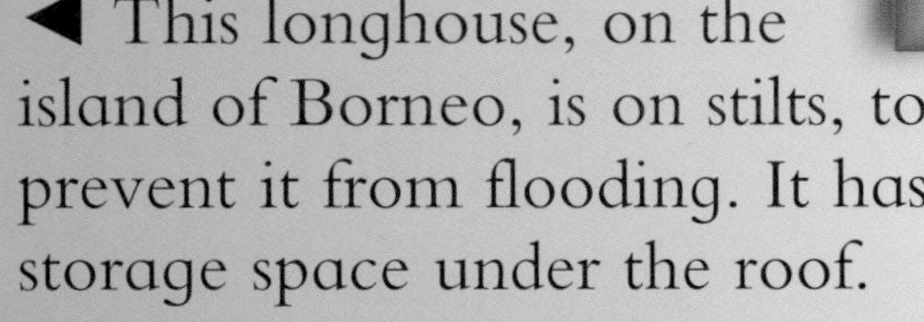

◀ This longhouse, on the island of Borneo, is on stilts, to prevent it from flooding. It has storage space under the roof.

◀ The nomads of Mongolia live in yurts. These round tents are made of thick felt. They are easy to put up and take down.

▲ In deserts and other dry areas, homes are often built of mud. Thick walls and small windows keep them cool.

Baba Yaga

In Russian myths, Baba Yaga is a wild old woman who lives in a cabin built on chicken legs, with no windows or doors. In fact, Siberian nomads build huts for storing food on the stumps of trees, which look rather like chicken legs. This is to stop bears getting in!

WHAT ARE HOMES MADE FROM?

Homes can be made from all kinds of materials. Bricks, wood and concrete are often used. However, igloos are made from ice and yurts from felt.

▲ In hot countries, houses are often painted white, to reflect the sun's heat. In Spain, people take a siesta (nap) when it is too hot to work.

▲ Brick houses like this one in Boston, USA, were originally built for one family to live in. Today, many have been divided into flats.

▲ Some people live on houseboats. These are often permanently moored, or tied up, where fresh water and electricity are available.

▲ The Inuit people of the Arctic still make bricks from ice to build their dome-shaped igloos. They do this when they go hunting.

▲ In the Alps and other snowy, mountainous regions, houses like these chalets have sloping roofs, to prevent the snow building up.

▲ This large wood-frame house is in Belize, in Central America. The timber was taken from local forests and cut into planks.

Clothes

The clothes we wear depend on where we live and what the weather is like, as well as what we are planning to do. They may keep us warm or cool, or protect us while we work. They can even show that we belong to a particular group of people.

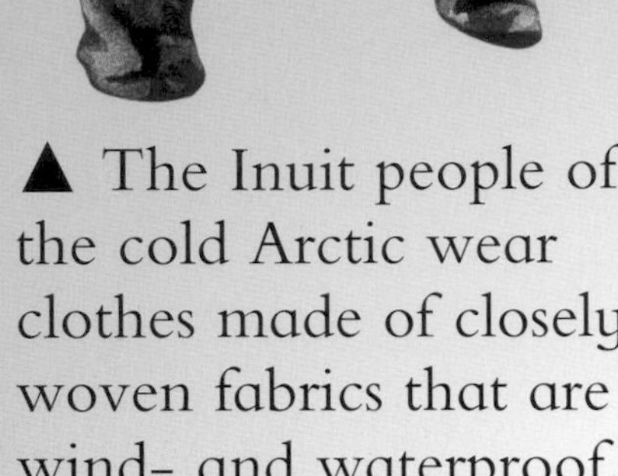

▲ The Inuit people of the cold Arctic wear clothes made of closely woven fabrics that are wind- and waterproof.

► This group of women is pounding maize to make flour for bread. Their clothes are colourful, and the baby is carried in a piece of cloth on the mother's back.

Leprechauns
There are many stories about leprechauns. These fairy shoemakers live on the island of Ireland. It is said that, if you listen very carefully, you can hear the sound of their hammers as they tap, tap, tap.

► Today, we mostly dress in casual clothing. This is practical and comfortable for all sorts of activities. It protects us, and is easy to move or run around in.

VOCABULARY

woven
Interlaced threads, for example to form a fabric or material.

traditional
The customs or habits in a country that are kept from generation to generation.

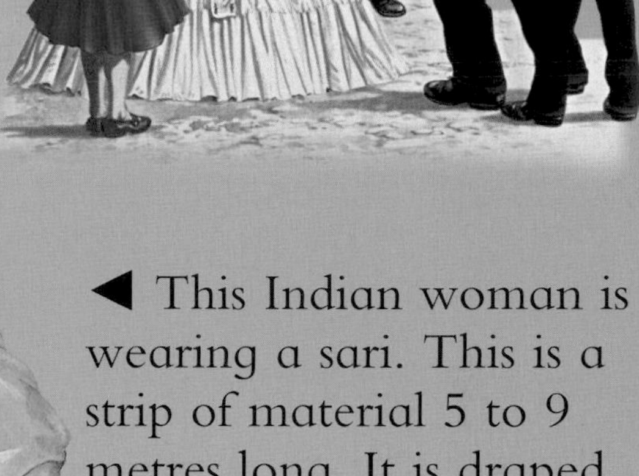

▶ At weddings in many countries, the bride is often dressed in white. In Greece, a bride traditionally has money pinned to her dress as a gift.

◀ This Indian woman is wearing a sari. This is a strip of material 5 to 9 metres long. It is draped around the body and can be worn in various styles.

▲ Fishermen need waterproof clothing to protect them from sea spray. The bright yellow clothes shown here also make them easy to spot should they fall into the water.

CREATIVE CORNER

Make a doll's dressing up box

Cover an old shoe box with plain or coloured paper. Now find pictures of interesting outfits, such as pirates, fairies or sportspeople, in magazines. Cut them out and stick them on the box for inspiration. Glue a white label onto the lid and write on your name.

Food and farming

Early people had to rely on what they could find or hunt. They often had to travel to find enough food. But, about 10,000 years ago, some people in the Middle East began to grow cereals, such as wheat. Farming allowed people to settle in one place, and build villages and towns.

► Today, huge fields of cereal crops such as wheat, corn and barley are harvested using efficient machines, such as combine harvesters.

◄ Today, there are fewer cowboys than there used to be. However, on large ranches, lassoes are still used to catch animals.

Animal farming
Like many farm animals, sheep are useful to us in more ways than one. We use the milk to drink or make cheese, the wool for clothing, and the meat for food. Sheep are easy to keep as they graze on grass in open fields.

◄ Farmers often sell their produce in markets. These Mexican women are setting up their stalls ready for the busy market to open.

▶ Fields of sunflowers are a glorious sight. They are grown mainly for their seeds, which we eat as snacks and use in animal feed. We use oil from the seeds to cook.

◀ Cereals are often made into bread. There are many different kinds of bread. Some are light and airy, while others are flat and dense, like the flatbread shown here.

▼ Fishermen using nets can bring in millions of fish at a time. In many places, fish are reared in farms, where they are kept in pens in the water until they are big enough to sell.

▲ Large farms often send their produce to factories, where they are sorted and packaged for sale in supermarkets, or made into other products. These Albanian women are sorting apples.

Traditions

Cultures all over the world have special traditions, or ways of doing things, that are important to them. The traditions of a society are some of the things that make people feel they belong together. They often involve music, dancing and feasting.

The Day of the Dead
This is celebrated in Mexico and other Latin American countries. It celebrates the fact that, although people die, they are also born and the cycle of life continues.

◀ The Chinese Moon Festival is held in autumn. Families gather together to watch the full moon. They also eat special moon cakes, and sing moon poems.

La Befana
In Italy, on the eve of 6 January, La Befana visits all the children to fill their socks with sweets if they are good, or a lump of coal if they are bad. She comes down the chimney and sweeps the floor before she leaves on her broomstick.

▲ Caribbean people celebrate many festivals. They parade through the streets in costumes, dancing and singing.

▶ Halloween is an ancient festival celebrating the night on which spirits are said to contact the living. Many children go trick-or-treating with pumpkin lanterns. They knock on neighbours' doors asking for treats, and threatening to play tricks on people who do not give anything!

▲ Carnival in Venice, Italy, has ancient origins. It is held in spring and has a different theme every year, but masks are always worn.

▶ The New Year in China falls in late January or early February. Chinese people all over the world celebrate it with firecrackers and parades led by people in gigantic dragon costumes.

Religions

Since ancient times, many people have believed in a god or gods. Their belief helps them to explain the world and their lives. Other religions are based around the individual, rather than a god. Religions are closely bound up with traditions and help people to feel part of a group.

The Kaaba in Mecca
Muslims believe this cube-shaped building was built by the prophet Abraham. Once in their lifetime, all Muslims who are able to do so are supposed to make the journey, or hajj, to Mecca.

► Islam is the religion of Muslim people. Muslims believe in one god, Allah, and try to follow the rules they believe he would like them to follow. Muslims say prayers in buildings called mosques.

▼ Christians believe in one god, who sent his son Jesus Christ to save humankind from sin. They build churches and cathedrals to worship in, like this one in Florence, Italy.

▲ Diwali is the Hindu festival of lights. It is held in either October or November, and celebrates the triumph of good over evil, and hope for humankind.

WHICH IS RIGHT?
We cannot say that any religion is the right one. Many people do not believe in a god of any kind. Most people believe we should live our lives in the way we choose.

▲ Judaism is the religion of the Jews. It was the first religion whose members believed in only one god. Hannukah is the celebration of lights, held in winter.

▲ Many religions, including Hinduism, Buddhism and Jainism, believe in a way of life rather than a god or gods. People often bring offerings to Buddhist monks (above).

The story of Buddha
A Hindu prince called Guatama Buddha thought that people who were truly good and pure would not have to be reborn. He decided to give up being a prince and live as good a life as he could. He had many Buddhist followers while he was alive, and even more after he died.

Arts and music

People like to express themselves, and the arts provide very good ways to do this. Painting, drawing, playing or writing music, dancing, singing and acting are all classed as arts. Today, some kinds of art are even used in therapy, to help people overcome illness.

Carving wood
The Makonde people of Tanzania are famed for their carving in a wood called mpingo. They shape figures from their tribal myths, as well as animals and ceremonial masks.

▼ Some of today's films use modern technology and special effects. However, films are mostly made with actors and traditional film sets.

Mermaids
These mythical sea creatures have the head and upper body of a woman and the tail of a fish. They are sometimes said to sing so sweetly that sailors become entranced, fall into the sea and drown.

▲ India has a strong dance tradition. Indian dance is also enjoyed all over the world because of its use in popular 'Bollywood' films.

Shadow puppet theatre

Javanese folk stories are acted out in shadows on a screen. Highly skilled puppeteers move puppets, which can be more than a metre tall, using long rods. A light behind the puppets casts shadows onto a screen.

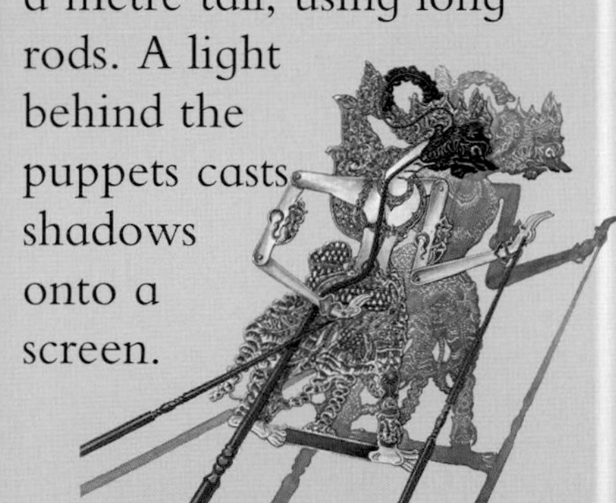

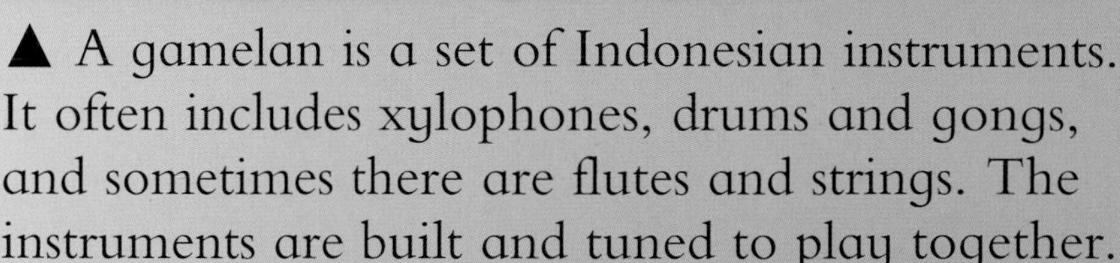

▲ A gamelan is a set of Indonesian instruments. It often includes xylophones, drums and gongs, and sometimes there are flutes and strings. The instruments are built and tuned to play together.

◀ Valuable works of art and old objects are often kept in a museum or art gallery. The staff look after the items to preserve them. Everyone can visit to see and learn more about them.

▲ Ballet is a formal style of dance that began in Europe over 300 years ago. It uses special gestures, developed from mime, to tell a story.

▶ An orchestra is a group of different types of instruments and the people who play them. It is directed by a conductor.

Sports

Sports are games that involve physical skill of some kind. People take part in sports for many reasons – to keep fit, to compete against others, or just for fun. Many modern sports, such as running, wrestling and archery, have developed from skills that people had originally needed to survive in the world.

Olympic games
The modern summer Olympics are based on games held in ancient Greece more than 2,000 years ago. They take place every four years.

◀ Cycling is a popular sport for all ages, partly because it does not need a special stadium, track or equipment apart from the bicycle itself and a safety helmet.

▲ In events, runners compete over different distances. Only in the shortest races do the runners sprint, or run as fast as possible, for the whole race.

▶ The world record for speed skiing is over 250km/h. It is the second fastest non-motorized sport, after skydiving.

▶ Grand Prix racing cars are designed for speed. They are very light, with powerful engines, and so low that the drivers have to lie almost flat in their seats.

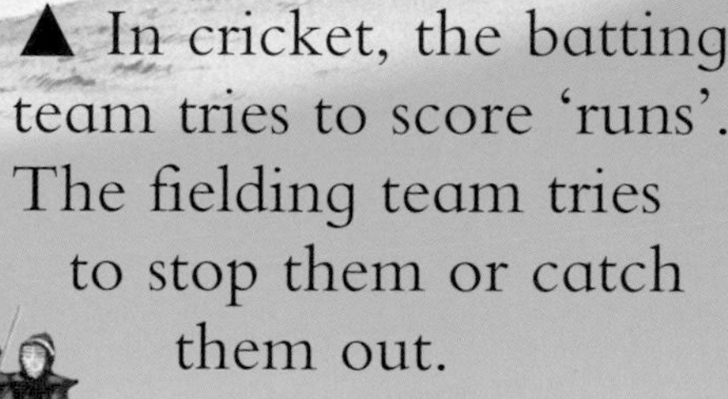

▲ In cricket, the batting team tries to score 'runs'. The fielding team tries to stop them or catch them out.

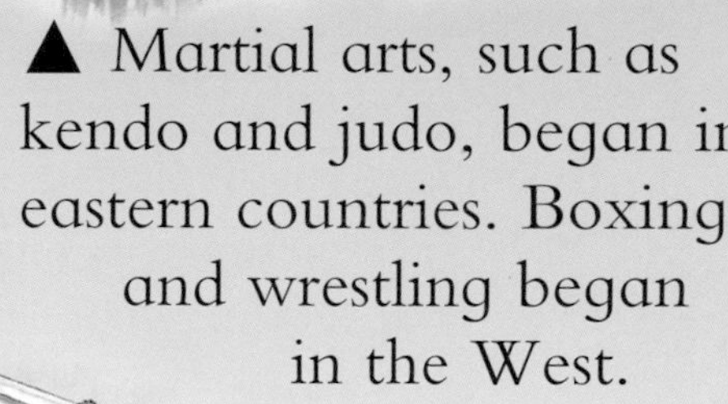

▲ In basketball, two teams of five players compete to score points by throwing a ball through a basket.

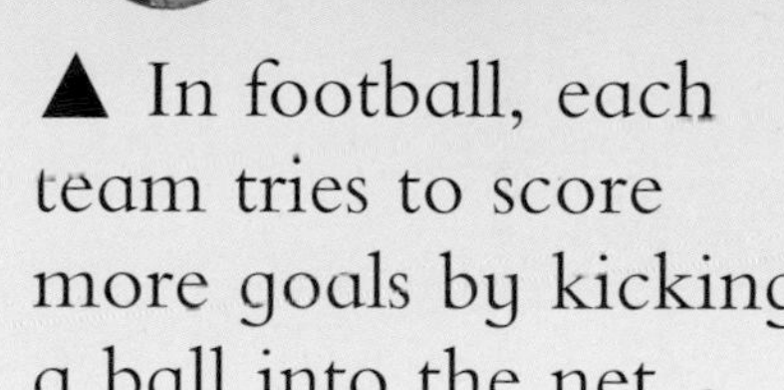

▲ Martial arts, such as kendo and judo, began in eastern countries. Boxing and wrestling began in the West.

▲ In football, each team tries to score more goals by kicking a ball into the net.

CREATIVE CORNER

Make a bowling alley outdoors

Half fill some empty plastic bottles with water or sand, and replace the tops. Stand them upright in front of a wall. Play with a friend and see how many pins you can knock over in one go by rolling a ball at them.

Now you know!

▲ Many celebrations involve music and dance. They often have festive clothes and masks as well.

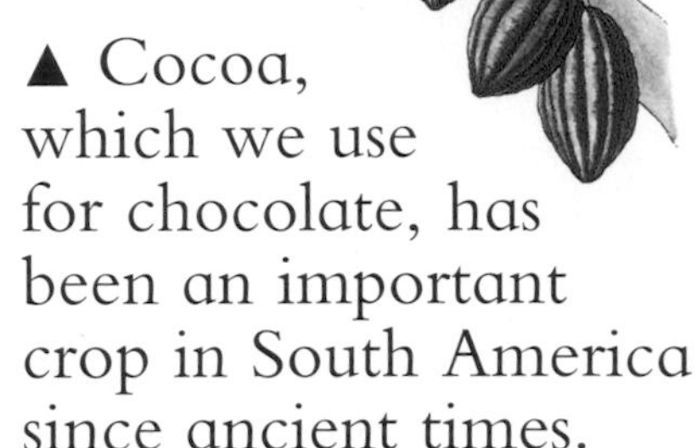

▲ Cocoa, which we use for chocolate, has been an important crop in South America since ancient times.

▲ Venezuela's Angel Falls is the highest waterfall, at almost 1,000 metres high.

▲ The Mounties are a special police force in Canada. They use horses to travel around.

▼ Nomads are people who move from place to place in search of food.

▲ People have learned to cope with extreme temperatures, such as cold in the Arctic or far northern regions of Earth.

► The Great Rainbow Snake is an ancient god said by the aboriginal people of Australia to have created rivers.

◄ People all over the world celebrate some of the same things, for example Halloween on 31 October.

People through time

We find out through history how people lived long ago, discovering and exploring the world around them. It tells us how they ate, dressed, made music and art, or told stories. This helps us understand why we live as we do today.

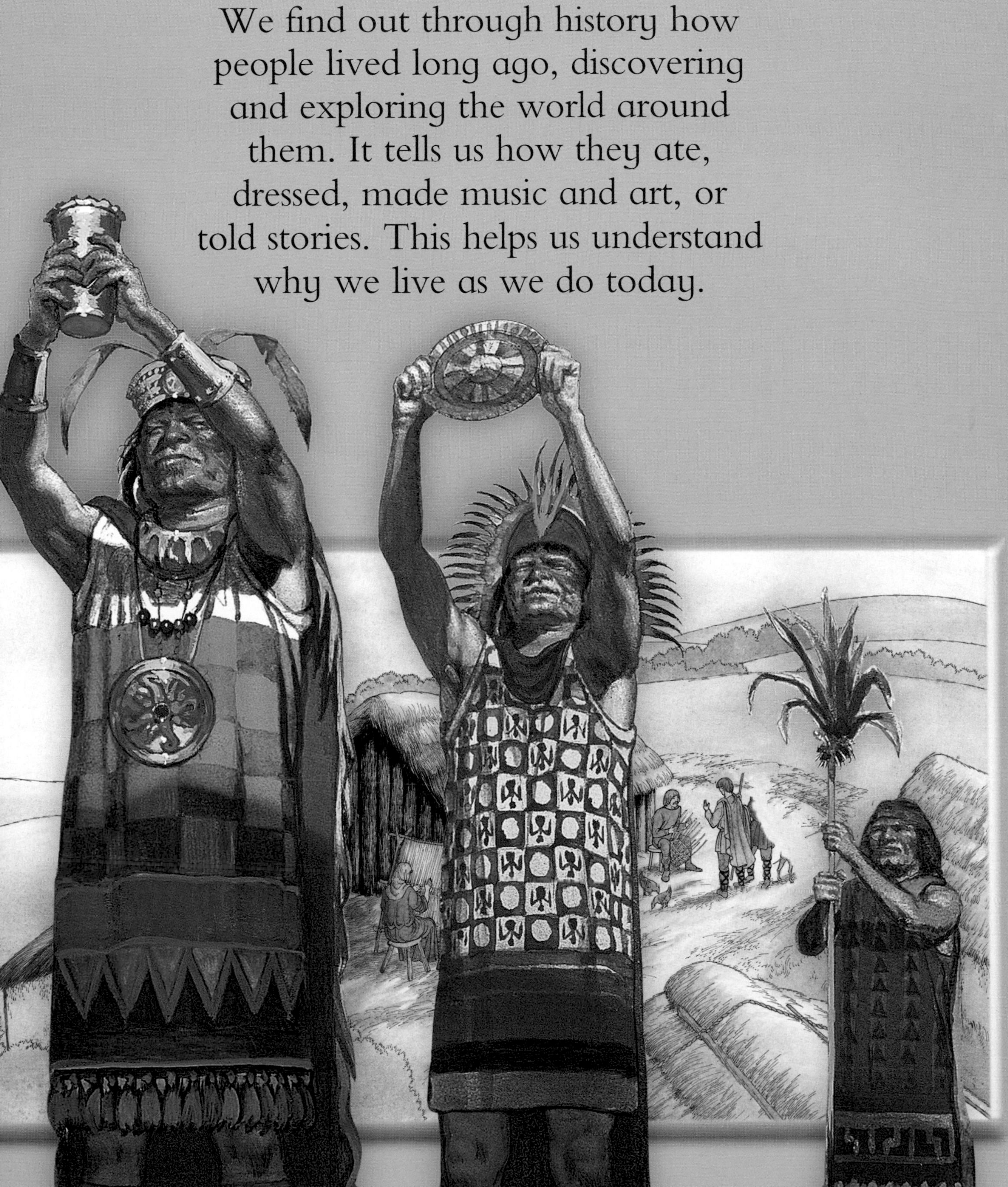

Prehistory

Ape-like creatures developed in Africa millions of years ago. Several learned to walk on two legs and even use tools. After about 400,000 years ago, some of these creatures developed into early forms of human being. Around 130,000 years ago, modern types of human had appeared. They then spread to other parts of the world.

Stone Age
The first people chipped hard stones such as flints until they were sharp. That is why this period is called the Stone Age. They also used wood, bone and horn.

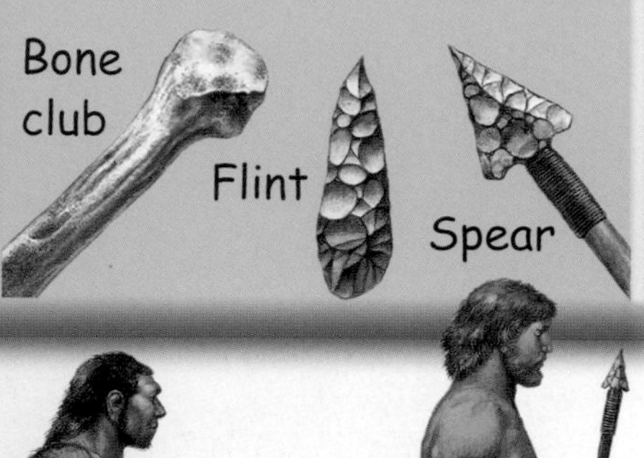

Australopithecus (southern ape) 5 to 1 million years ago

Homo habilis (handy human) 2.2 to 1.6 million years ago

Homo erectus (upright human) 2 to 0.4 million years ago

Neanderthaler (early wise human) 200,000 to 30,000 years ago

Homo sapiens (modern wise human) 130,000 years ago to the present

▲ Early creatures in the human family could run and climb. They were clever, with big brains. They were good at gripping objects. They made simple tools and weapons, and used them to hunt and gather food.

Is anybody out there?
Did prehistoric ape-men survive into modern times? There are many tales of strange beasts living in remote forests or mountains. A legend from the Himalayas tells of a creature called the Yeti, or 'abominable snowman'.

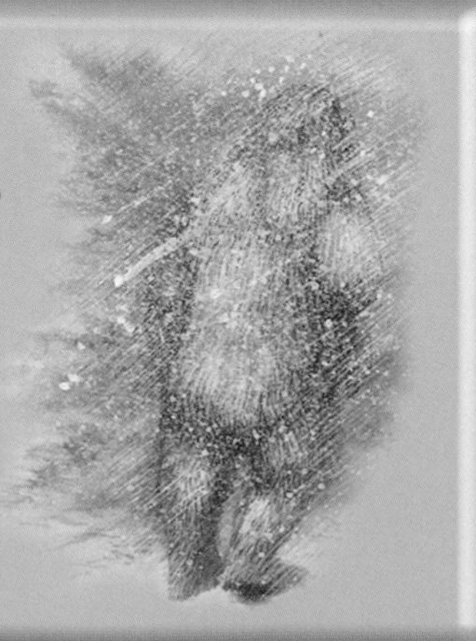

▼ At these caves in France, people made paintings of wild animals more than 15,000 years ago. Many early people made their homes in caves.

▲ In prehistoric times there were long ice ages across the world. People survived by hunting animals, such as the woolly mammoth.

CAN YOU FIND?

1. a lamp burning animal fat
2. clothes made from animal skins
3. colours being mixed
4. wooden poles

INTERNET LINKS: www.culture.gouv.fr:80/culture/arcnat/lascaux/en/ • http://museums.ncl.ac.uk/flint/menu.html

First civilizations

People learned to tame animals and grow crops in western Asia over 12,000 years ago. Villages grew into busy towns and cities. Some cities conquered others, creating countries and empires. People learned to write and understand mathematics, to trade, govern and pass laws. These were the world's first civilizations.

Clever inventions
Inventions that changed the world were made in ancient Iraq over 5,000 years ago. The first writing was made up of marks pressed into soft clay. The first carts used heavy wheels made of wood.

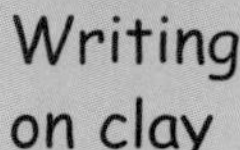

Writing on clay

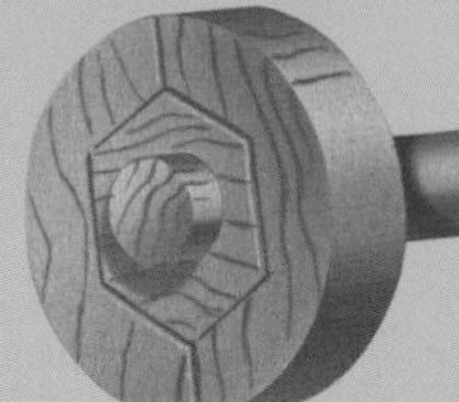

Wooden wheel

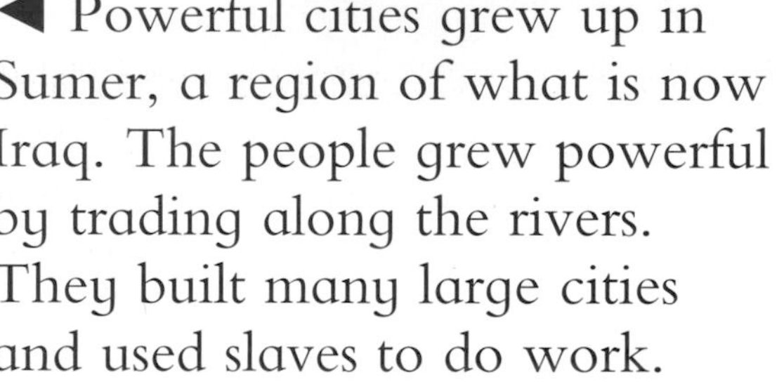

◀ Powerful cities grew up in Sumer, a region of what is now Iraq. The people grew powerful by trading along the rivers. They built many large cities and used slaves to do work.

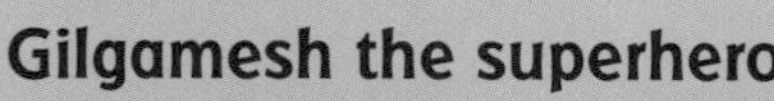

Gilgamesh the superhero
The people of Sumer liked to tell stories about Gilgamesh, the powerful and proud king of Uruk city. Among other adventures, he attacked the monster Humbaba and killed the Bull of Heaven that had been sent to destroy him. But he never found out the secret of how to live forever.

▲ This is the oldest known board-game in the world. It was made before 2600BCE and placed in a royal tomb in Ur, one of the greatest cities of Sumer.

◀ Copper and tin were mined and traded in western Asia. By 3500BCE these metals were being heated and mixed to make bronze.

Pin Tweezers Bracelet

◀ Iron is a tougher and harder metal than bronze. It was used in what is now Turkey by about 1300BCE. People called the Hittites conquered large areas of west Asia at this time using iron weapons.

▶ The Assyrians were a western Asian people who conquered many lands from the 1100s to the 600s BCE. Their fierce armies attacked city walls with archers, ladders, towers and battering rams. The Assyrian kings built fine palaces with libraries and gardens.

The Egyptians

The River Nile flows through the deserts of Egypt, in North Africa. The river flooded each year, leaving a rich mud. Farmers grew crops on the river banks, providing food for people in the towns and cities. Egypt was a powerful kingdom, with great tombs and palaces.

Nut of the stars
The Egyptian sky goddess was called Nut. Egyptian wall paintings show her arching over the Earth god, Geb. Her body is covered with stars. Egyptians believed that each morning Nut gave birth to the Sun god, Ra, and swallowed him again each evening.

◀ Over 4,500 years ago the Egyptians buried their kings, the pharaohs, in huge pyramids. These pointed stone monuments were built by thousands of labourers, who toiled in the hot desert sun.

CAN YOU FIND?

1. an injured worker
2. a ramp
3. a wooden sled
4. a wooden box
5. a dog

▲ Tutankhamun was a young pharaoh who died in 1325BCE. His body was preserved to make a mummy. It was wrapped, and covered with a gold mask. Then it was put inside human-shaped coffins in a stone box.

▲ In front of the pyramids at Giza is a sphinx, a statue of a lion with a human head. The head may show the face of the pharaoh Khafra.

▼ The Egyptians used reed boats to hunt hippopotamuses in the River Nile. The animals were a nuisance because they trampled crops along the river banks.

◄ The Egyptians worshipped hundreds of gods. Ra was the Sun god and Osiris the god of death and rebirth. Isis, his wife, was the mother goddess, while Anubis was the god of funerals.

The ancient East

Great civilizations grew up around the River Indus, in what is now Pakistan, as well as in India, China and southeast Asia. For thousands of years, this area produced great inventions, works of art, books, statues, temples and palaces, and scientific discoveries. There was also long-distance trade in spices, silk, jade and ivory.

▲ From about 3300 to 1600BCE Harappa was one of the great cities of the Indus valley. It had houses made of brick, drains, toilets, baths and wide streets. About 40,000 people lived there.

▼ The first emperor of all China, Qin Shi Huangdi, died in 210BCE. Placed around his tomb were thousands of life-sized model soldiers. He thought they would guard his body against evil spirits. The ghostly army was discovered again in 1974.

Mother of Dragons

The Chinese tell of a woman who found a magic egg by the river. Five dragons hatched out and she became known as Long Mu, Mother of Dragons. After she died the dragons turned into wise men called the Five Scholars.

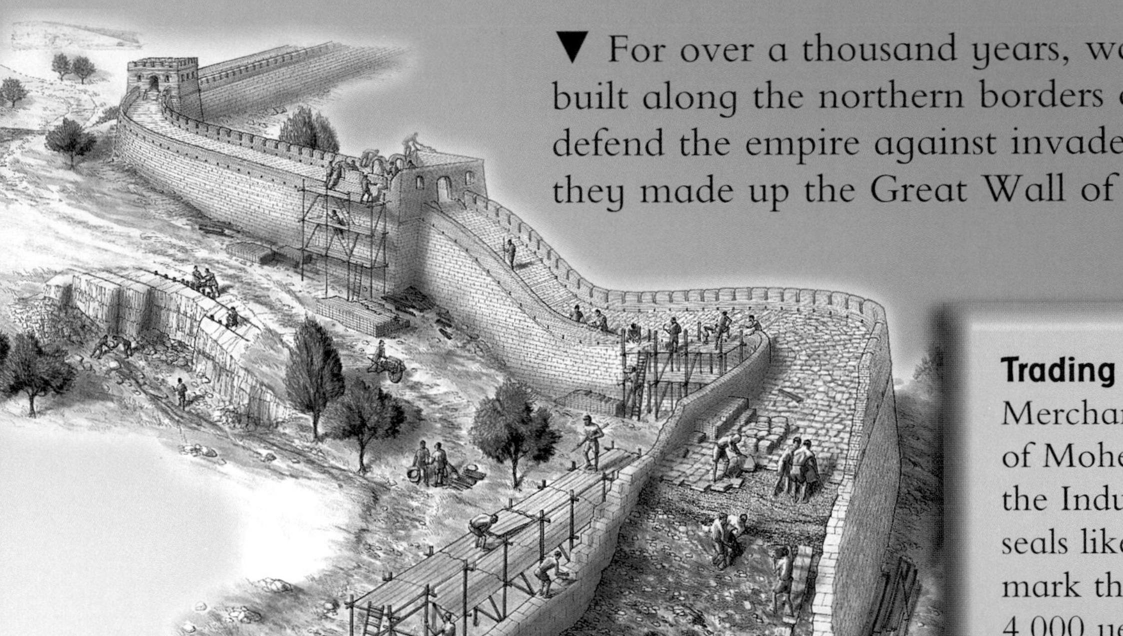

▼ For over a thousand years, walls were built along the northern borders of China to defend the empire against invaders. Together they made up the Great Wall of China.

Trading seal
Merchants from the city of Mohenjo-Daro, in the Indus valley, used seals like this one to mark their goods about 4,000 years ago. They traded with the cities of western Asia.

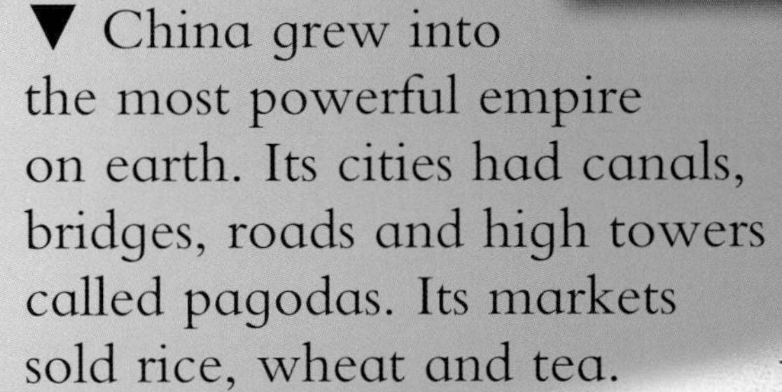

CAN YOU FIND?

1. a vegetable seller
2. a pagoda
3. merchants with camels
4. the canal
5. a horse-drawn wagon
6. a bridge

▼ China grew into the most powerful empire on earth. Its cities had canals, bridges, roads and high towers called pagodas. Its markets sold rice, wheat and tea.

INTERNET LINKS: www.ancientindia.co.uk/ • http://library.thinkquest.org/J002388/chinawall.html

The Greeks

Between about 2000 and 146BCE great civilizations grew up in Greece. Greeks also settled around the Mediterranean Sea and the Black Sea. They were great thinkers, politicians, writers, athletes, sculptors, sailors and warriors. In the 300s BCE, Greeks ruled much of western Asia and also Egypt.

Time's up!
Athens allowed its citizens to govern themselves. This was called democracy. There were assemblies, councils and public law courts. Speakers in court had a time limit. They could speak until the water ran out of a pot that had a hole in it.

◀ Athens was one of the greatest Greek cities. At the centre of Athens was a rocky hill called the Acropolis. Here stood a splendid temple called the Parthenon, in which there was a giant statue of Athene, the Greek goddess of wisdom.

▶ The Greeks had many gods. Hermes was their messenger, and Aphrodite goddess of love, Zeus king of the gods and Hera queen. Demeter was goddess of earth and Hades god of the underworld.

Hermes Aphrodite Zeus Hera Demeter Hades

◀ A fleet of Greek ships prepares for war. These ships were called triremes, and had three banks of oars as well as sails. The pointed front of the ships was used to ram enemy boats and sink them.

▶ The Greeks built open-air theatres in many cities. The actors wore masks. All the parts were played by men. Sad plays were called tragedies. Funny plays were called comedies.

▲ One Greek country was called Sparta. Spartan children were raised to be tough. The boys were trained to be soldiers.

CREATIVE CORNER

Make a Greek shield

Draw a circle on card. Cut it out. Now draw a leaping dolphin and paint it blue and the background yellow. Use a black marker to outline the dolphin. Cut a band of card and paste it to the back as a handle.

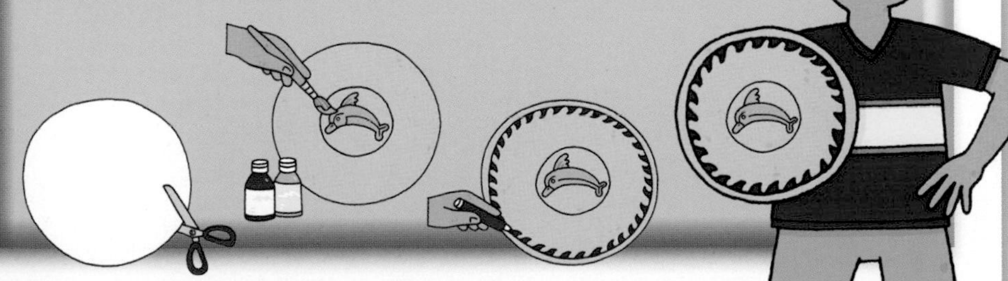

The Romans

The Italian city of Rome was first settled in about 753BCE. Within 500 years, the Romans had conquered most of Italy. They went on to rule a huge empire which stretched across Europe, western Asia and North Africa. They built long, straight roads from one city to another. The Roman empire lasted until 476CE.

▲ Roman dress included cloaks, tunics, shawls, long dresses, leather boots and sandals. Most clothes were made from wool.

◀ Much of Europe was the home of Celtic peoples such as the Gauls and the Britons. The Romans fought against the Celts and conquered many of their lands.

Saturn's holiday

The Romans believed the god Saturn was driven from the heavens by Jupiter and hid himself in Rome. Every winter, a holiday called Saturnalia was held in Rome in his honour. It was marked by feasting, merry-making, tricks and presents. Slaves and masters swapped places for a day.

▲ The Romans loved the public baths. There they could plunge in cold tubs and hot pools, and have massages. They could take exercise or just talk to friends

▲ Important men wore long robes called togas. These two are doing business in Rome's forum, the city centre.

Making a tortoise

The Roman army was divided into groups called legions. When soldiers of the legion were attacking a fort, they sometimes formed a tight band and placed shields around and over their bodies. This was called making a 'tortoise'.

▼ The Colosseum was a big stadium in the middle of Rome. It could hold about 50,000 spectators. Instead of sport they watched horrible shows, in which wild animals and people were cruelly killed.

◀ Gladiators were trained fighters who fought to the death in the arena. The emperor would decide if their lives were to be spared.

The Vikings

Scandinavia is a name given to Sweden, Denmark and Norway. The people who farmed and fished there around 1,200 years ago were called Vikings. They were great explorers, reaching North America and trading from Russia to Baghdad.

Runestones
The Vikings raised stone memorials carved with their own sort of writing and decorated with swirling patterns. They used a 16-letter alphabet, with letters called runes.

Sleipnir the swift
The Vikings loved to tell stories about gods, giants and magical beasts. Sleipnir was the horse ridden by Odin, father of the gods. Sleipnir had eight legs and could ride like the wind, over land or through the air. He was said to have been born from Svadilfari, the horse of the giants, and Loki the mischief-maker.

◀ The Vikings were fierce warriors, feared all over Europe. They carried swords, axes, spears and round shields. When two Vikings quarrelled, they might have been ordered to settle the argument with a fight to the death!

CAN YOU FIND?
1. a cauldron
2. hearth stones
3. wooden bowls
4. a brooch on a dress strap
5. rushes on the floor
6. a wooden tub

▲ The Vikings built trading vessels and longships to sail the oceans. They were seafarers and pirates. They raided towns along coasts and rivers, carrying off gold, cattle and slaves.

▲ The Vikings lived in farming settlements and built long, low houses. There was a fire for cooking indoors. Smoke escaped through a hole in the roof. Families gathered round the fire after a hard day's work.

► Viking warriors loved to feast and drink. Poets would sing the praises of the chief at the feasts, in the hope of a reward. They would also tell stories and riddles.

INTERNET LINKS: www.cdli.ca/CITE/v_childhood.htm • www.bbc.co.uk/schools/vikings/

The Middle Ages

In Europe, the thousand years between the end of the Roman empire and the beginning of the modern age are known as the Middle Ages. This was a time when kings and queens built castles and big churches called cathedrals. Most people followed the Christian faith, although the Moors of southern Spain were Muslims, and Jews lived in many towns.

VOCABULARY

cathedral
The most important church in a region, run by a bishop.

plague
A terrible disease that spreads from one person to another.

◀ Poor peasants had to work hard in the fields. They had to provide food for the lord in the local manor house or the castle. In times of war, they had to fight for him. In return, he promised to protect them from attack.

DID CHILDREN GO TO SCHOOL?
Many children worked on the land or learned a trade. Most could not read or write. A few were taught by monks at church schools.

▲ The Black Death was a terrible plague that swept across Asia and Europe in the 1340s. It was spread by rat fleas. Bodies were carted away by the thousands.

▲ Churches were built in every town and city. The head of the Church was the Pope, who lived in Rome, in Italy. People called pilgrims travelled long distances to pray at holy places such as Rome, or Compostela in Spain.

► Many long and terrible wars were fought during the Middle Ages. Here, a Spanish army led by a famous knight called El Cid is capturing the city of Valencia from the Moors. The year is 1094.

Knights and castles

During the Middle Ages, wars were fought by horsemen in armour. They were called knights, and they carried shields, swords and long spears called lances. Kings and lords lived in castles, which were hard to attack. Many castles were built with thick walls of stone.

VOCABULARY

tournament
A mock battle fought between knights with blunted weapons.

siege
Surrounding a castle and cutting off its supplies, forcing it to surrender.

◀ At festivals called tournaments, knights would show off their fighting skills in mock battles. Each would try to knock the other off his horse. The knights would wear fancy armour and helmets.

King Arthur and the knights of the Round Table
Arthur was probably a warrior who lived in Britain in the 500s. After he died, fantastic stories were told about him. By the 1100s, Arthur was being described as a great king, whose knights sat at a Round Table. They were said to be adventurous, brave and honourable. Many real-life knights wanted to be like the ones at King Arthur's court.

CAN YOU FIND?

1. a well
2. a musician
3. a bed
4. a spiral staircase
5. a monk
6. a knight on horseback

► During a siege, one army would surround and try to capture a castle, using ladders and giant catapults. The other army would shoot arrows and throw rocks.

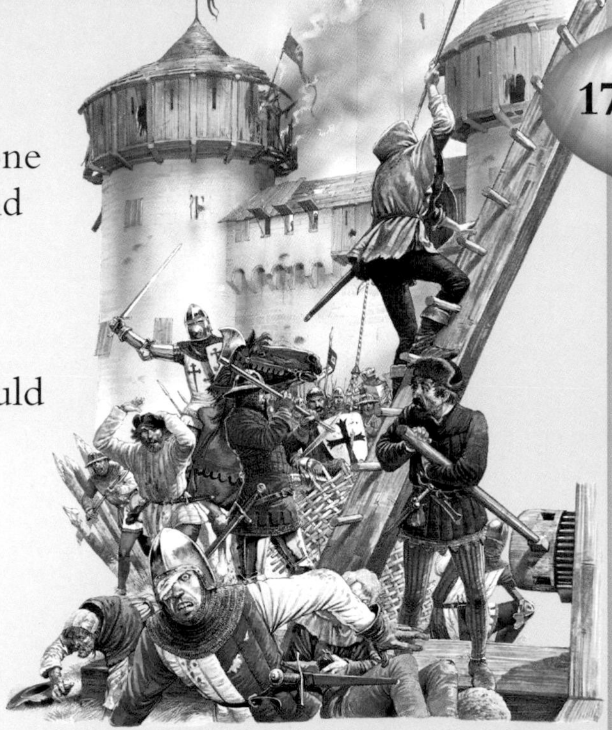

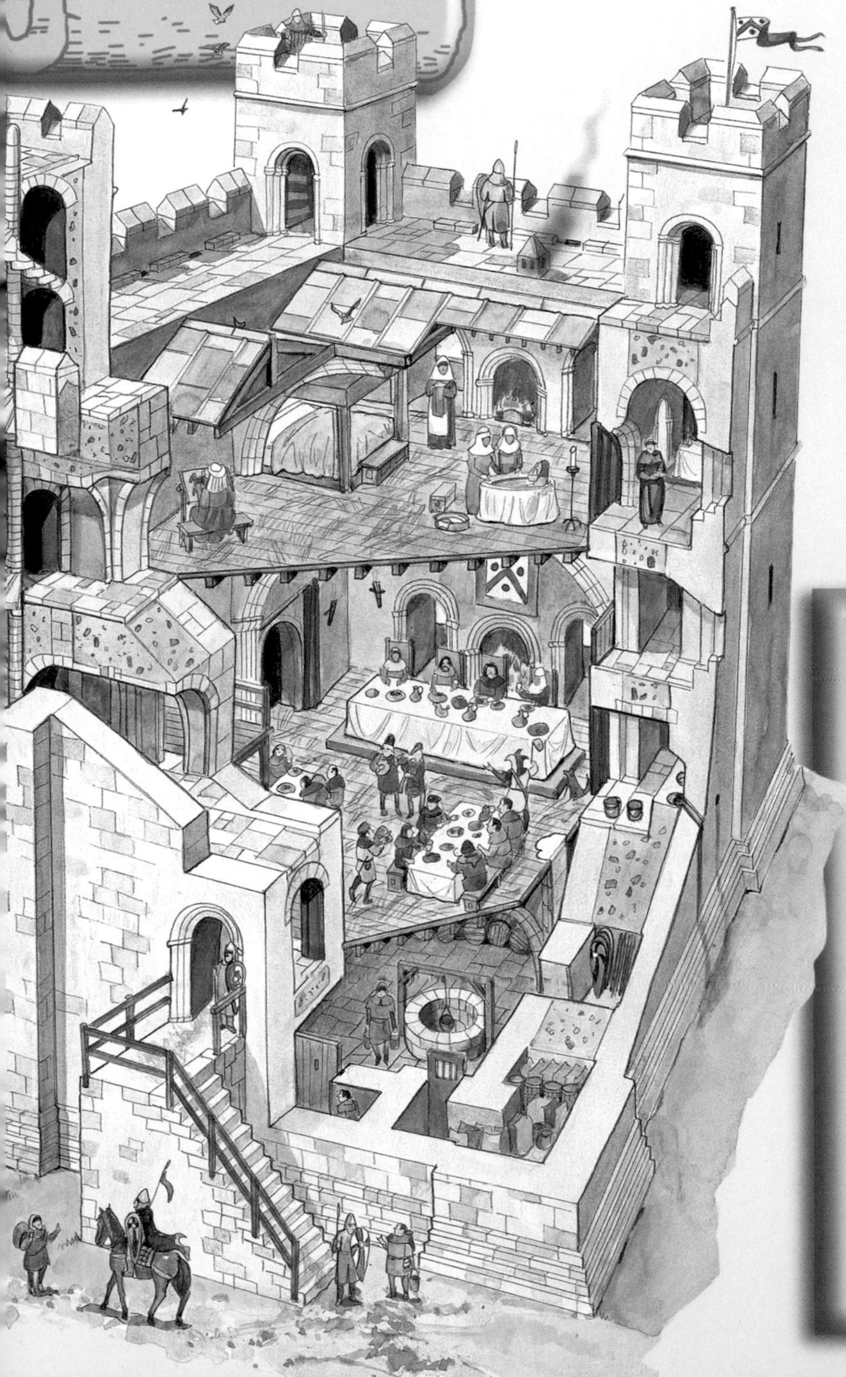

◄ A castle was a home as well as a place for fighting. This is an early castle that is a simple, strong tower. Later castles had round walls with many layers of defence.

CREATIVE CORNER

Design your coat-of-arms

Copy a shield shape onto paper and divide it into four parts. Draw a ribbon underneath and an emblem in each quarter. Then colour them and the background. Now write your motto in the ribbon.

INTERNET LINKS: www.castles.org/Kids_Section/Castle_Story/ • www.knightsandarmor.com/

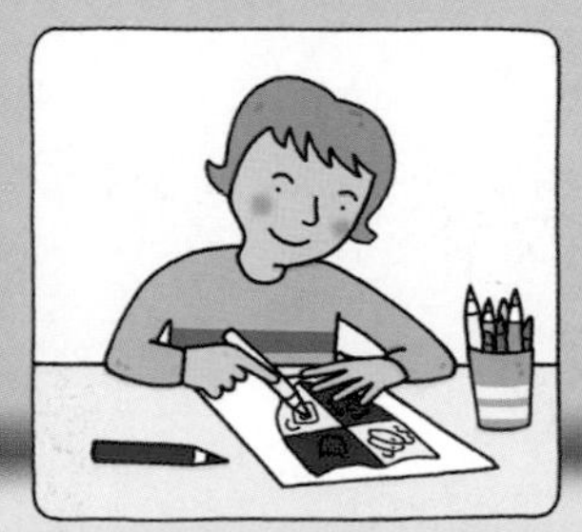

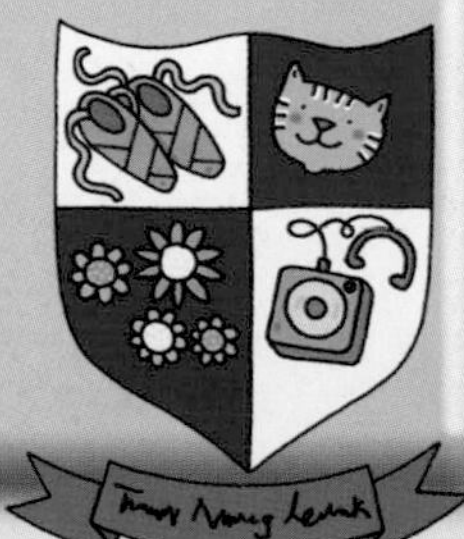

Explorers

During the Middle Ages, Arab and Chinese seafarers explored the Indian ocean and the coast of East Africa. Polynesians explored the islands of the Pacific ocean. Europeans sailed around Africa to India. By the 1500s, Europeans were sailing around the world.

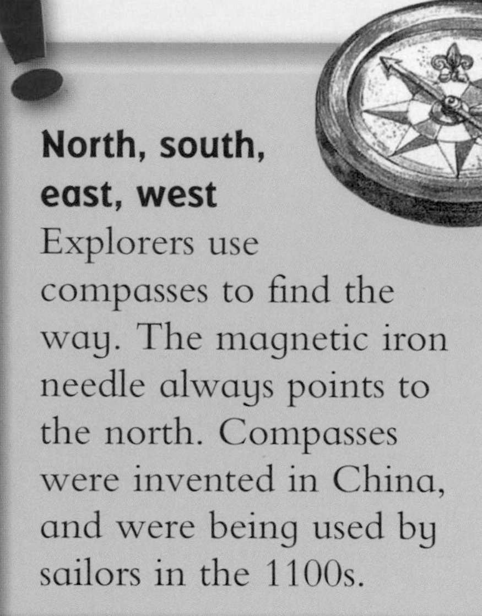

North, south, east, west
Explorers use compasses to find the way. The magnetic iron needle always points to the north. Compasses were invented in China, and were being used by sailors in the 1100s.

▲ Marco Polo (1254–1324) and his family were merchants from Venice in Italy. They travelled all the way to China. They were presented to the emperor and saw many marvels.

► Ibn Battuta was born in Morocco in 1304. He spent nearly 30 years of his life exploring Egypt, Arabia, India, southeast Asia, China and West Africa. He wrote about his adventures.

Dreaming of El Dorado
In the 1500s, Spanish soldiers were exploring South America. They heard rumours of a ruler called El Dorado, 'the Golden One', whose body was covered in gold dust. His kingdom was said to be full of fabulous riches... but really no such land existed.

▶ Ferdinand Magellan left Spain in 1519. He travelled through icy seas off South America before reaching the Pacific ocean. His crew sailed right around the world, but he was killed on the way.

▲ This Spanish ship was called *Santa Maria*. Its captain was an Italian called Christopher Columbus. In 1492, he sailed across the Atlantic ocean to discover the New World – America.

◀ For hundreds of years, pirates attacked ships in the Caribbean and other parts of the world. They stole any treasure they could find on board. They were often very cruel and violent people.

CREATIVE CORNER

Make a Treasure Island map

Draw the outline of your imaginary island. Mark in beaches, bays, palm trees, hills and a river. Give them all names. Draw in compass points. Decorate the map with pictures of old sailing ships or sea monsters.

The Incas

Many great civilizations developed in South America. In the 1400s, the empire of the Incas ruled much of the Pacific coast and the Andes mountains. It was conquered by Spanish soldiers in the 1530s.

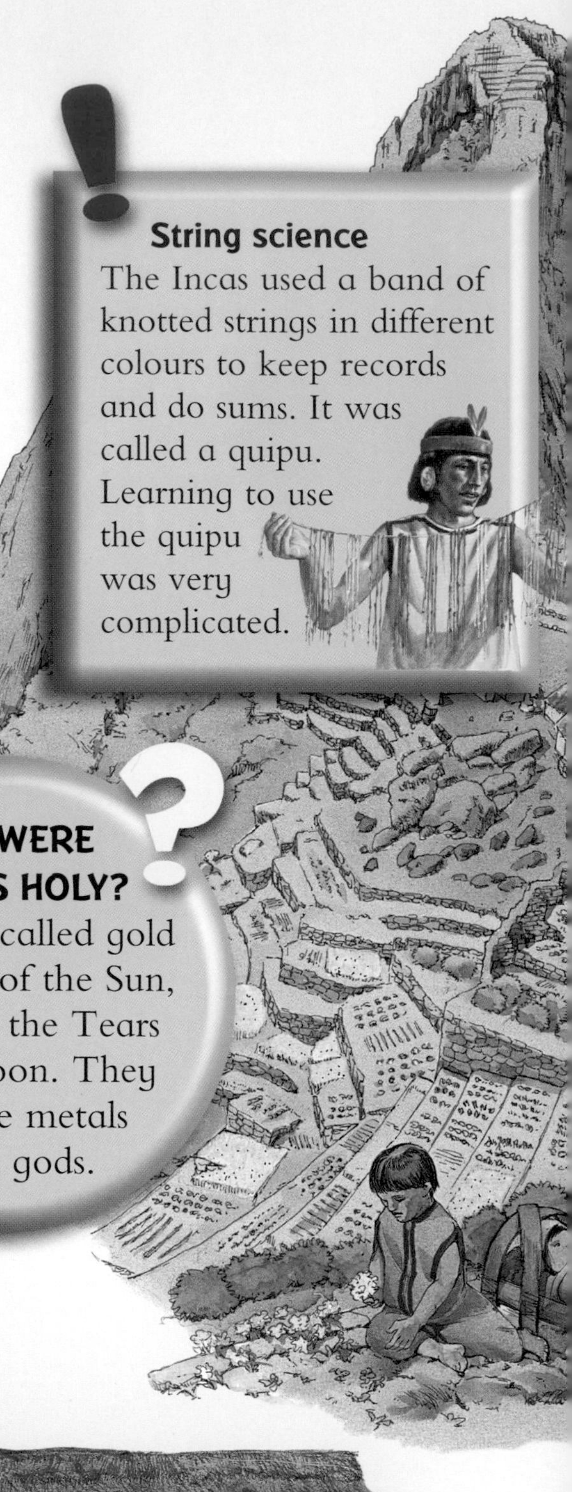

String science
The Incas used a band of knotted strings in different colours to keep records and do sums. It was called a quipu. Learning to use the quipu was very complicated.

▼ The Inca emperor made offerings to Inti, the Sun god. People believed that the emperor was descended from the Sun, and the empress from the Moon.

WHY WERE METALS HOLY?
The Incas called gold the Sweat of the Sun, and silver the Tears of the Moon. They were the metals of the gods.

► Tunics and shawls were woven from the hair of animals. Llama fibre was quite coarse, but alpaca hair was soft and silky.

▲ The Inca town of Machu Picchu was built high in the mountains. It had houses for farmers, craft workers and soldiers, a square, a temple and a palace. Fields were cut from the mountainside.

▲ The Inca emperor Atahualpa was captured by Spanish soldiers in November 1532. His people gave the soldiers a fortune in gold, but the Spanish still murdered him the following summer.

CREATIVE CORNER

Make a golden mask

Draw the outline of the mask to the size of your face. Cut out eye holes. Mark in the eyebrows, nose, mouth and ear holes. Make holes for strings.

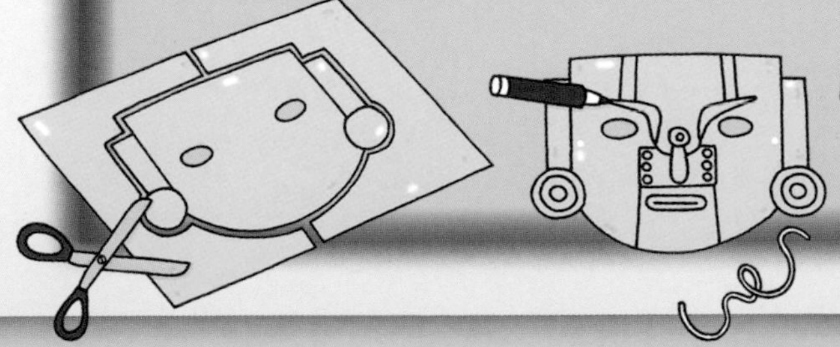

The Aztecs

The lands of Mexico and Central America also saw many civilizations grow up. The most powerful empire in the 1400s was ruled by the Aztecs. Their capital city, Tenochtitlán, was built on an island in a lake. Over 250,000 people lived there. It was destroyed by Spanish soldiers in 1521.

Worship

The Aztecs worshipped many gods. There were gods of war, of rain, of springtime and death. There were goddesses of lakes, of maize and of the hearth.

◀ The Aztecs built up platforms of mud, sticks and reeds in the lake and turned them into farmland. They grew maize, sweet potatoes, beans, tomatoes and chilli peppers.

The eagle and the cactus

The Aztec people lived far to the north. They were told by the war god to travel south. The god told them to make their home wherever they saw an eagle land on a cactus plant. At last they saw their eagle – on a swampy island in Lake Texcoco.

► Aztec nobles lived in splendid houses and palaces. These had courtyards, bedrooms and kitchens. Aztecs liked to entertain important guests with splendid feasts.

◄ The weapons of an Aztec warrior were edged with a sharp black stone called obsidian. There were two top fighting groups called the Eagles and the Jaguars. This is an Eagle warrior.

▼ A great pyramid towered over the centre of Tenochtitlán. Steps led up to temples on the top, where thousands of prisoners of war were sacrificed to the gods on stone altars.

▲ The Aztecs liked to play a ballgame called tlachtli. The rubber ball could not be handled or kicked. It had to be bounced off the body. The aim was to get it through a high stone ring.

Age of empires

Between the 1500s and the 1900s, the Europeans created huge empires in Africa, Asia and Australia as well as the Americas. Sometimes they settled in the lands they ruled. Sometimes they mined metals or planted crops to make themselves rich. The people they ruled often stayed poor.

▲ The Turkish Ottoman empire lasted from 1299 to 1922. It ruled the Middle East, North Africa and southeast Europe. One of its greatest rulers was Süleyman the Magnificent. Here, he is attacking the city of Vienna.

▼ Napoleon was a French emperor who conquered much of Europe in the 1800s. He was defeated in 1815, but even so France went on to gain a huge empire in Africa and Asia.

CAN YOU FIND?

1. a rifle
2. a bayonet
3. a French flag
4. a soldier's pack
5. a sword
6. a tricorne hat

► Britain founded colonies in North America. During the American Revolution, the colonists broke away from British rule. The rebels captured Fort Ticonderoga in 1757.

◄ In South America, the colonists also fought European rule. Rebels waged a big battle against the Spanish at Ayacucho in Peru in 1824 and defeated them. Famous fighters for freedom included Simón Bolívar.

▼ Big, fast sailing ships called clippers carried tea from China and wool from Australia back to Britain in the 1870s to 1890s. Soon the clippers were being replaced by steamships.

Queen Victoria

This queen ruled over Britain from 1837 to 1901. She also became Empress of India. She ruled over the British empire, the largest the world had ever known. At its height, the British empire covered a quarter of all the land on Earth.

Age of industry

In the 1700s and 1800s, new machines were invented, many powered by steam. Coal was mined and engineers worked out new ways of making iron and steel. This was the age of industry, when smoky cities and big factories grew up near the new canals and railways.

VOCABULARY

industry
The world of work, the making and selling of goods.

factory
A building where products are made or processed on a large scale.

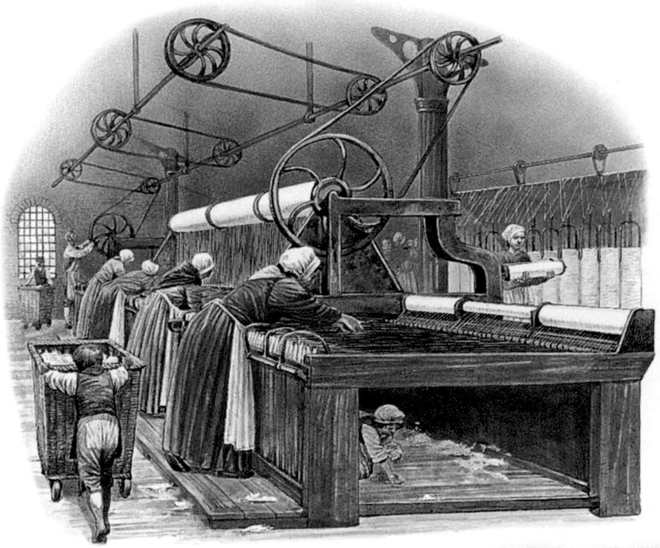

▲ Cloth was no longer woven at home, but in mills that could produce large amounts very quickly. Men, women and children worked long hours for very little pay.

▶ The Eiffel Tower was built of iron in 1887. It rose high above the city of Paris, in France. People learned new ways of building. The first skyscrapers were being built in North America.

◀ Locomotives were first used to pull steam trains in 1804. Railways were soon crossing the world. This 'iron horse' puffed its way across North America.

▲ This cast iron bridge was the first of its kind. It was built across the River Severn at Ironbridge in England, and opened in 1781. The age of industry began in Britain but soon spread across northern Europe and North America.

▲ This massive steam hammer was invented in 1842. It could beat and shape red hot iron.

▼ In Europe many people were poor and hungry during the 1800s. Some left their homes to make a new start in distant lands. These people have crossed the ocean to the United States. Their ship is passing the Statue of Liberty, in New York City.

Modern world

The last 100 years have seen the age of the motor car, the aeroplane and the space rocket. It has seen the birth of radio, cinema, television and computers. New medicines have saved millions of lives. However, this has also been an age of terrible wars.

▲ An armour-plated tank crosses a muddy battlefield in France during World War I. Millions of young men from many parts of the world died between 1914 and 1918.

Albert Einstein

▲ In the 1900s, scientists such as Albert Einstein made discoveries about how our universe works. This knowledge was used to design fearsome new weapons. Nuclear bombs were dropped (above, left) at the end of World War II (1939–1945).

▼ People dreamed of flying for hundreds of years. At last in 1903, in the United States, that dream came true. Today's big jets can take passengers huge distances in just a few hours.

▶ This weather satellite circles our planet, keeping an eye on storms down below. The first space satellite was launched in 1957. By 1969, humans were standing on the Moon. The next great space challenge is to send people to Mars.

◀ Many of the things in this bedroom would have been unknown to a girl of the 1800s. They include the computer, a radio and an electric light, as well as plastic and nylon.

▶ Cars and trucks have also made our lives much easier, but like other kinds of transport they fill the air with harmful gases. These are damaging our planet.

CREATIVE CORNER

Make a time capsule

Choose items such as photographs that will tell people in the future how we live today. Put them in a piece of pipe. Write your name, age and address inside the time capsule. Bury it underground or place it under floorboards.

Now you know!

▲ In prehistoric times people lived by hunting. They used tools and weapons made of stone.

▲ By 5,500 years ago, people in western Asia were building towns, writing, and using wheels to travel.

▲ The ancient Egyptians lived in North Africa. They built great pyramids over 4,500 years ago.

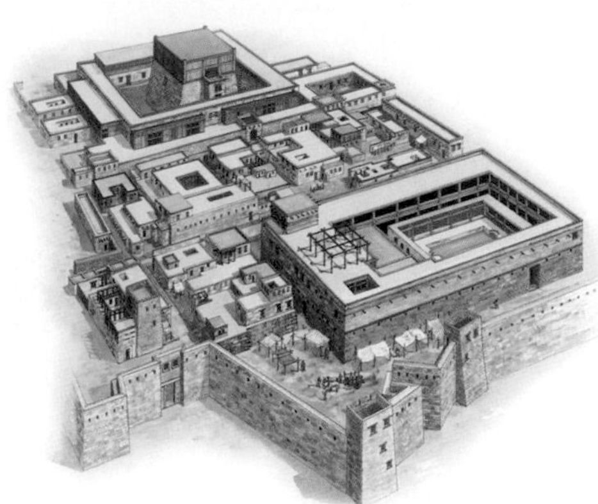

▲ The ancient Chinese built canals, walls and great cities. They created many useful inventions.

▲ More than 2,000 years ago, the Greeks and Romans produced many thinkers, sculptors, poets, mathematicians, soldiers, engineers and athletes.

▲ Castles and cathedrals were built in Europe during the Middle Ages. At this time, the Incas and the Aztecs were building cities in the Americas.

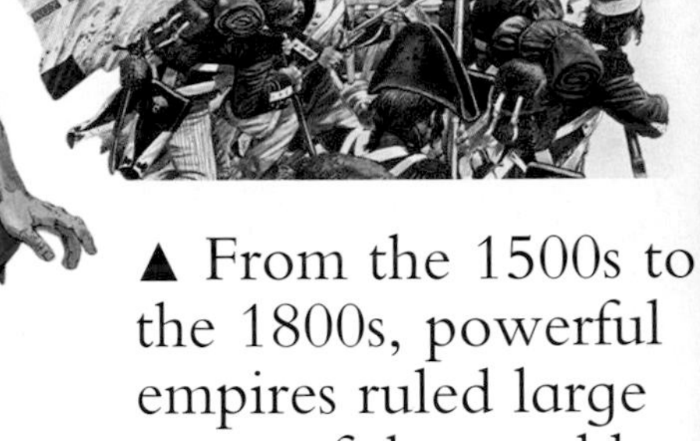

▲ From the 1500s to the 1800s, powerful empires ruled large areas of the world.

▼ In the 1700s and 1800s, many new cities, factories and railways were built. Amazing new technology was developed in the 1900s.

My body

Have you ever wondered how your body works? Your body is a complicated machine, with all the parts working together. Your body never stops working, even when you are fast asleep at night. Your heart and brain keep going 24 hours a day, for the whole of your life.

The human body

Your body is an incredible machine. It has thousands of parts that work together to keep you alive. Each group of parts, also called a system, has a particular job. For example, your muscles keep your body moving, and your blood carries oxygen and nutrients around your body. All the different systems must work properly so you can stay fit and well.

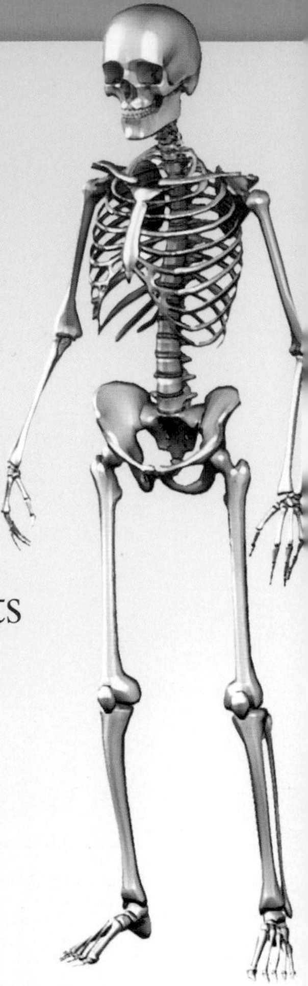

◀ The colour of our hair, skin and eyes may be different, but whatever we look like, our bodies work in exactly the same way. We are all humans.

▲ Your bones make up a structure called a skeleton. This protects your soft body organs.

VOCABULARY

organ
A part of your body that does a particular job to make it work.

nerve cell
A tiny living unit that carries messages to and from your brain.

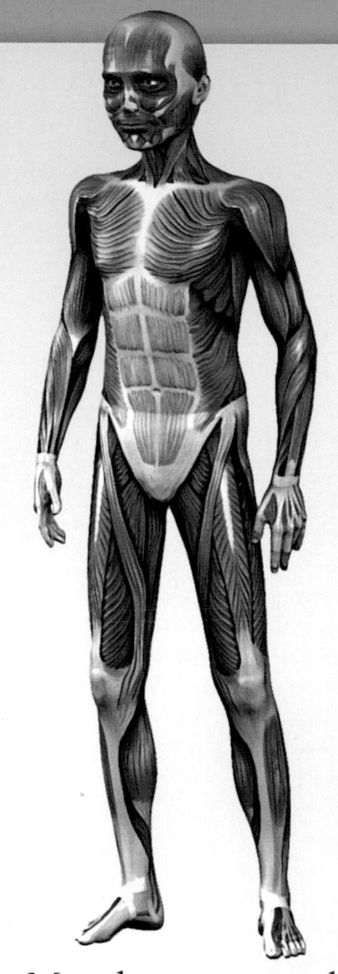

▲ Muscles are attached to your bones. They pull on the bones and this makes you move.

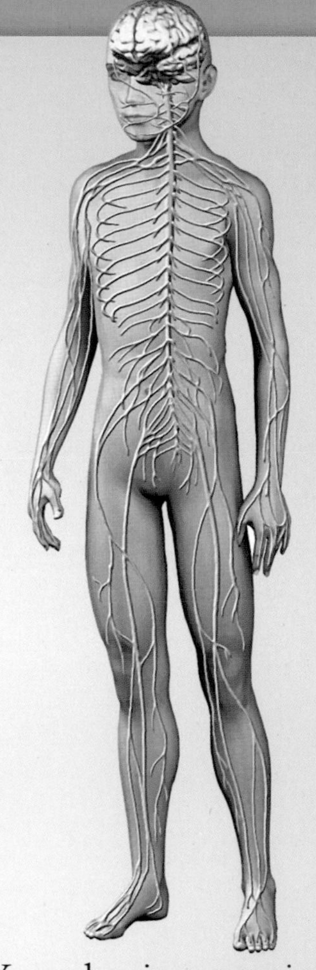

▲ Your brain contains billions of nerve cells, called neurons, that send messages around your body.

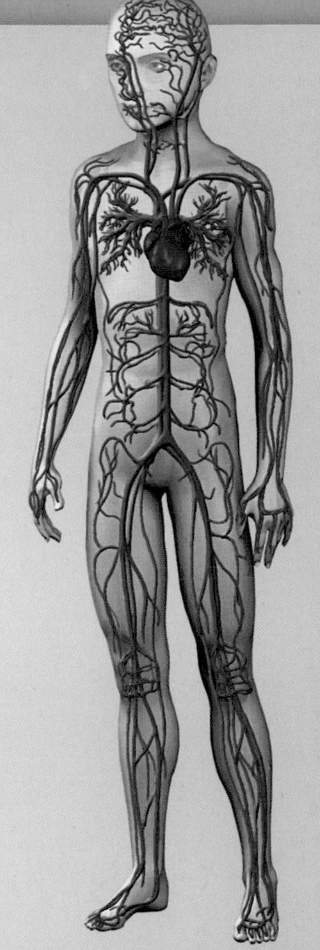

▲ Arteries carry blood away from your heart, and veins carry blood back to your heart.

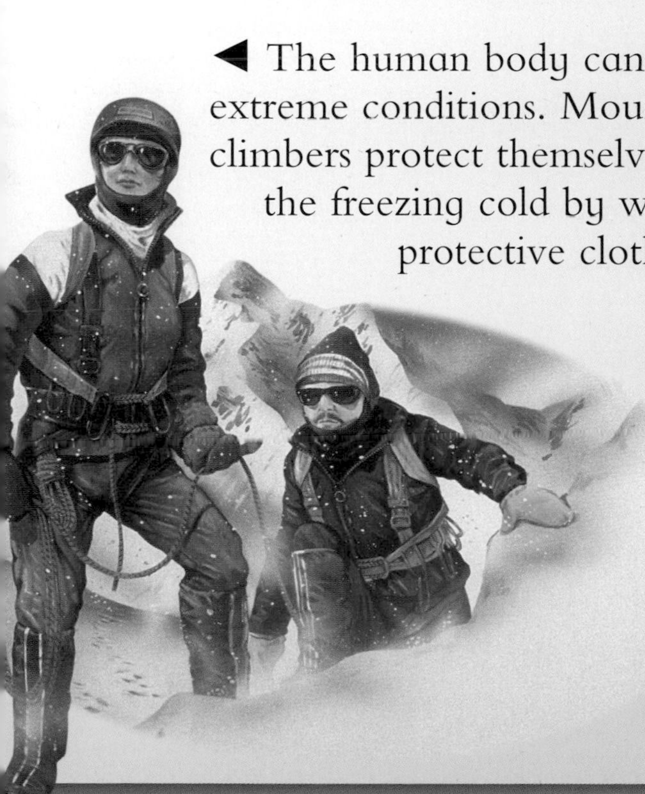

◀ The human body can survive extreme conditions. Mountain climbers protect themselves from the freezing cold by wearing protective clothing.

Pinocchio

In the story of Pinocchio, a toy-maker called Geppetto wishes for his wooden puppet to become a real boy. His wish comes true, and Pinocchio comes to life. He has lots of amazing adventures.

Skin

Your skin covers your whole body, protecting it and keeping it at the right temperature. Skin is actually your body's biggest organ. It is alive on the inside, but dead on the outside. The dead layer keeps your body waterproof, and stops it from being attacked and invaded by harmful bacteria.

HOW MUCH SKIN HAVE I GOT?

Your skin grows with you. When you are an adult, you will have about two square metres of skin.

▼ The outer layer of your skin is called the epidermis. It is covered with hairs and pores, which are tiny holes to let out your sweat. Underneath the epidermis is a living layer of skin called the dermis.

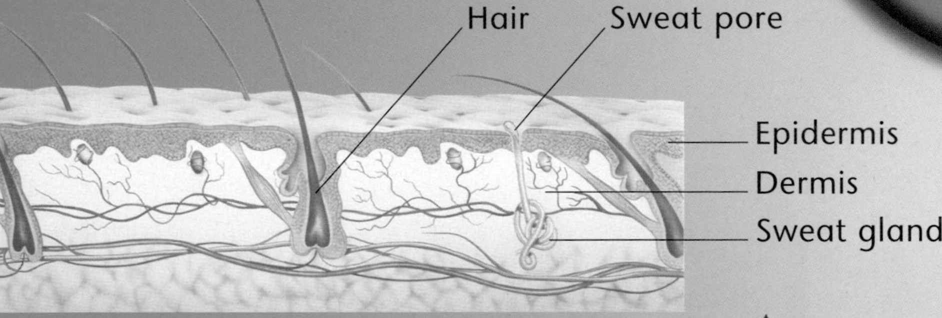

Skin colour

Everyone's skin contains a colouring substance called melanin. This tans the skin a darker colour. Dark skin contains more melanin than fair skin.

▲ As skin ages, it gets wrinkly and less elastic. Pinch yourself to see how quickly your skin goes back into place. Old skin takes much longer.

▲ Freckles are made where there are concentrated amounts of melanin in the skin. They increase and get darker in sunny weather, then fade during the winter.

▼ When you are cold, the muscles at the base of your hairs contract, making your hairs stand up on end. Small bumps, called goose bumps, appear all over your skin.

▲ Your skin is the part of your body that is exposed to the outside world. It is easy to scratch, cut or bruise your skin. However, your skin heals very quickly when it is damaged.

CREATIVE CORNER

Taking fingerprints

Use an inkpad to make your fingertip inky. Then look at the finger through a magnifying glass. The swirling pattern of lines on your fingerprint is unique. This means that no one else in the world has exactly the same fingerprint as you.

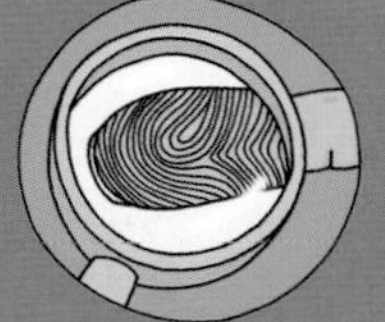

INTERNET LINKS: www.bbc.co.uk/science/humanbody/body/factfiles/skin/skin.shtml

Hair

Hair grows all over your body, except on the soles of your feet, the palms of your hands and your lips. Your hair grows from tiny pockets in your skin, called follicles. The shape of these affects how curly your hair is. Hair dies when it grows out from your skin, so it does not hurt when it is cut.

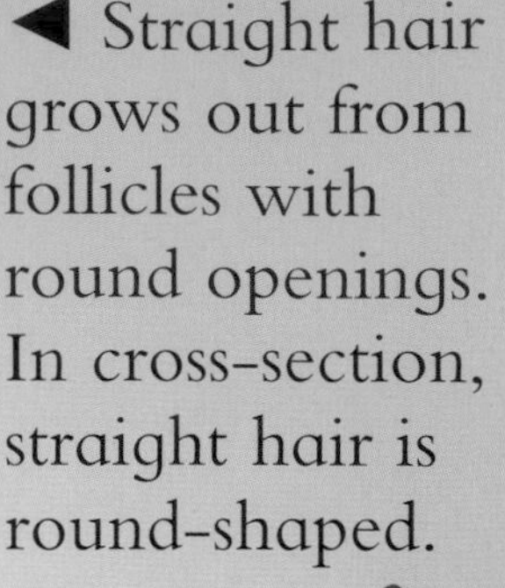

◄ Straight hair grows out from follicles with round openings. In cross-section, straight hair is round-shaped.

◄ Wavy hair is oval when seen in cross-section. This is because it grows out of oval hair follicles.

◄ Curly hairs are flat in shape, because they grow out from follicles that are shaped like slots.

Rapunzel

In the fairy-tale of Rapunzel, an evil witch traps a beautiful princess at the top of a tall tower. Rapunzel lets down her long, fair hair so that a brave prince can climb up the tower to rescue her.

HOW MANY HAIR FOLLICLES DO I HAVE?

You have hair follicles all over your body. As you get older, you get more hairy! Adults have about 20 million hair follicles.

Nails

Your nails never stop growing and need to be cut, just like your hair. Boys' fingernails usually grow faster than girls' fingernails, and everyone's nails grow more in the summer. As you get older, your nails do not grow as fast.

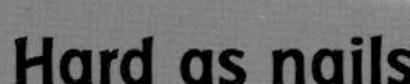

Hard as nails
The horns of a ram are like your hair and nails! Human hair and nails contain keratin. This tough protein is also found in animal horns, claws and hooves, as well as in the shafts of feathers.

VOCABULARY

cuticle
The protective flap of skin at the base of your fingernail.

circulation
The movement of blood around your body, when your heart pumps.

◀ Your fingernails grow about half a millimetre every week, and take six months to grow from base to tip. Fingernails grow faster than toenails.

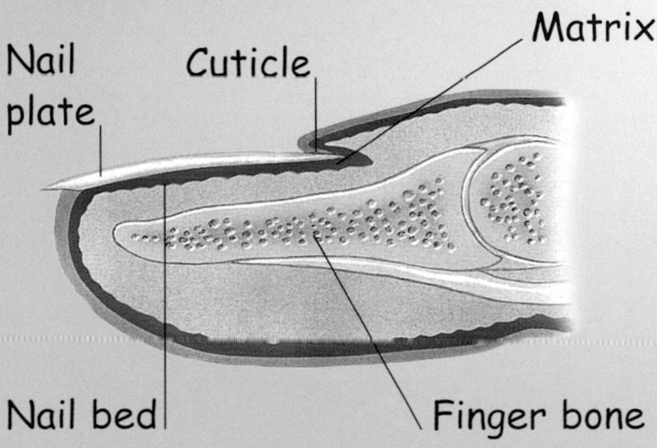

▲ Fingernails grow out from the matrix, which is underneath the cuticle. As new cells grow, older cells are pushed up and out in the form of a hard nail.

Healthy nails
Some people like to paint their nails, but this may cover up important clues about their health. For example, hard or brittle nails may mean a person has poor circulation. Or they may have an infection or a problem with their diet.

INTERNET LINKS: www.childrenfirst.nhs.uk/kids/health/body_tour/nails.html

Teeth

Children have 20 milk teeth, and grown-ups have 32 adult teeth. The part of a tooth that you can see is called the crown. It is covered with a hard, white material called enamel. The part of a tooth that is hidden under the gum is the root. The soft inside part of a tooth contains blood vessels and nerves, and is called the pulp. Everyone should look after their teeth – they have to last a very long time.

▲ Milk contains a substance called calcium, which helps teeth to grow. Drinking lots of milk and water, and eating healthy food, strengthens teeth.

The Tooth Fairy
In many countries, there is a popular tradition. If a milk tooth falls out, the child puts it under their pillow. The Tooth Fairy will take it away to her castle, and leave them some money in return.

Milk teeth
Gum
Adult teeth
Jaw bone

▲ Your first teeth are called your milk teeth. These teeth start to fall out from about the age of six. They are gradually pushed out by the adult teeth which move up or down from the gums.

Cleaning teeth
Small bits of leftover food in the mouth mix with saliva to form plaque. This sticks and can cause tooth decay. Brushing teeth after every meal stops this happening.

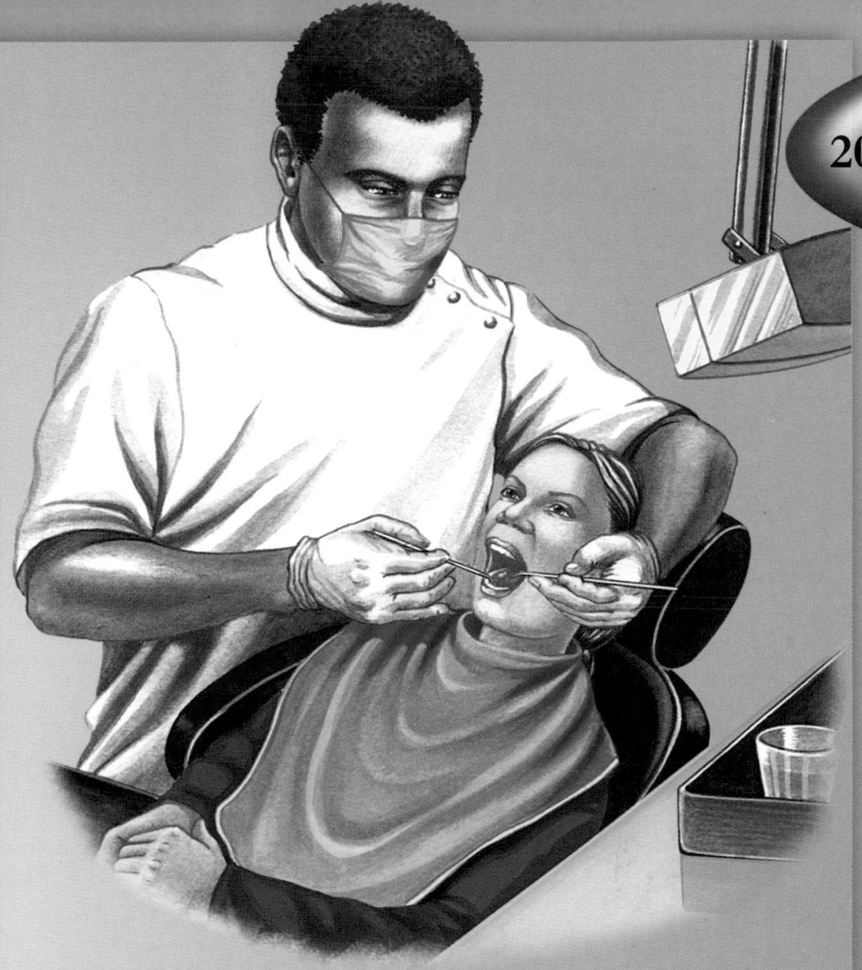

▲ Regular visits to the dentist for check-ups are vital. Dentists can spot if there is something wrong with your teeth or gums. They can give the right treatment or advice before the problem gets worse.

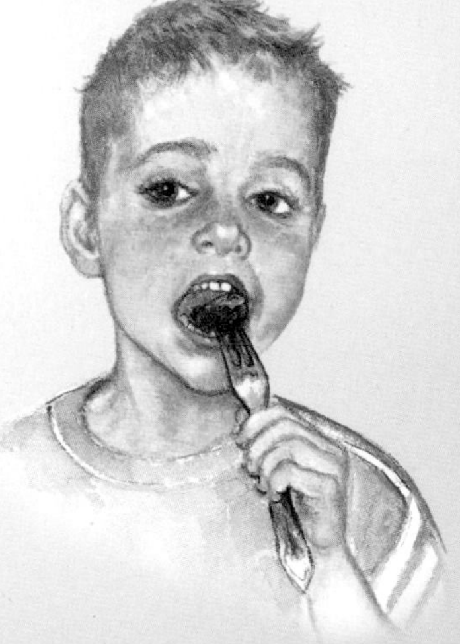

▲ The incisor and canine teeth at the front of the mouth bite into food. The strong, flat molars at the back are used for chewing. Food is easier to digest if it is chewed properly.

CREATIVE CORNER

Tooth experiment
When a milk tooth falls out, put it in a glass. Then pour in some cola. See what happens to the tooth after a day, and again after a week. You will see why sweet fizzy drinks like cola are so bad for your teeth.

INTERNET LINKS: www.bbc.co.uk/schools/scienceclips/ages/7_8/teeth_eating.shtml

Bones

All your bones link up to form your skeleton, which supports your body and protects its organs. Some of the bones are very big, while others are tiny. You were born with about 300 bones, but as you grow up, some of the bones fuse together. Adults have about 200 bones.

VOCABULARY

X-ray
A special photograph of the inside of the body.

cartilage
Tissue found in joints and in the soft parts of the skeleton.

▲ The point where two bones meet is called a joint. A layer of tissue called cartilage covers the bones in a joint so they move together smoothly. The biggest joint in your body is your knee.

◀ Bones are strong, but they can break. Doctors take X-rays to look at broken bones. Children's bones are growing, so they mend more quickly than adults' bones.

CREATIVE CORNER

Make a dancing skeleton

Draw a skeleton on some card, leaving a gap between the main joints. Cut out the joints, then use butterfly clips to fix them together again. Make your skeleton move its arms and legs.

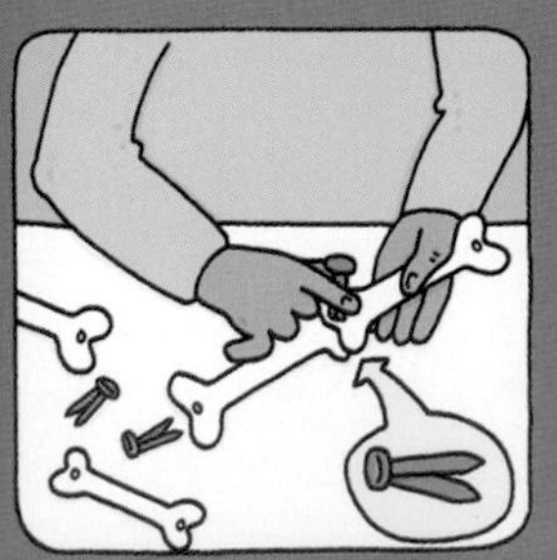

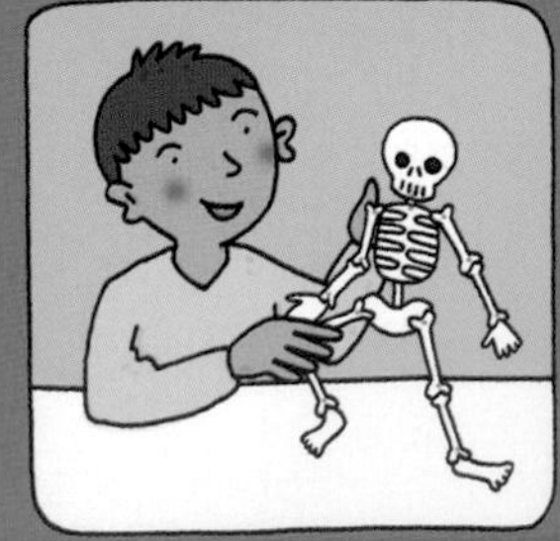

Muscles

Muscles are attached to your bones, and they make your body move. They pull, but they cannot push, so most of the muscles have to work in pairs or groups. When you take a step, you use about 200 different muscles! When you are sitting still, muscles are making organs work inside your body.

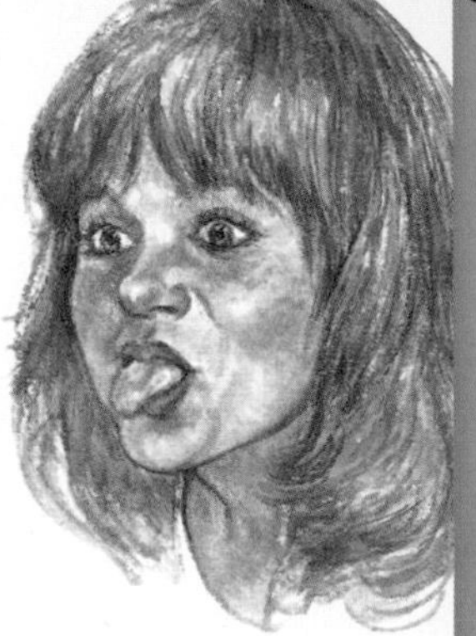

▶ Your tongue is made up of a group of very strong and flexible muscles. You can move your tongue to speak, eat and pull silly faces!

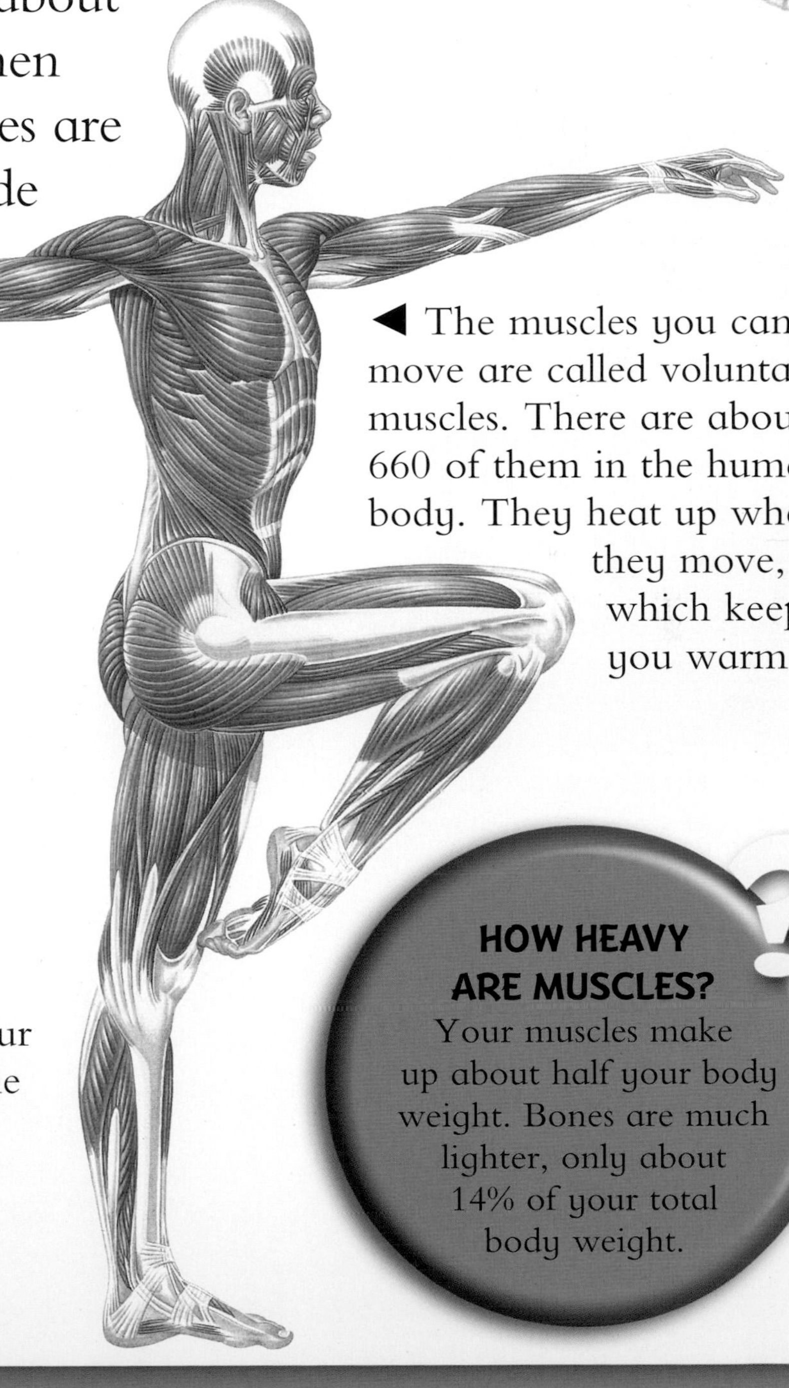

◀ The muscles you can move are called voluntary muscles. There are about 660 of them in the human body. They heat up when they move, which keeps you warm.

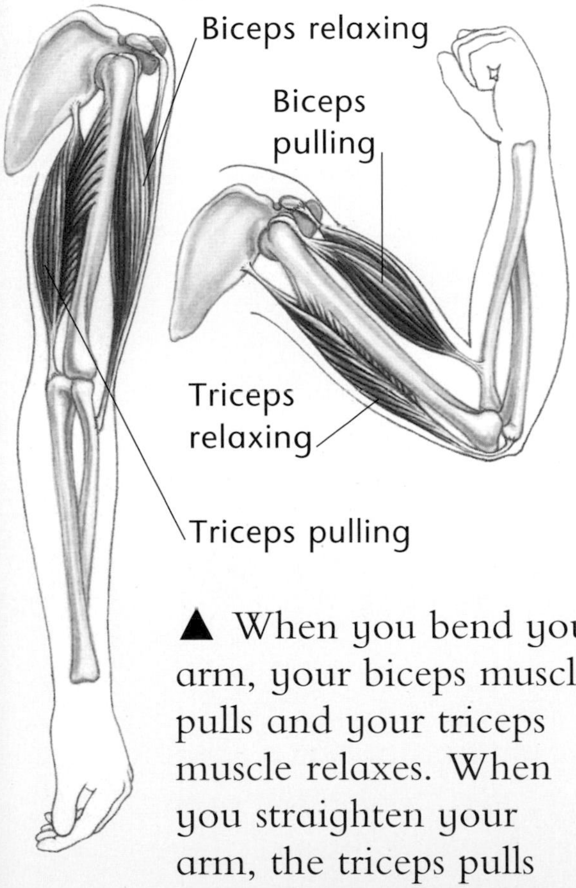

Biceps relaxing

Biceps pulling

Triceps relaxing

Triceps pulling

▲ When you bend your arm, your biceps muscle pulls and your triceps muscle relaxes. When you straighten your arm, the triceps pulls and the biceps relaxes.

HOW HEAVY ARE MUSCLES?

Your muscles make up about half your body weight. Bones are much lighter, only about 14% of your total body weight.

The body organs

The organs inside your body all work together to keep you alive and well. Your lungs help you to breathe, your heart pumps blood around your body and your brain controls every move that you make. Your liver, kidneys, stomach and intestines process everything you eat and drink.

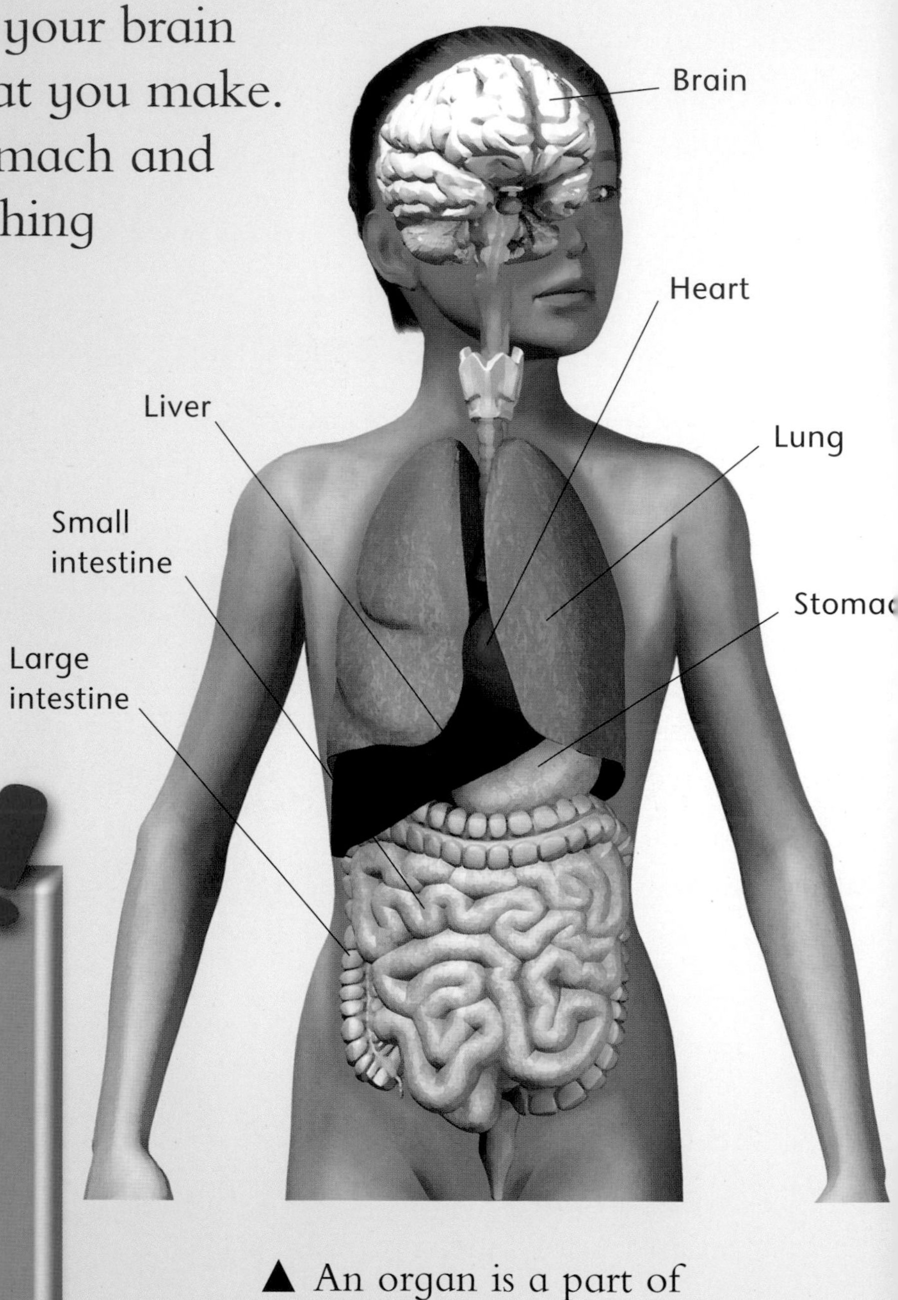

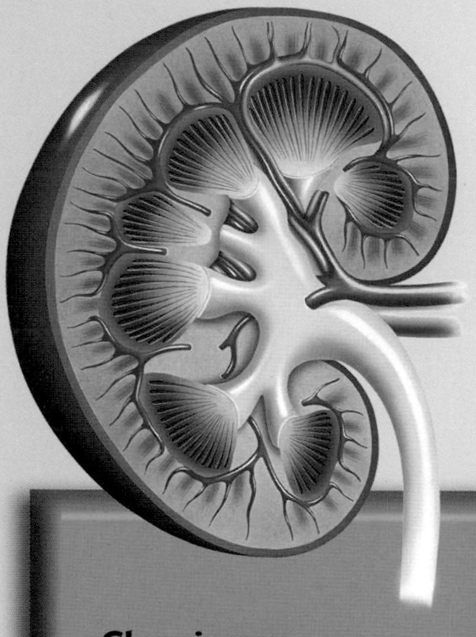

Cleaning up
You have two kidneys and each one is the size of your fist. Your kidneys filter blood, taking out unwanted water and chemicals. Urine is made from this waste, and passed down to your bladder. You empty your bladder when you go to the toilet.

▲ An organ is a part of your body that has a special job to do. Your body organs work hard all the time, even when you are asleep.

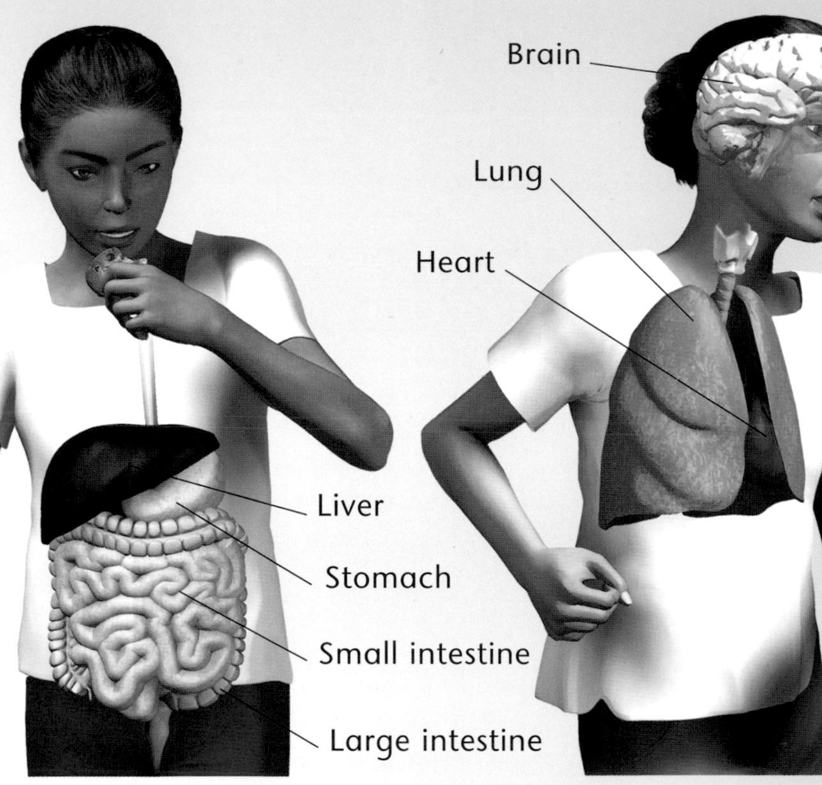

VOCABULARY

chemical
A substance that can change if mixed with another substance.

bladder
A bag inside your body that collects urine from both your kidneys.

◀ When you run, your brain tells your arms and legs to move, your lungs breathe in oxygen and your heart pumps blood to your muscles.

▲ Your stomach and small intestine digest food. Your liver sorts chemicals and stores nutrients. Undigested food is held in the large intestine, and passed out as waste.

CAN YOU FIND?

1. brain
2. lung
3. heart
4. liver
5. stomach
6. kidney
7. small intestine
8. large intestine

CREATIVE CORNER

Heart rate experiment
Find your friend's pulse and feel it for one minute. Ask your friend to run around the park, then feel the pulse again. It will be faster than before. This is because the exercise has made your friend's heart beat faster.

Lungs and breathing

You never stop breathing, even when you are asleep. This is because your body needs oxygen, one of the gases in the air. A strong muscle called the diaphragm pulls downwards to make you breathe in. Air is sucked into your lungs. They absorb oxygen, and then your diaphragm moves upwards to make you breathe out again.

▼ When you blow up a balloon, or blow out candles, you are breathing out a gas called carbon dioxide. This is a waste gas that your body does not need.

► When you exercise, your breathing speeds up. The extra oxygen you breathe in is absorbed into your blood and pumped fast around your body.

Apache creation story

An Apache story from North America describes how the creator of all things made a small brown ball, about the size of a bean. He asked the wind to go inside the ball and blow it up. The ball became Earth, the planet we live on now.

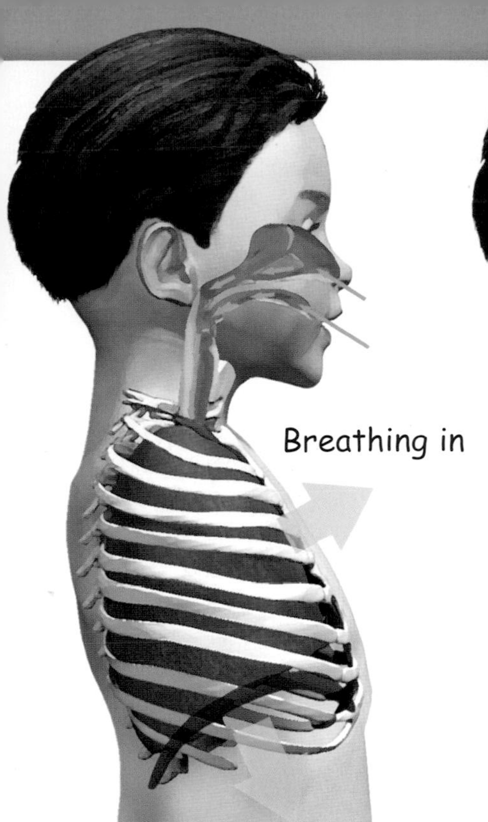

▲ You breathe in through your windpipe, or trachea. You can feel your chest expand as your lungs fill with air.

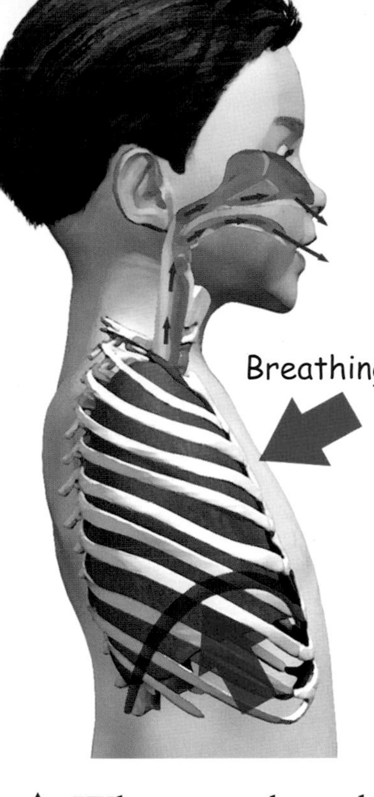

▲ When you breathe out, you can feel your chest go down again. If your lungs were empty, they would collapse.

▲ You cannot breathe under water because there is no oxygen. This is why scuba divers use oxygen tanks. Without the oxygen, they would die very quickly.

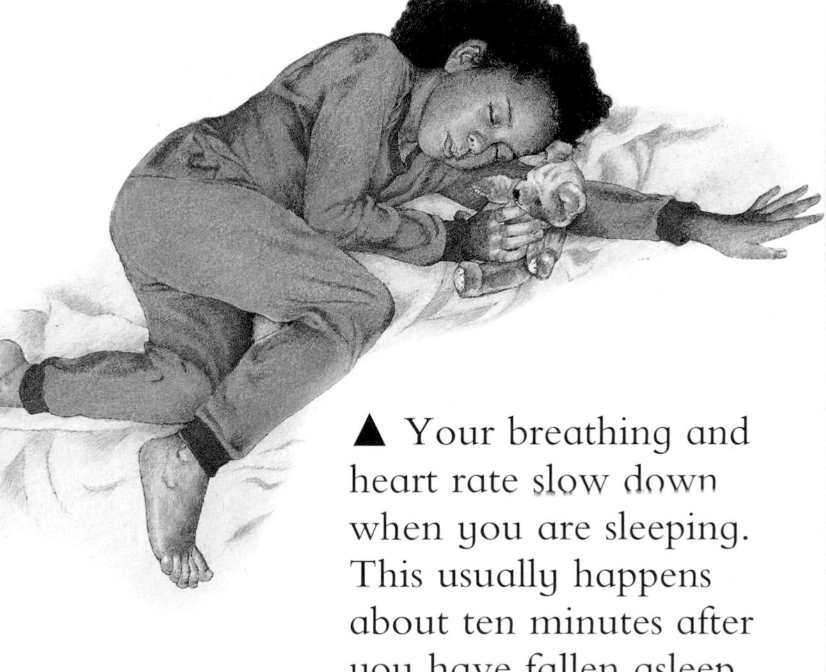

▲ Your breathing and heart rate slow down when you are sleeping. This usually happens about ten minutes after you have fallen asleep, when you begin to go into a deep sleep.

Inside your lungs

Air goes into each lung through a tube called a bronchus. The bronchus divides into many smaller tubes, which end in tiny stretchy sacs, called alveoli. Oxygen passes through the alveoli into the blood, and carbon dioxide passes back through the alveoli into the lungs.

Group of alveoli

INTERNET LINKS: www.kidshealth.org/kid/body/lungs_SW.html

Heart and blood

The heart is a powerful muscle that pushes blood around your body. In one minute, the heart can pump a single drop of blood down to your toes and back up again. The blood is constantly moving around your body through long tubes, called blood vessels. Blood carries oxygen from your lungs, and nutrients from your food, to all your body organs and muscles.

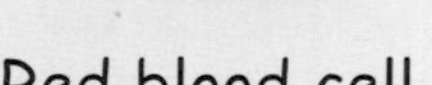

Red blood cell

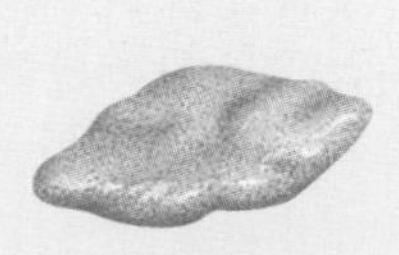

Platelet

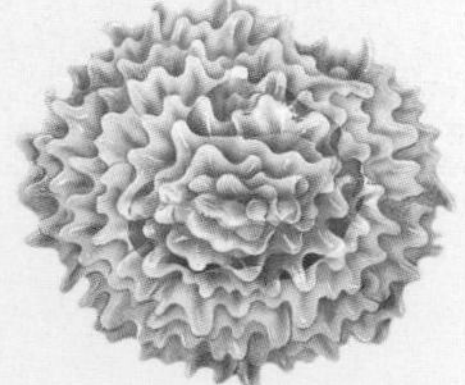

White blood cell

▲ One drop of blood contains millions of cells. Most of them are red, but some are white. Blood contains platelets, which help clots to form. Blood cells and platelets float in a liquid called plasma.

The Tinman

In the story 'The Wizard of Oz', the Tinman is sad because he is made of metal and has no heart. He goes in search of one, along with a scarecrow who needs a brain, a lion that needs courage and a girl called Dorothy who needs to find her way home.

Largest artery (aorta)

Largest vein (vena cava)

Wall of muscle (septum)

▲ The heart has two upper and two lower chambers, divided in the middle by a wall of muscle. Blood flows in through veins and out through arteries.

VOCABULARY

cell
The smallest unit that there is of any living thing.

clot
Blood that thickens and sticks together, often to heal a wound to the body.

▲ Exercise makes your heart stronger, helping it to pump more blood with every heartbeat. This brings more oxygen to your muscles and body organs, so they can work better. It is important to take exercise to keep your heart healthy.

Upper chamber (atrium)

Lower chamber (ventricle)

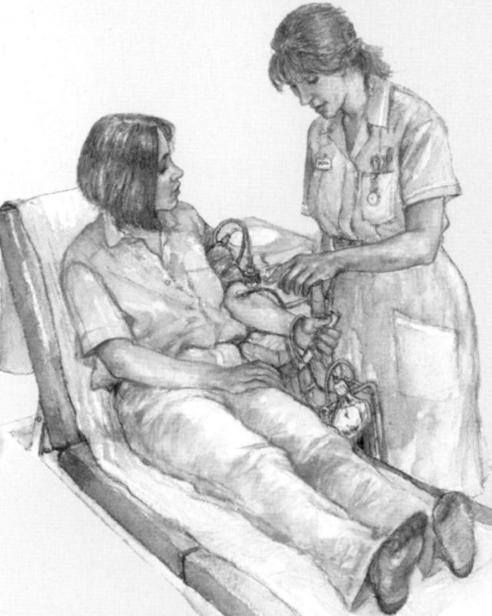

◀ You have about four litres of blood. Adults have more, and babies have less. You can give blood to help people who are sick, or who have had serious accidents.

WHAT IS CIRCULATION?

Circulation is the movement of blood around your body. As your blood moves, it carries oxygen away from your lungs, and brings carbon dioxide back.

Heart beat
Your heart rate is the number of times your heart beats in one minute. Babies up to the age of one have a heart rate of 120–160 beats per minute. By the age of 12, this falls to about 70–80 beats per minute.

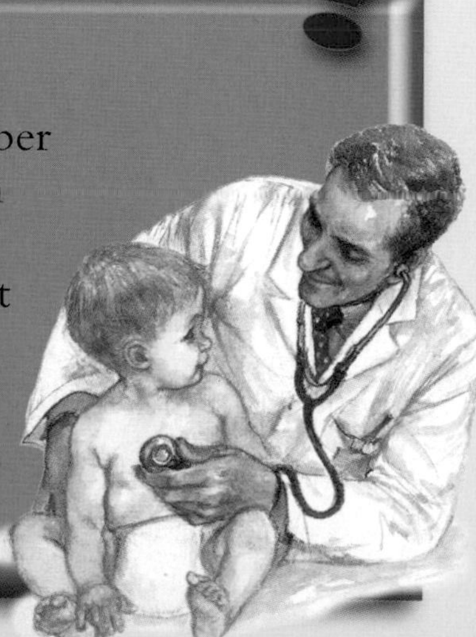

INTERNET LINKS: www.kidshealth.org/kid/body/heart_noSW.html

Food and digestion

The food you eat takes a long journey through your body. The way your body processes this food is called digestion. Some food is digested and turned into energy to keep your body active. Nutrients from the food help your body to grow, keep healthy and repair itself. Some food is not digested, and is passed out of your body when you go to the toilet.

► When your food reaches your stomach, it is churned up into a liquid. The liquid then flows through your small intestine. Goodness from the food is passed into your blood, and pumped around your body.

HOW DO I SWALLOW?

When you swallow your food, strong muscles squeeze it along your digestive system. This process is called peristalsis.

Oesophagus

Liver

Stomach

Small intestine

Large intestine

► You get rid of undigested food when you go to the toilet. When you were a baby you had to wear a nappy to catch this waste.

Fats keep you warm, but you only need a small amount. Eat fewer fats than other foods.

◀ Some foods are much better for you than others. This food pyramid shows the balance of the foods that you should eat to stay healthy. Avoid too many snacks full of fat and sugar.

Foods that contain protein help your body to mend itself, so eat plenty.

Vitamins, minerals and fibre keep your body healthy. You should eat plenty of fresh vegetables and fruit every day.

Foods that are rich in carbohydrates give you energy and are important in your diet.

◀ Food gives you energy, and that energy is measured in kilojoules. When you play sport, you use lots of energy.

CREATIVE CORNER

Make a food poster

Divide a piece of paper into five sections. At the top of each section, write the name of a food group: fats, vitamins, minerals, proteins and carbohydrates. Cut out some food pictures and stick them on the correct section of your poster.

INTERNET LINKS: www.kidshealth.org/kid/body/digest_SW.html

Senses

You have five senses, and each one of them is important. Your senses help you experience the world around you, and keep you safe by warning you of danger. You use your senses of sight and hearing to see and hear things. Smell and taste help you enjoy good food, and you feel things with your sense of touch. Your clever brain controls all of your senses.

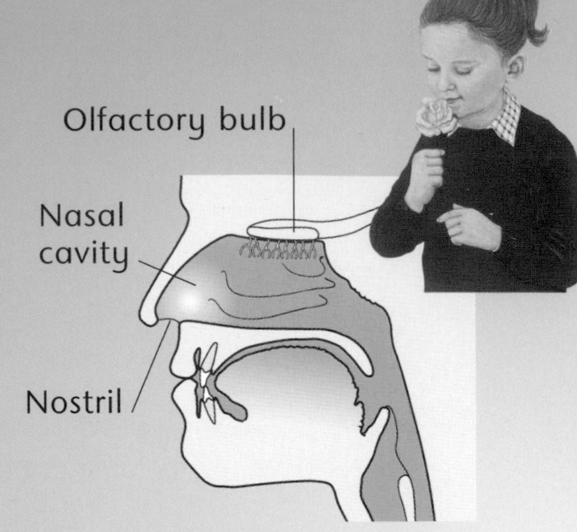

▲ Smell sensors in the olfactory (smelling) bulb in your nose send messages to your brain to tell you whether something, like a rose, smells nice.

Reading by touch
Blind people use their sense of touch to read. Braille is an alphabet of raised dots that can be read by feeling the page. It is named after its inventor, a Frenchman called Louis Braille.

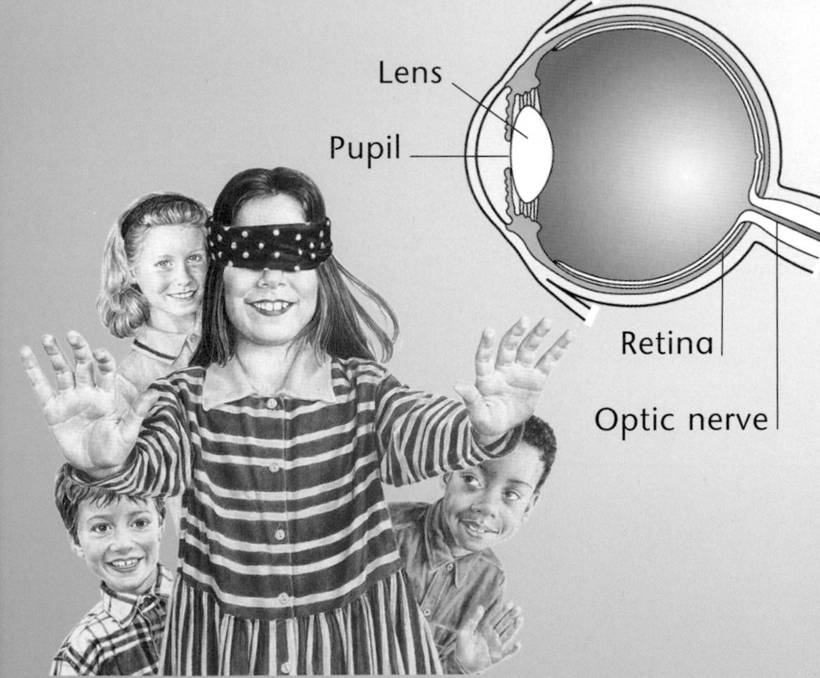

▲ You need your eyes to see! Light enters your eye through the pupil. An image is projected upside down onto the retina. Your brain turns this image around, so you see it the right way up.

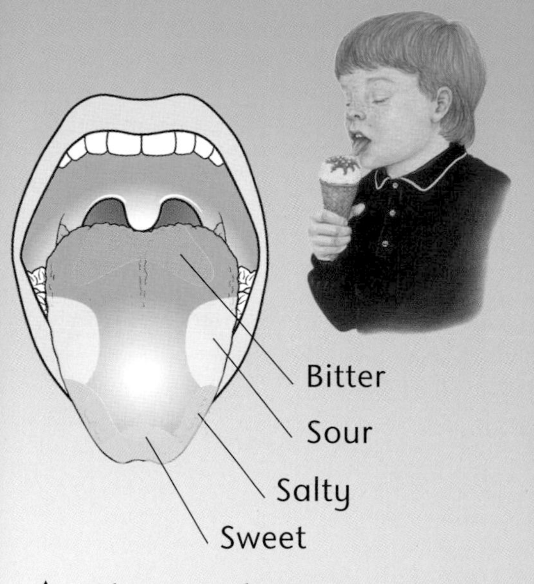

The Emperor's New Clothes
A silly emperor tells his people that he is wearing a fine robe, when he is completely naked! Everyone believes him, except one boy. This boy trusts what he can see with his own eyes, and tells the emperor the truth.

▲ The tiny bumps on your tongue are called tastebuds. Different areas of your tongue detect sweet, sour, salty and bitter flavours.

► Waves of sound travel through the air to reach your ears. The loudness of a sound is measured in units called decibels. If you listen to a very loud sound for too long, you may damage your hearing.

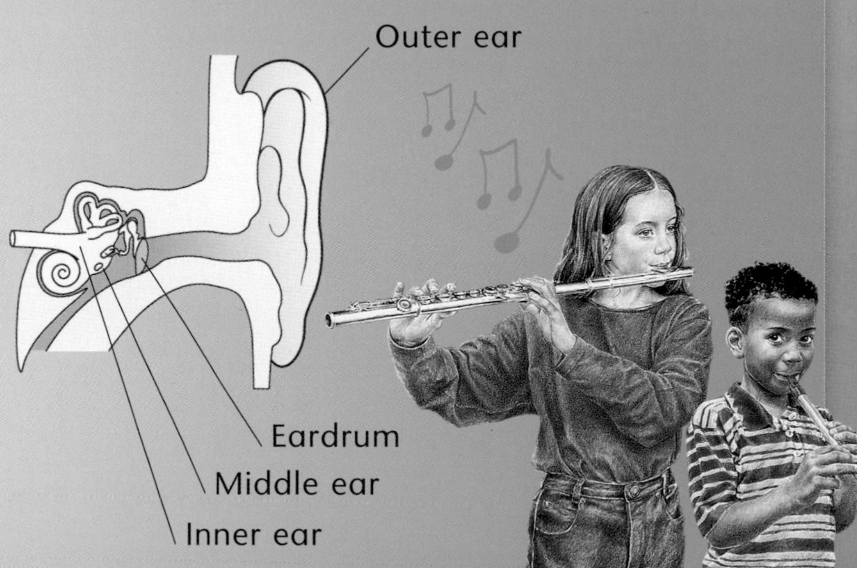

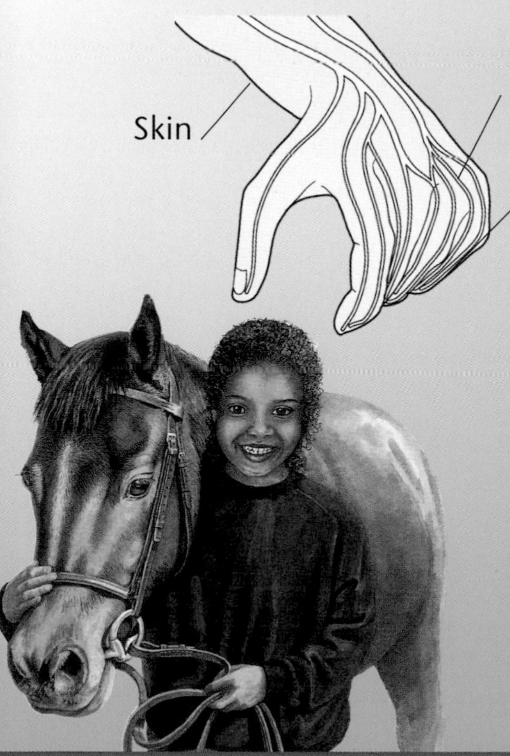

◄ When you touch something, receptor cells under your skin send messages to your brain through sensory nerves. Your brain interprets these messages, and makes you react to whatever you touch.

VOCABULARY

receptor cell
A cell that reacts to something by sending a message through the body to the brain.

optic nerve
This nerve takes messages from your eye to your brain.

Brain and nerves

Your brain is one of the most important organs in your body. It is your body's control centre. Your brain works by using a very complicated system of nerves. These nerves carry signals to and from your brain, reaching every single part of your body. The human brain looks a bit like a wrinkly walnut. It has two halves, called hemispheres, and each half controls different kinds of activities that the body carries out.

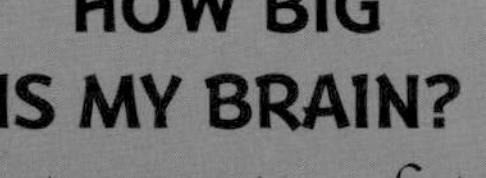

HOW BIG IS MY BRAIN?

Put your two fists together. Your brain is about that big. It is protected by a hard, bony case, which is your skull.

Thoughts

Speech

▲ The left hemisphere of your brain controls all five senses. Your body sends signals to this part of your brain to process what you see, hear, touch, smell and taste. The left side of your brain also controls thought, speech and skilled movement.

Super brain

Your brain controls every action and reaction that you have. It helps you to think, speak, feel emotions and do countless different things. Believe it or not, scientists think that most people use only about 10% of their full brainpower!

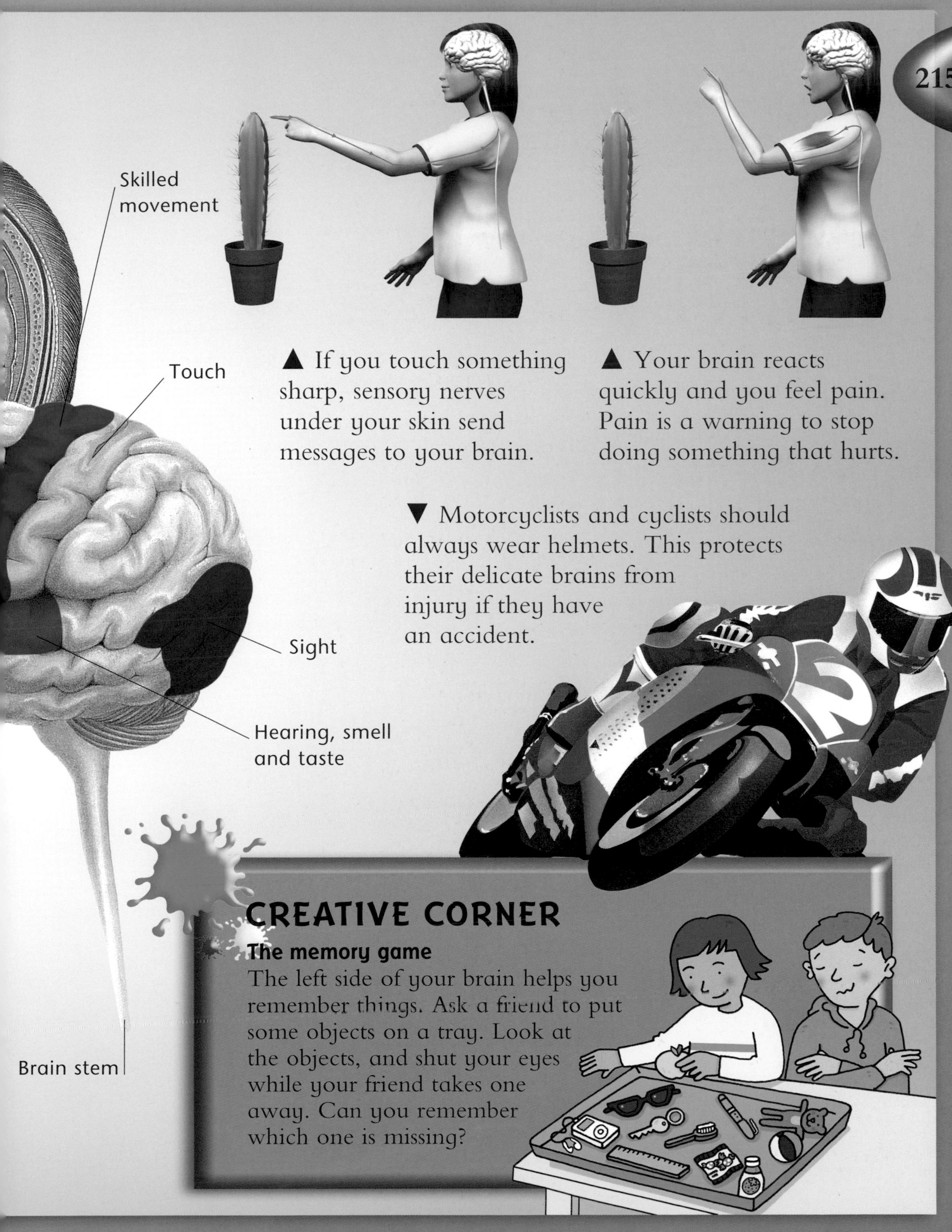

▲ If you touch something sharp, sensory nerves under your skin send messages to your brain.

▲ Your brain reacts quickly and you feel pain. Pain is a warning to stop doing something that hurts.

▼ Motorcyclists and cyclists should always wear helmets. This protects their delicate brains from injury if they have an accident.

CREATIVE CORNER

The memory game

The left side of your brain helps you remember things. Ask a friend to put some objects on a tray. Look at the objects, and shut your eyes while your friend takes one away. Can you remember which one is missing?

A new life

Your amazing body is made up of billions of living units, which are called cells. But you began your life as one single cell, a fertilized egg inside your mother's body. You grew in her womb, or uterus, for about nine months, until you were ready to be born.

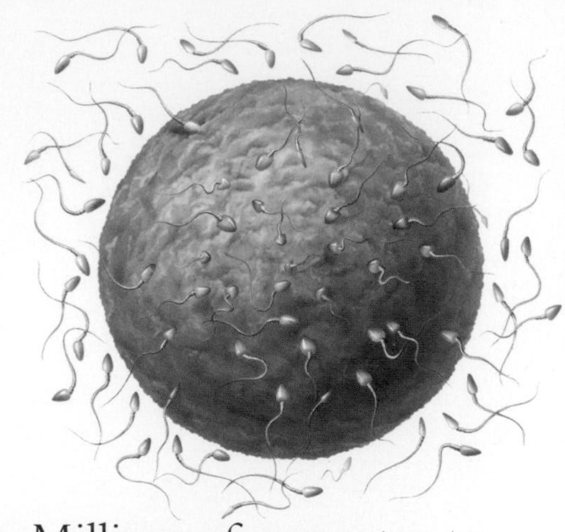

▲ Millions of sperm try to fertilize an egg, but only one is successful. A new cell is created. This divides many times and slowly grows into a human baby

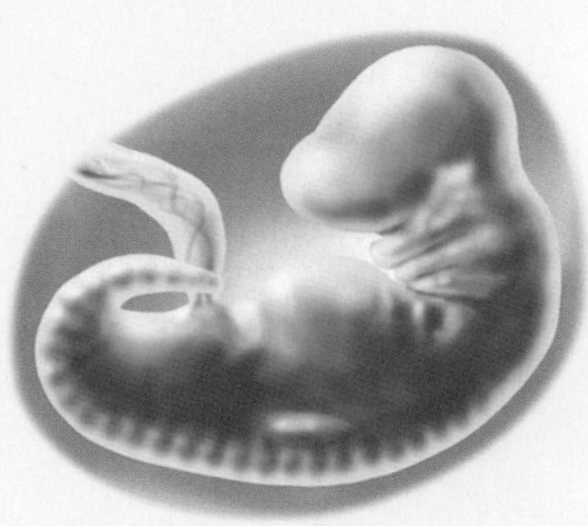

◀ The fertilized egg travels to the mother's uterus and attaches itself. The new human life is called a foetus. At four weeks, it is the size of your thumbnail.

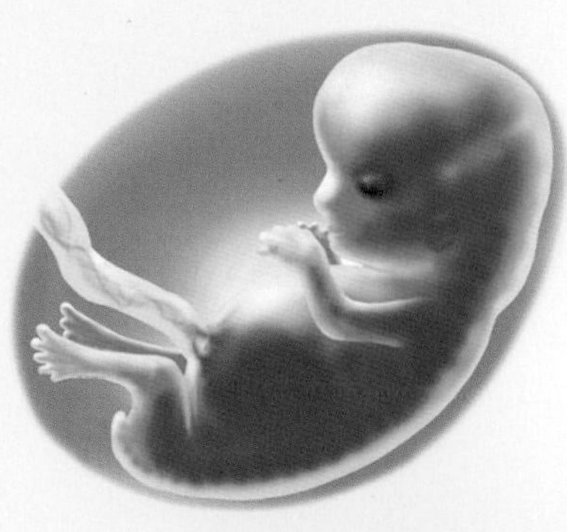

◀ The foetus grows, and after about 8 weeks it is about the size of your ear. It is already starting to look like a baby.

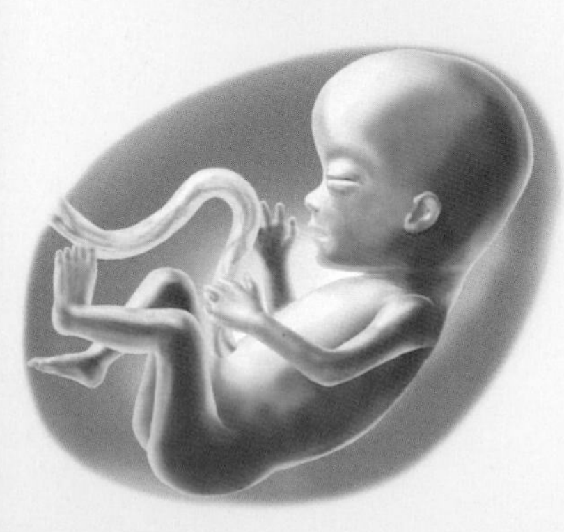

◀ The baby continues to grow inside a bag of watery liquid. A tube, called the umbilical cord, carries oxygen and nutrients from the mother to the baby. By 12 weeks, the baby is as big as your fist.

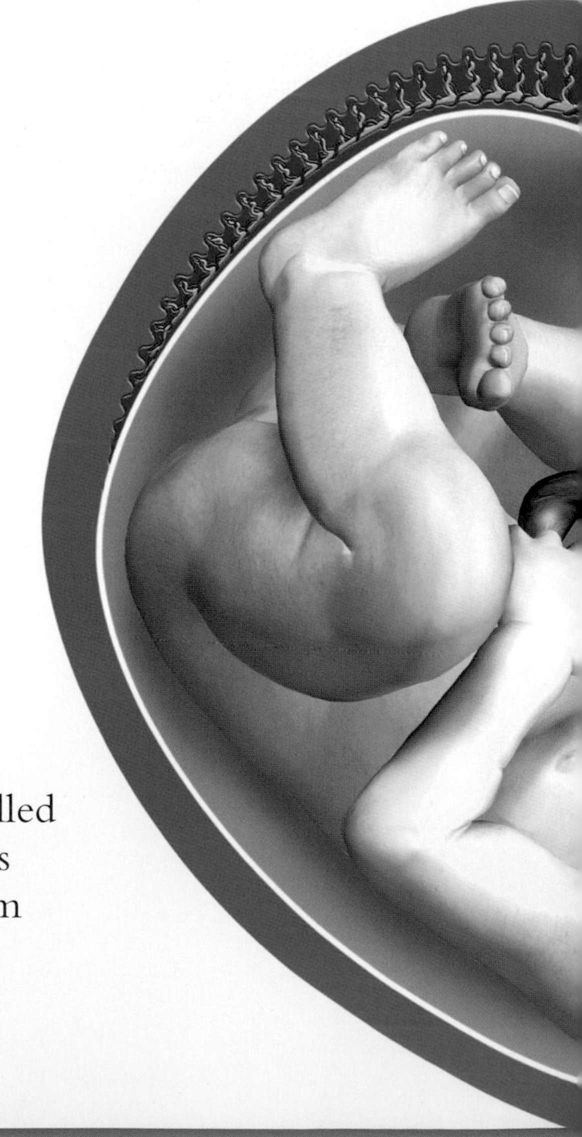

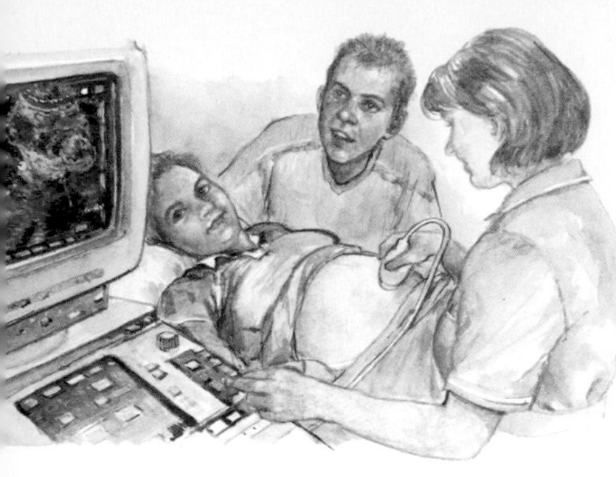

▲ A pregnant woman can see her baby when she has a scan. Doctors check that her baby is well, and may tell her whether it is a boy or girl.

The founders of Rome

Romulus and Remus are twins in a famous Roman legend. Their mother abandoned them when they were babies, and a female wolf looked after them. Years later, they decided to start building the city of Rome where the wolf had found them.

▼ There is not much space inside the uterus, so the growing baby lies with its arms and legs tucked up close to its body. After about 40 weeks, the baby leaves the womb, usually head first.

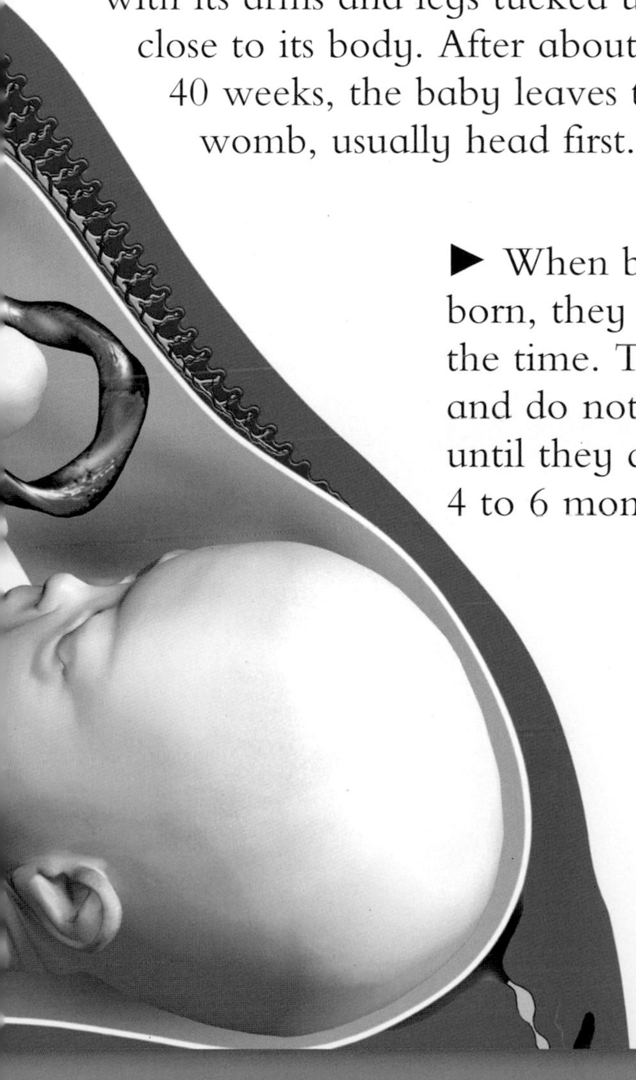

WHY DO I LOOK LIKE MY FAMILY?

Genes are the body's instructions for the creation of a new person, and parents pass them on to their children.

► When babies are first born, they sleep for most of the time. They drink milk, and do not eat solid food until they are about 4 to 6 months old.

INTERNET LINKS: www.kidshealth.org/kid/feeling/home_family/mom_pregnant.html

Growing older

As you get older, your body grows. During the first year after birth, the body grows very quickly. The growth is controlled by hormones, which are carried by your blood to different parts of your body. When you are an adult, you will stop growing. Some old people get shorter as their bodies lose muscle and fat.

VOCABULARY

hormone
A substance that makes a part of your body react. Growth hormones make you grow.

teenager
A young person aged between the ages of 13 and 19 years.

Growing pains
Have you ever wanted to grow to be as big as a giant, or shrink to be as small as a mouse? In a famous children's story, a little girl called Alice drinks a potion that makes her become tiny, and then eats a cake that makes her huge. These strange things happen in a place called Wonderland.

▲ By the time they are one year old, most toddlers have learned to crawl or walk.

► As children get older, they learn to control their muscles and hop, skip or ride a bike. When they go to school, they learn to read and write.

HOW FAST WILL I GROW?

Children grow at different speeds, and by the age of 10, some are taller than others. They usually 'catch up' by the time they are adults.

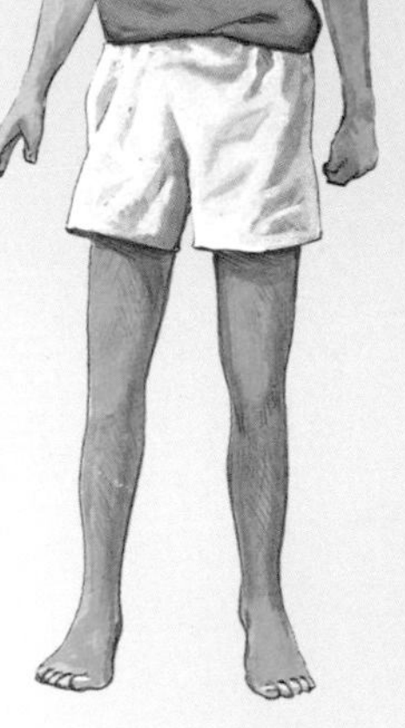

6 years old 12 years old 21 years old 65 years old

◀ Hormones make you grow at particular times, for example when you are a teenager. They also stop you from growing when you are about 21.

▼ Around the world, people now live twice as long as they did 200 years ago. It is more common for people to live to 100 years old.

CREATIVE CORNER

Make a height chart

Draw a straight line on a piece of paper. Write 50cm at the bottom, and mark every 5cm up to the 1.5m mark. Paint a picture next to the line. Fix your height chart 50cm above ground level, and then measure how tall you are.

Health and fitness

You must look after your body to stay fit and well. If you neglect your body, you become ill. It is vital to make sure you eat the right kinds of food, and do not have too much fat or sugar in your diet. It is also very important to enjoy the things you do. Keep active, and remember to take exercise if you want to live a long, healthy and happy life.

◀ Exercise keeps you fit, and is fun! Walk, run and play sports as much as you can, and get lots of fresh air.

▲ To stay healthy, you need to wash properly and clean your teeth regularly. Always wash your hands after you go to the toilet.

The weight of the sky
In the Greek myth, super-strong Atlas fought against the gods of Mount Olympus. As a punishment for upsetting the gods, he was forced to stand at the edge of the Earth and bear the weight of the sky on his shoulders. In pictures and statues of Atlas, the sky is often shown as a celestial sphere.

VOCABULARY

physical
To do with the body and how all the parts of the body work together.

mental
To do with the mind and the way the brain works.

◀ If you eat the right food, you are giving your body the nutrients it needs to stay well and to fight illness. You should eat at least five portions of fruit and vegetables every day as part of a healthy diet.

▼ It is good to hug the people you love because it makes you feel happy. Your emotional and mental health is very important, because it is linked to your physical health.

CREATIVE CORNER

Keep a sleep diary

Did you sleep well last night? Keep a sleep diary for a few weeks. Write down how many hours of sleep you get during the night. When you wake up each morning, make a note of how you feel. Do you think there is a link between feeling good and sleeping well?

Fighting disease

If germs get inside your body, they multiply and cause an infection, which makes you ill. Your body is always fighting germs to keep you well. Sometimes you do not even know it is happening. For example, when you cry, your tears are cleaning out the germs in your eyes.

▲ Sneezes and coughs are often symptoms of a common cold. You can take medicine to ease the symptoms of a cold, but there is no cure for the common cold virus.

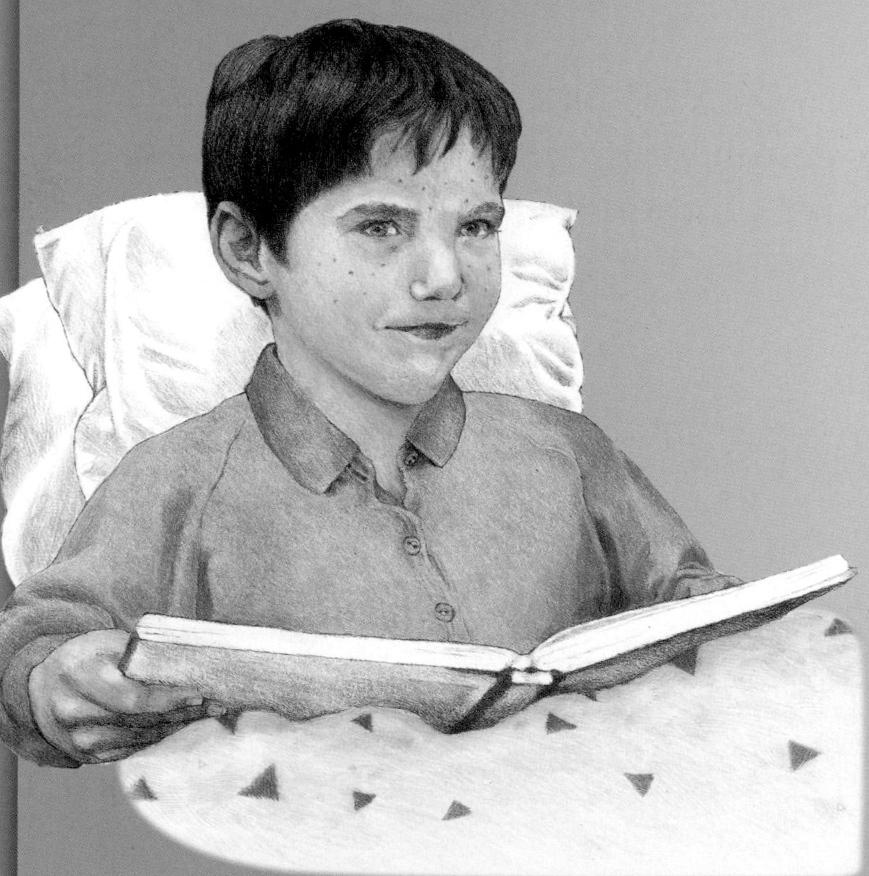

▲ When you are ill, you may have a high body temperature. You may not have your usual amount of energy, and need to rest in bed. You feel very tired because your body is working hard to get better again.

Pandora's Box

Hermes, the Greek god, gave a box to Pandora, but told her never to open it. One day, she felt curious and looked inside. Disease, Misery and Death flew out, but then came Hope, to heal the sadness caused by suffering.

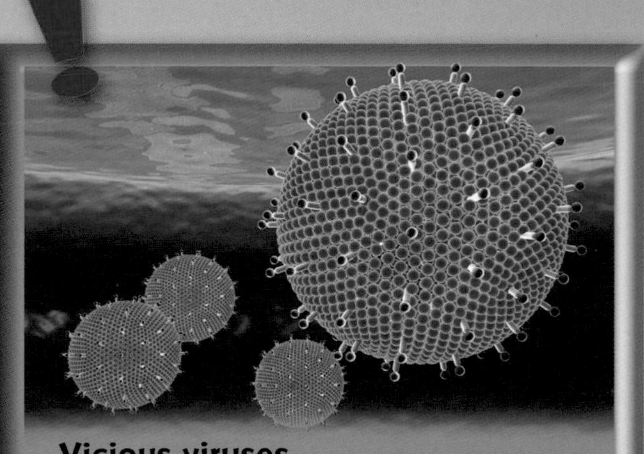

Vicious viruses

Some illnesses, such as chicken-pox, are caused by viruses. Viruses live inside body cells, and cannot be treated with antibiotics. Antiviral drugs may be used instead to stop viruses from reproducing inside the body.

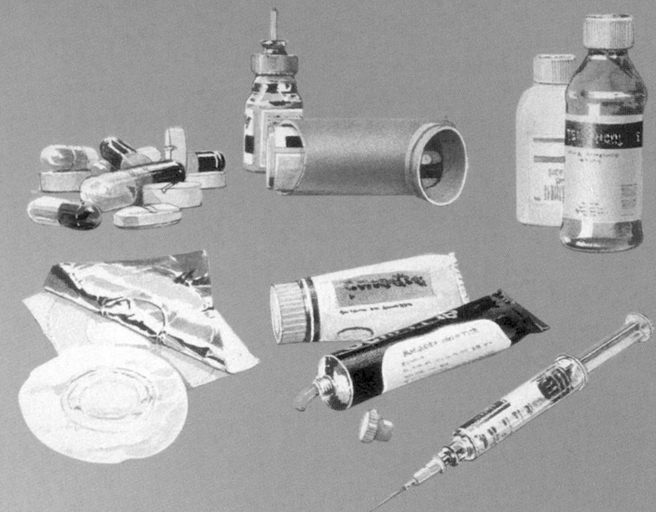

▲ Medicines are also called drugs. They are made in different forms, including liquids, tablets, inhalers and creams. Doctors prescribe different drugs for different health problems.

▲ Babies and children are given vaccinations to stop them getting some illnesses, such as measles and mumps. Some vaccinations are given as an injection, and others as pills or liquids.

WHAT ARE ANTIBIOTICS?

Infections are caused by harmful bacteria. Antibiotics are chemicals that can attack and kill these bacteria.

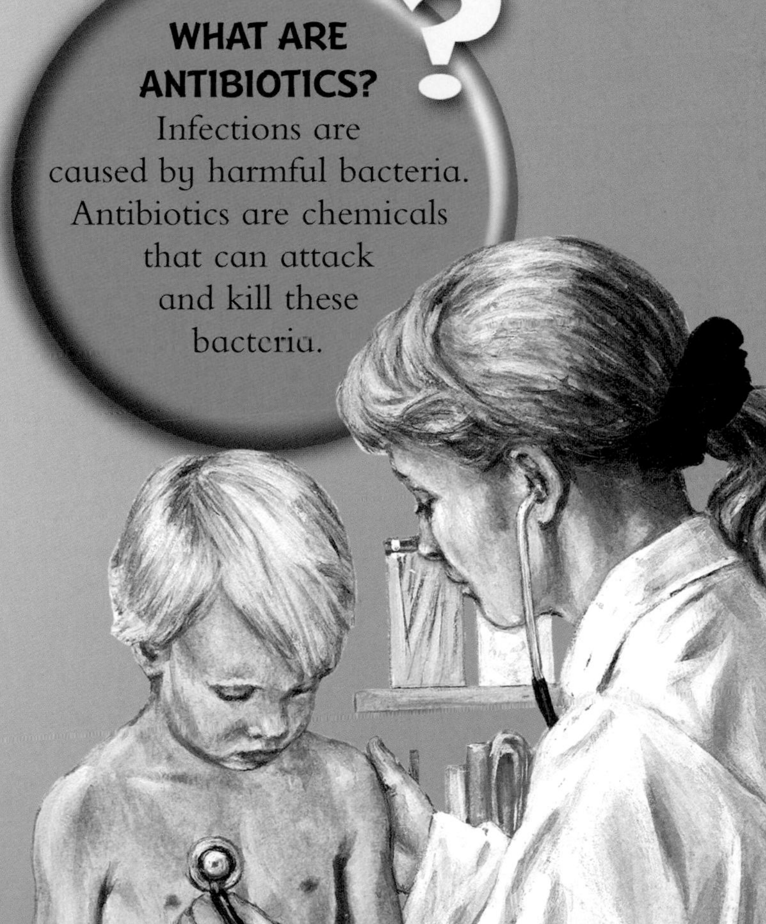

► If you feel unwell, you should visit your doctor. He or she will examine you to diagnose, or work out, what is wrong with you.

Now you know!

► Your skeleton holds up your body and protects your organs. You were born with about 300 bones. Some fuse together as you grow.

▲ You have five senses, which help you see, hear, smell, taste and feel things. Your brain controls your senses.

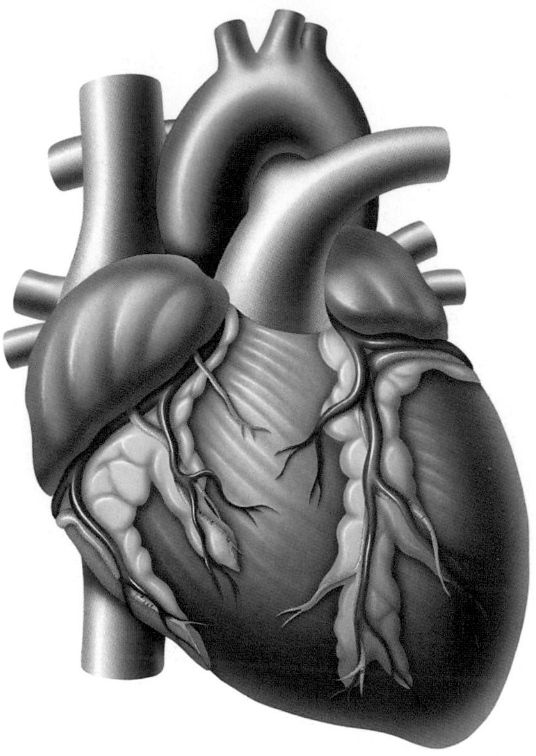

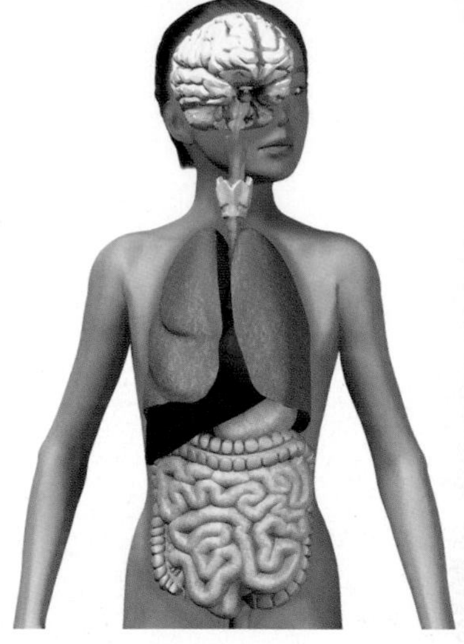

▲ The food you eat is digested by your stomach and small intestine. Your large intestine stores food you do not need.

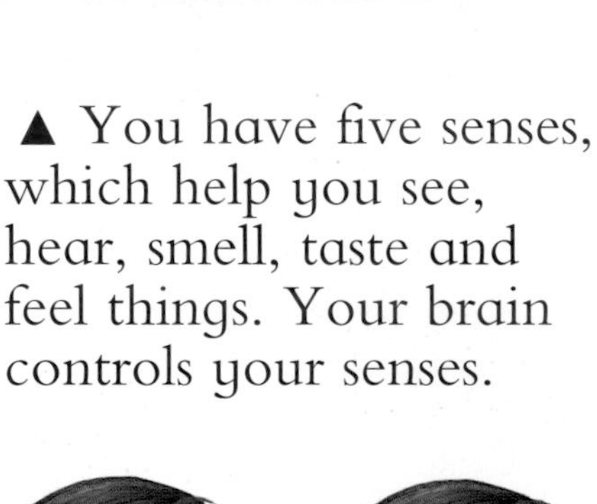

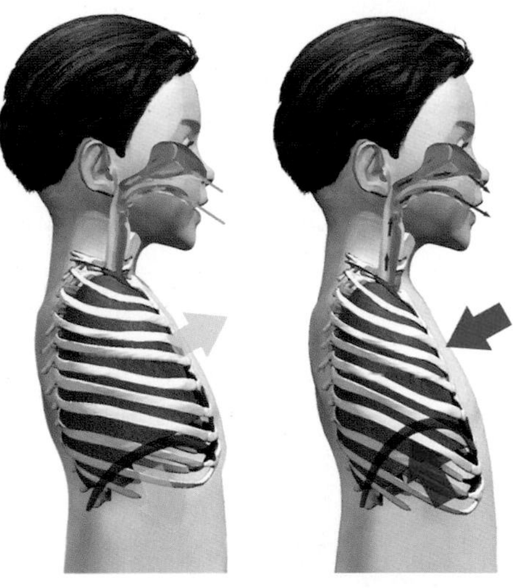

▲ Your heart is a muscle that pushes blood round your body. You need to keep fit so your heart can pump lots of blood.

▲ You breathe oxygen in through your lungs. Your blood carries oxygen round your body. You breathe out carbon dioxide.

► Your brain is your body's central control centre. It works by using a complex system of nerves, carrying signals all over your body.

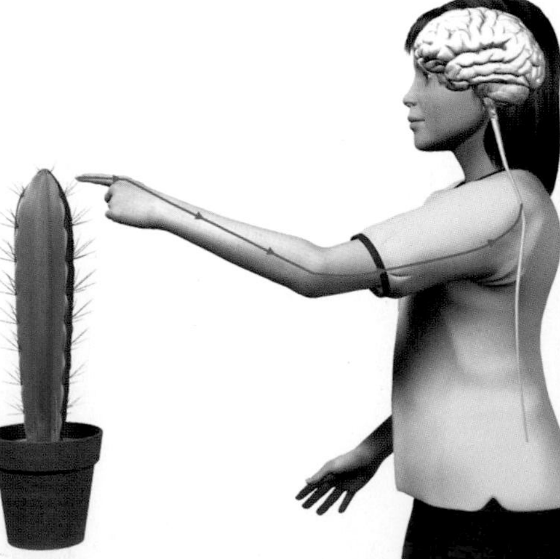

Science

Science helps us to answer questions about our world, such as 'What makes things start, go and stop?' This chapter contains the answers to all these questions, and much more besides. It will help you to make sense of your surroundings and understand why things happen in your everyday life.

What is science?

Science is all about how and why things happen in the world around us. It explains simple things, such as why a ball bounces, as well as more difficult ideas, such as the speed of sound. Scientists try to answer questions by observing and experimenting to test out their theories.

▲ Scientific equipment includes many complicate machines. Among them c microscopes (above) that are used to look at things too small for the naked e

▼ Geologists study volcanoes by measuring temperatures and taking samples of the boiling hot rocks. They find out what it is like deep inside the Earth.

WHY IS SCIENCE IMPORTANT?

By studying our world, scientists find ways to increase our knowledge, improve our lives and help people who are suffering.

▲ One of the main branches of science is biology, the science of living things. Biological scientists study the bodie of plants and animals.

VOCABULARY

chemistry
Study of matter, its properties, and how it behaves and changes.

biology
Study of living things.

physics
Study of energy, force and matter.

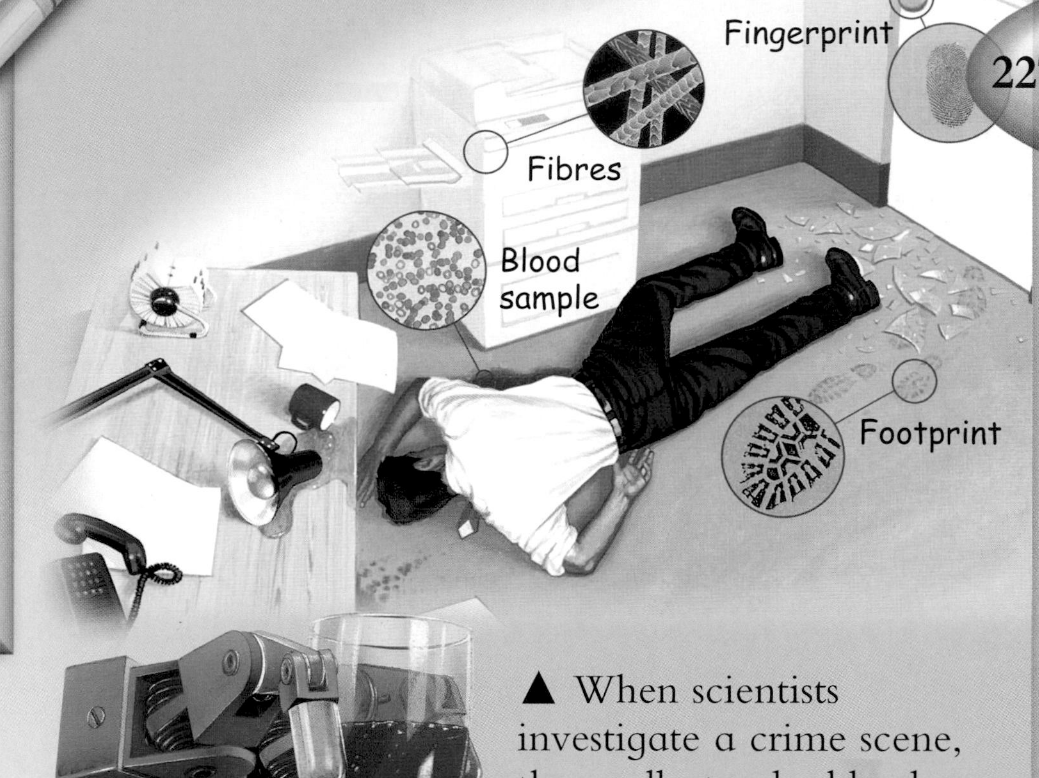

► When science is put to some sort of practical use, such as building robots, this is called technology. Practical science like this is referred to as applied science.

▲ When scientists investigate a crime scene, they collect valuable clues. The evidence includes clothing fibres, samples of blood and fingerprints.

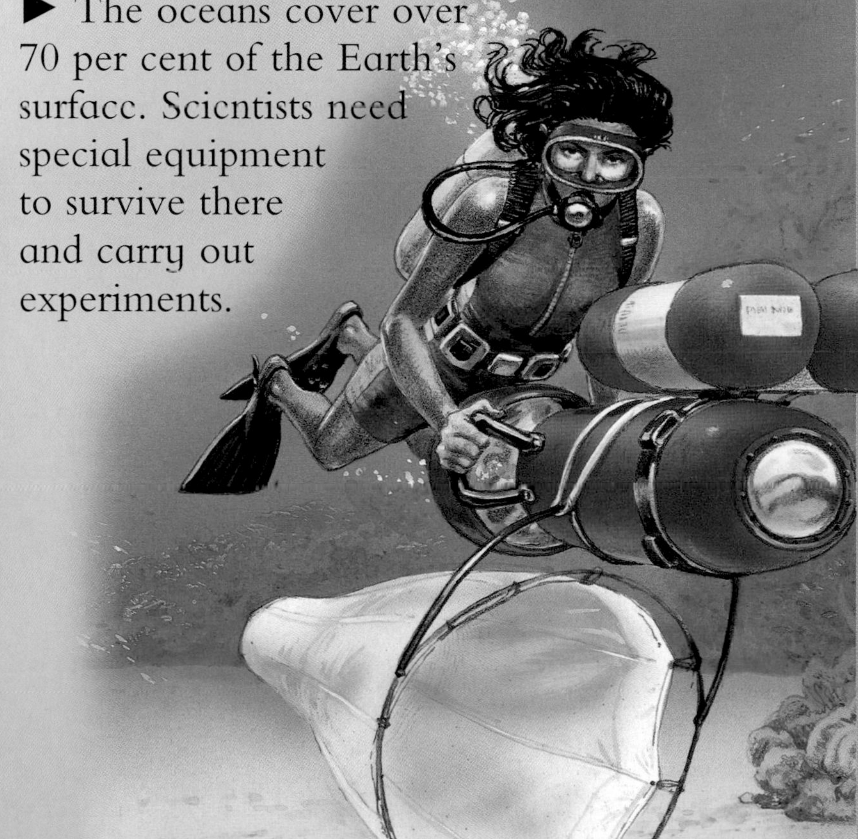

► The oceans cover over 70 per cent of the Earth's surfacc. Scicntists need special equipment to survive there and carry out experiments.

▲ When you watch a firework display, you are watching the chemical energy in the fireworks as well as physics in action.

INTERNET LINKS: www.sciencenewsforkids.org/pages/search.asp?catid=12 • www.sciencemadesimple.com

Materials

Materials, such as wood, metal and glass, are the basic substances that everything is made from. There are hundreds of thousands of different materials, some of which are natural materials and some of which are man-made. Materials have different properties which make them suitable for different purposes.

VOCABULARY

man-made
Artificial materials made by people.

properties
The characteristics of a particular material, which affect the way it behaves and how it is used by people.

◀ Some natural materials, such as wood, come from plants, and animals provide us with wool and leather. Others, such as stone, clay and gold, are found in the ground.

► People use chemical processes to change raw materials, such as oil or sand, into new materials, such as plastic.

The three little pigs

Three little pigs build houses of different materials – straw, sticks and bricks. A big, bad wolf blows down the flimsy straw and stick houses, and eats the pigs. However, he cannot blow down the sturdy brick house.

▶ A skyscraper is built around a skeleton of strong steel rods and girders (beams). Skyscrapers need strong foundations, such as steel and concrete pillars, to support their weight.

CAN YOU FIND?

1. a man welding
2. cage
3. girder
4. crane
5. surveyor
6. hard hat

◀ The Louvre pyramid in Paris, France, is made from one of the oldest man-made materials – glass. Glass is made by heating together sand, washing soda and limestone.

CREATIVE CORNER

Make a stained-glass window

Draw a pattern of shapes on a piece of black paper. Cut out the shapes, leaving a frame around each one. Next, glue coloured tissue paper behind the space in each frame. Tape the finished window to a real window so the light shines through.

Solids, liquids and gases

Everything around us is made from matter. The most common types, or states, of matter are solids, liquids and gases. Most solids are hard and have a definite volume and shape. Liquids have a definite volume but no definite shape, while gases have no definite volume or shape.

Moving particles

Particles in a solid are packed tightly together and cannot move. In a liquid, the particles move about more. In a gas the particles are far apart and move about even more freely.

Solid

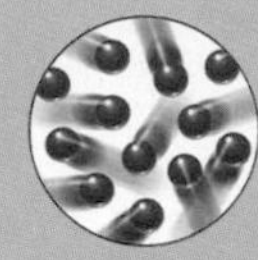
Liquid

Gas

► If you pour a liquid into a container, it takes on the shape of that container. When you boil liquid water, it changes into a gas called water vapour.

▼ Rocks are typical solids. These columns of rock formed from rivers of lava (below right) from inside the Earth. When the lava cooled down, it set into hard, solid shapes.

Aladdin and the genie

One day, a poor boy called Aladdin discovers he can make a powerful genie appear by rubbing a magic lamp that apparently has nothing but air inside it. The genie grants Aladdin's every wish. He becomes rich, marries the daughter of the Sultan and lives happily ever after.

WHAT IS OXYGEN?

Oxygen is a gas that has no colour and does not smell. It makes up about one-fifth of the atmosphere of Earth. We need to breathe oxygen to stay alive.

▲ The most important gases on Earth are the mixture of gases in the air. Air moves faster over the top of a plane's wings than it does underneath. This lifts the plane up into the air.

▼ Sounds are made when the air moves to and fro very quickly, which is called vibration. Big vibrations have a lot of energy and produce loud sounds.

Lava flow

CREATIVE CORNER

Air pressure

Fill a beaker to the brim with water. Now carefully slide a smooth piece of card, such as a postcard, over the top. Hold your hand on the card and slowly turn the beaker upside down. Take away your hand, and the air pressure will keep the water in the glass.

INTERNET LINKS: http://library.thinkquest.org/J001539/ • www.chem4kids.com/files/matter_intro.html

Mixing and reacting

Some substances, such as the salt and water in sea water, can be mixed together without changing chemically. This means it is usually possible to separate mixtures into their different parts. When other substances come together, they break apart and change into new substances in a process called a chemical reaction. Baking a cake is a type of chemical reaction.

Burning
A common type of chemical reaction is burning. When substances burn, they combine with a gas called oxygen in the air and give out energy as heat and light. Fuels, such as coal and oil, burn well.

◀ Oil and water do not mix. The oil is lighter than water, so it floats on top. Oil sometimes spills from damaged oil tankers and is washed onto beaches. Seabirds with oily feathers cannot keep warm and dry.

CAN YOU FIND?
1. oily birds
2. oily seaweed
3. protective clothing
4. men digging

HOW DO YOU DIGEST?

Chemicals called enzymes help to speed up the chemical reactions that break down your food. Enzymes can change the speed of a chemical reaction without changing themselves.

▲ In hot climates, salt can be separated from sea water. Heat from the Sun makes the water disappear into the air, leaving the salt behind to be collected.

▶ When a cake mixture is heated in the oven, there is a reaction. Bubbles of air and carbon dioxide gas make the cake rise as it cooks.

▲ When you shake salad dressing, you make an emulsion. The oil breaks into little drops that hang in the vinegar. The same thing happens with peanut butter and mayonnaise.

CREATIVE CORNER

Fizzing volcano

Use modelling clay to shape a tall volcano with a large dip in the top. Spoon baking soda into the dip and mix in a few drops of red food colouring. Add some drops of vinegar, and watch your volcano fizz as the vinegar and baking powder react, giving off bubbles of carbon dioxide.

Energy

Energy makes things happen. It is invisible, but you can see, hear or feel what it does to things around you. Energy can take many different forms, such as heat, light, sound and movement. All living things need energy to survive.

▲ Plants, such as sunflowers, use the energy in sunlight to make their own food. They use this energy to stay alive.

▼ You use up energy all the time, especially when you run around. You burn food inside your body to release energy.

▲ Energy is never made or lost. When this pole vaulter leaps, the chemical energy stored in his muscles changes into movement and heat energy.

Power and energy
The world's stores of oil and gas will probably last for about another 70 years. The energy that we get from these natural resources will then not be available. New oil and gas reserves may be discovered in the future. We do not know how quickly we will use up any newly found energy.

► The wind turns the blades of these wind turbines and the movement energy is turned into electricity. Wind farms do not cause pollution.

Making cars move
The petrol that we put into our cars gives them the energy to move. When the petrol burns in the car engine, the stored energy is released.

► The solar panels on the Hubble telescope capture the Sun's energy and turn it into electricity. This is used to run the computers and scientific equipment that keep the telescope working.

► Nuclear power stations use the energy given out by natural radioactive materials when their atoms split. This produces heat, which is used to turn water into steam and generate electricity.

Heat and temperature

Heat is a form of movement energy because the hotter something gets, the faster its particles move. Heat is the energy something has because its particles are moving. A temperature scale measures heat energy and tells us how hot something is.

VOCABULARY

thermometer
A device for measuring how hot or cold it is.

Celsius scale
A temperature scale on which water freezes at 0° and boils at 100°.

► The air inside a hot air balloon is heated with a gas flame. The heat makes the particles in the air move further apart and become lighter, or less dense, than the air outside the balloon. This is why the balloon rises up into the sky.

Melting wings

A Greek myth tells how Daedalus and his son Icarus tried to escape from the island of Crete. Daedalus made wings from feathers glued with wax. Icarus flew too near to the Sun. The heat melted the wax, and he fell in the sea and drowned.

Thermometer in winter

Thermometer in summer

◄ We measure temperature with a thermometer. When the temperature rises, the mercury or coloured alcohol expands and rises up the tube.

Rainforest people

Native Americans in Canada

◀ In places with cold winters, people need warmer clothes and homes than people living in rainforests, where it is hot all year round.

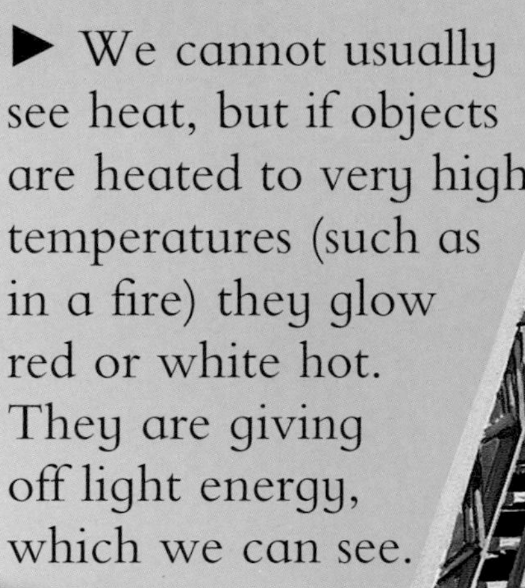

▶ We cannot usually see heat, but if objects are heated to very high temperatures (such as in a fire) they glow red or white hot. They are giving off light energy, which we can see.

HOW DOES HEAT TRAVEL?

In a liquid or a gas, heat is carried by the movement of the liquid or gas. This is called convection. Conduction is when, in a solid, heat spreads from particle to particle.

▲ The heat from a campfire helps us to keep warm. Several layers of clothes keep us warmer than one thick item of clothing. This is because air is trapped between the layers and does not let body heat pass through easily.

Changing states

Most substances will change from one state of matter to another when the temperature or pressure changes. As temperatures rise, solids melt into liquids, and liquids boil into gases. As temperatures fall, liquids freeze into solids, and gases turn back into liquids.

▼ Water is an unusual substance because it exists as a solid, a liquid and a gas in everyday life. It often changes its state. Liquid water changes into solid ice when it is frozen.

▲ When we boil water, bubbles of gas form in the liquid and escape up the kettle spout. This process is called evaporation.

WHAT IS CONDENSATION?

It is the process by which a gas cools down and turns into a liquid. As the gas cools, the particles move closer together, which makes the gas turn into a liquid.

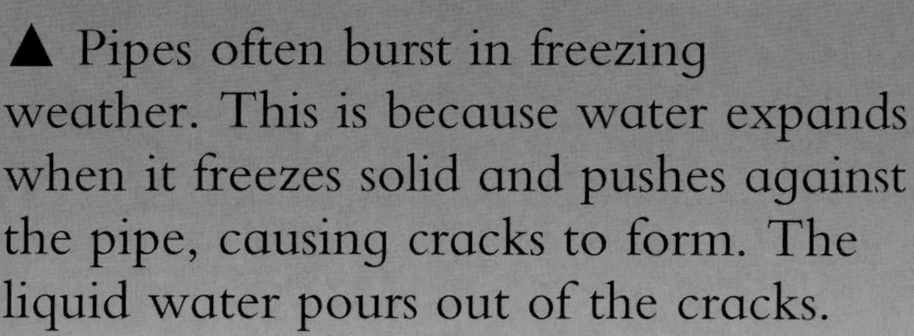

▲ Pipes often burst in freezing weather. This is because water expands when it freezes solid and pushes against the pipe, causing cracks to form. The liquid water pours out of the cracks.

▲ The metal used to build bridges changes size when it is heated or cooled by the weather. As the metal heats up, it expands. As the metal cools down, it contracts.

▲ When you heat popcorn kernels, the air inside them grows bigger, or expands. The outsides split and the kernels explode with a pop.

◀ Many solids and gases can dissolve in liquids and become part of the liquids. In fizzy drinks, the bubbles are carbon dioxide gas, which has been forced into the liquid drink under pressure.

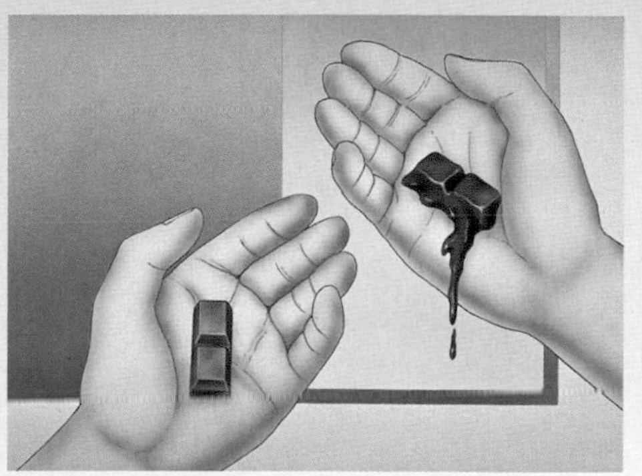

▲ The heat from your hands makes the particles in chocolate move freely over each other. This makes the chocolate melt.

CREATIVE CORNER

Make an ice balloon

Fill a balloon with cold water and tie the neck. Put it inside a large plastic bag and leave in the freezer overnight. Next morning, use scissors to cut the balloon away from the ice. Float it in a bowl of water. How much of the ice balloon is below the surface?

INTERNET LINKS: www.bbc.co.uk/schools/scienceclips/ages/8_9/solid_liquids.shtml

Electricity

Without electricity our lives would be very different. There would be no electric lights or computers, and machines such as kettles, cars and toasters would not work. Electricity is a very useful form of energy. It can be easily changed into light or heat.

▲ Electricity flows along a wire in a path called a circuit. Here, the bulb lights up when electricity stored in the battery travels along the wire.

▼ A virtual reality helmet allows this boy to enter a world created by computer. He can press buttons on the glove to change the images he sees.

▼ Electric toasters have timers, which make the bread pop up when it has cooked for a set time. It usually stops us from burning the toast!

Frankenstein's monster
In a story by Mary Shelley, Frankenstein creates an artificial man by fixing together pieces of dead bodies. In films, he brings his monster to life with the power of a huge lightning flash during a massive electrical storm.

◀ Cars need the electricity in their batteries to work. Electric sparks make the petrol burn inside the engine and this in turn makes the car move.

HOW HOT IS LIGHTNING?

Lightning heats up the air to very high temperatures – as much as five times as hot as the surface of the Sun! This makes the air suddenly expand, producing thunder.

▲ Static electricity is made by rubbing things together. If you rub a balloon against your jumper, it gives it a static electric charge, which pulls your hair and makes it stand on end.

VOCABULARY

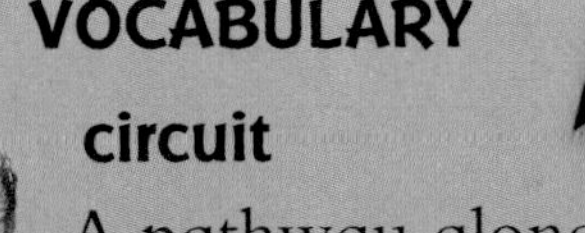

circuit
A pathway along which electricity flows.

static electricity
A form of electricity produced by rubbing things together. It can produce positive or negative charges.

▶ Lightning is a huge spark of static electricity that builds up inside storm clouds. When the electricity jumps down to the ground, it releases energy.

Magnets

Magnets are pieces of metal or stone surrounded by an invisible force. They may pull things towards them (attract them) or push them away (repel them). Magnets occur naturally in rocks in the ground, but some materials, such as iron, can be made into magnets.

▲ The Earth is like a giant magnet. Migrating birds are able to sense this magnetism. They use it to keep on course during long journeys.

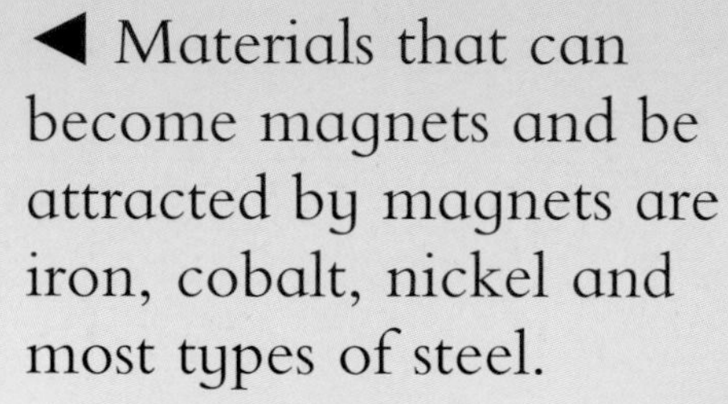

◀ Materials that can become magnets and be attracted by magnets are iron, cobalt, nickel and most types of steel.

WHAT ARE ELECTROMAGNETS?

Some materials act like magnets only when electricity is passed through them. When the electricity is switched off, they stop being magnetic.

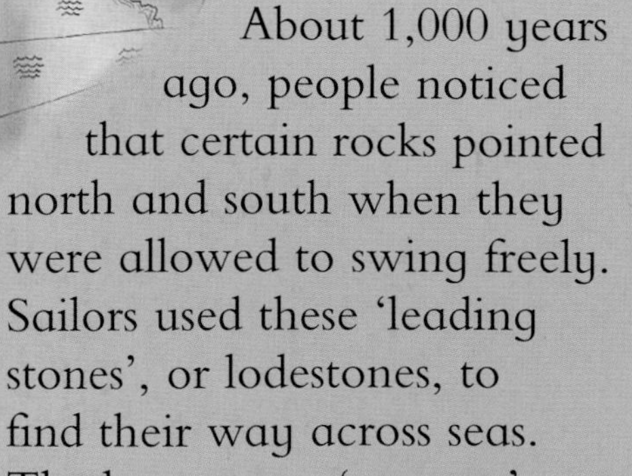

Lodestones

About 1,000 years ago, people noticed that certain rocks pointed north and south when they were allowed to swing freely. Sailors used these 'leading stones', or lodestones, to find their way across seas. The later name 'magnet' comes from Magnesia, in modern-day Turkey.

Magnetic guide

A compass needle is a tiny magnet. The needle always swings to point north–south because it is pulled by the strong magnetic forces inside the Earth.

▼ A Maglev (magnetic levitation) train and the track it runs on have electromagnets on them. The two magnets repel, or push each other apart. This means the train 'floats' above the track.

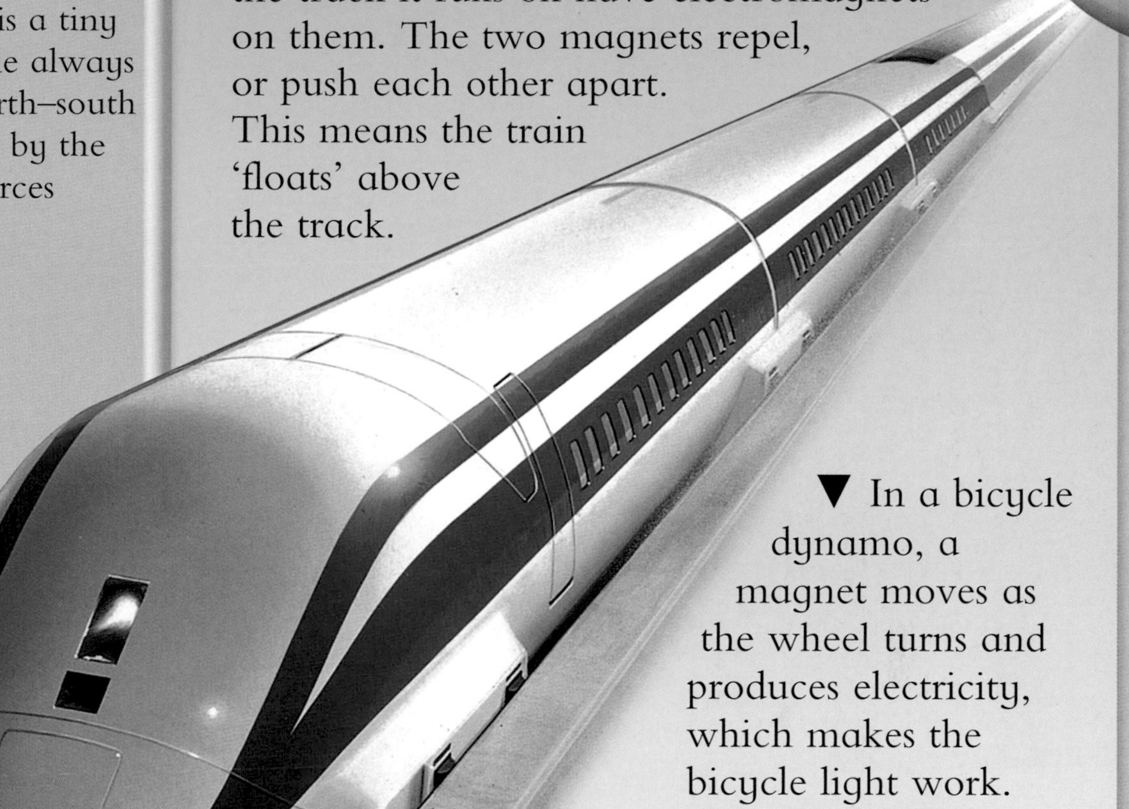

▼ In a bicycle dynamo, a magnet moves as the wheel turns and produces electricity, which makes the bicycle light work.

◀ Electromagnets are used to pick up heavy scrap iron and move it about. When the electricity is turned off, the iron falls off.

CREATIVE CORNER

Make a compass

Stroke a needle several times with one end of a magnet in one direction. Now put some water in a saucer and float a piece of cork on the surface. Put the needle on top of the cork. The needle will turn to point north–south.

Forces

Forces are the pushes and pulls that get things moving and change the way they move. Forces can make things speed up, slow down, or change direction, size or shape. Contact forces, such as kicking a ball, need objects to be touching. When energy is used, forces are involved.

Force of gravity
A pendulum is a weight that hangs from a fixed point and swings from side to side under the action of gravity. Gravity pulls things on Earth down towards the ground.

▲ We cannot see pushing and pulling forces, but we can see the effect they have on things around us. This miner feels his muscles getting tired as he uses up stored energy by pushing.

◀ The arrows on this tug and barges show when there is a force acting on something in one direction, the object applies an equal force in the opposite direction.

▲ A rubbing force called friction will try to stop moving objects. A bowling ball and alley are smooth, so there is little friction.

Tug-of-war
An African myth tells how a clever hare bet a big elephant that he could beat him in a tug-of-war. Then he hid behind some bushes and made the same bet with a hippo. Each thought they were competing with the hare.

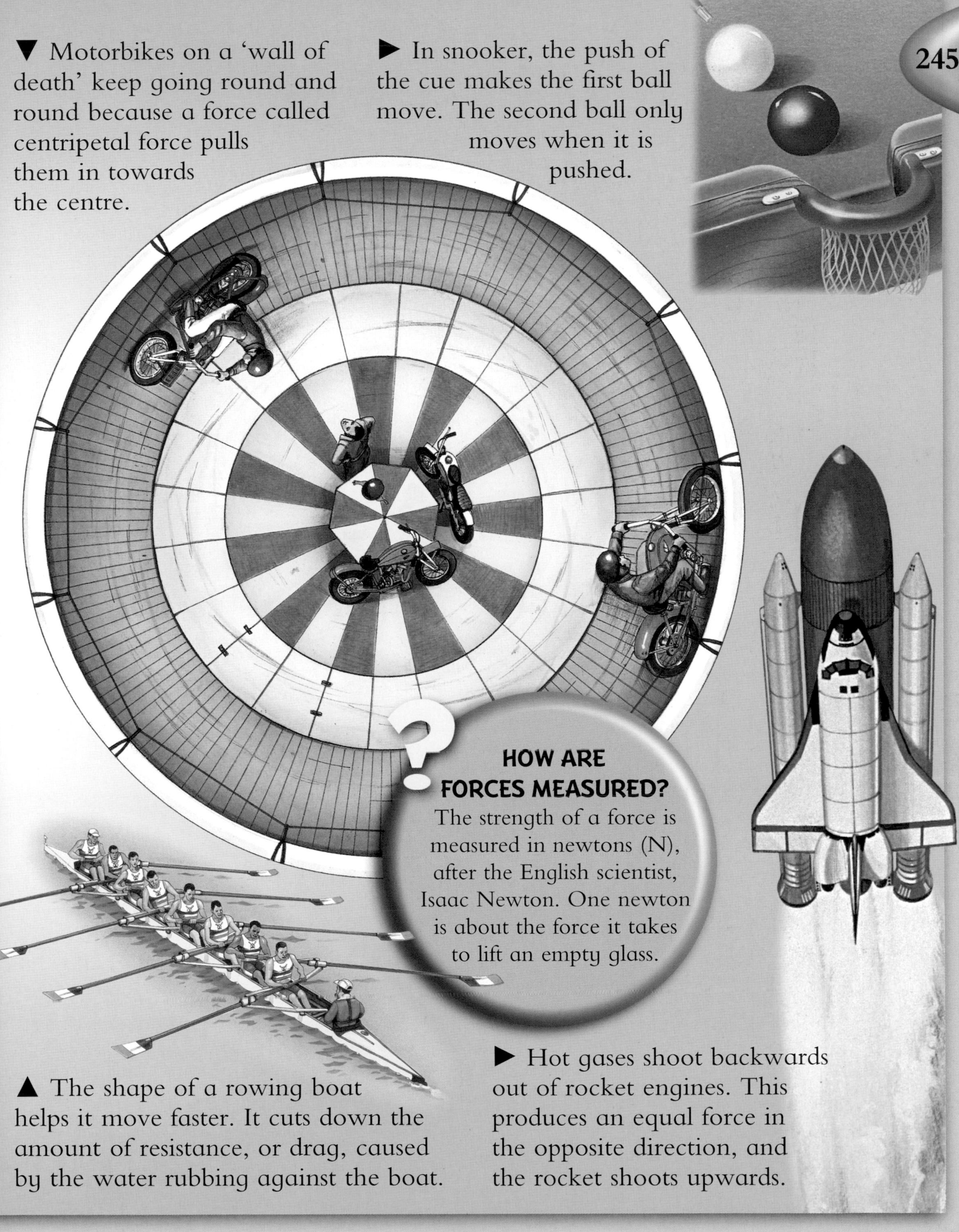

▼ Motorbikes on a 'wall of death' keep going round and round because a force called centripetal force pulls them in towards the centre.

► In snooker, the push of the cue makes the first ball move. The second ball only moves when it is pushed.

HOW ARE FORCES MEASURED?

The strength of a force is measured in newtons (N), after the English scientist, Isaac Newton. One newton is about the force it takes to lift an empty glass.

▲ The shape of a rowing boat helps it move faster. It cuts down the amount of resistance, or drag, caused by the water rubbing against the boat.

► Hot gases shoot backwards out of rocket engines. This produces an equal force in the opposite direction, and the rocket shoots upwards.

Floating and sinking

If you try to push a tennis ball under the water in a bowl and then let go, the water pushes the ball back to the surface. This upward push is called upthrust. An object will float if the upthrust is equal to its weight. It will sink if its weight is greater than the upthrust.

Salty sea
The very salty water in the Dead Sea is much denser than ordinary sea water. It pushes up more strongly against objects, helping them to float. This is why it is so easy.

▲ Small objects made from different materials act differently in a bowl of water. Metal objects sink, while cork, wood and plastic float.

◀ The armbands this girl is wearing are full of air. They help her to float because air is less dense than water.

▼ Our bodies have a lot of air inside them and are less dense than water. This is why we float. These divers wear heavy weights on their belts to resist the upthrust of the water.

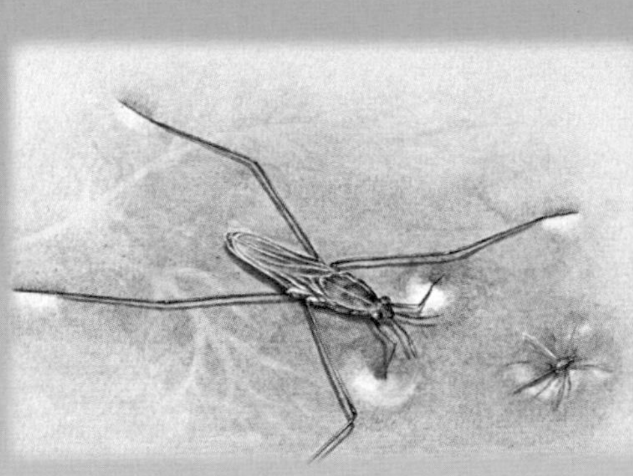

▲ The long legs of this pond skater spread its weight. It can walk over the stretchy 'skin' on the surface of the water without sinking. Its feet make little dips, but do not break through.

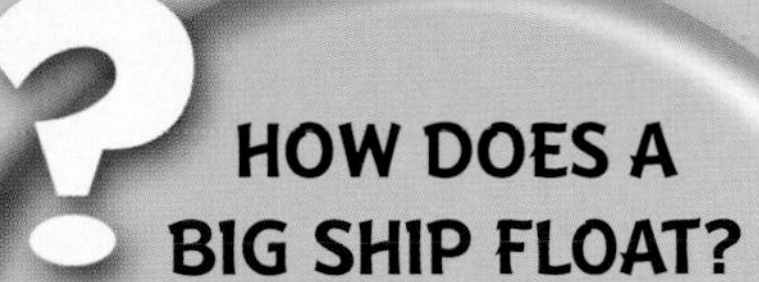

HOW DOES A BIG SHIP FLOAT?

A big ship will float because it is hollow. The water the ship pushes out of the way creates an upthrust that balances the downwards force of the ship's weight.

▲ After long periods of heavy rain, rivers burst their banks and flood dry land. People make rafts out of anything that will float!

▲ Submarines have special tanks that can be filled with either air or water. To dive, water is let into the tanks, making the submarine heavy enough to sink.

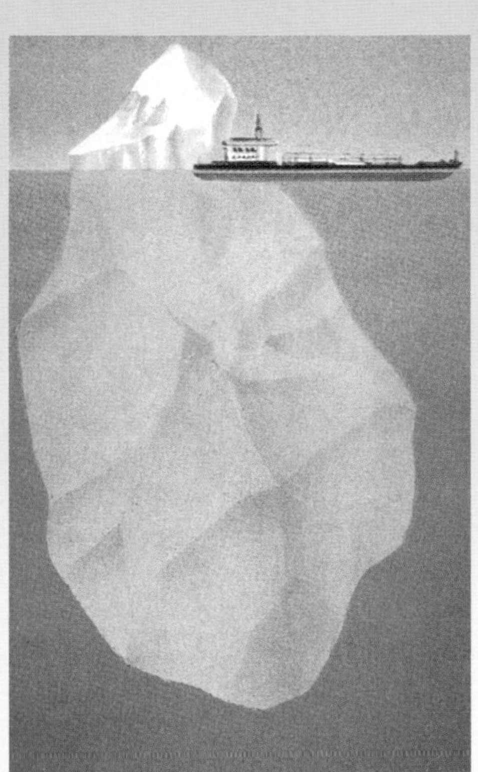

▲ Ice is slightly less dense than water, which means that it floats on the water. Most of the huge floating blocks of ice called icebergs are under the water.

CREATIVE CORNER

Test for surface tension

Pour some milk into a shallow dish. Add a few drops of food colouring. They float on the surface, not breaking through the 'skin' of the milk. Now add some detergent to break the skin and let the colours spread.

INTERNET LINKS: www.kids-science-experiments.com/cat_floating.html

Gravity and weight

An invisible pulling force called gravity attracts objects to each other. It is most obvious when one of the objects is much larger than the other. The Earth is a huge planet and its gravity pulls all the objects on Earth down to the ground. If the Earth had no gravity, objects there would not weigh anything.

▲ The scientist Isaac Newton thought about gravity when he saw an apple fall from a tree. He said the Earth's gravity could also pull the Moon and keep it circling around the Earth.

► When we weigh apples, we are really measuring what they are made of. To a scientist, the word for this is 'mass', and it is measured in grammes.

WHAT DOES THE SUN'S GRAVITY DO?

The huge pull of the Sun's gravity holds the Earth and all the other planets in our Solar System in place. It keeps them circling around the Sun.

▲ To lift and balance these weights, the boy has to push upwards with a strong force to overcome the downward pull of gravity. When he holds steady, the forces inside and outside are evenly balanced.

▲ The Moon is smaller than the Earth. It has only one-sixth of the gravitational pull. Astronauts can jump six times higher on the Moon than on the Earth because there is less gravity pulling them down.

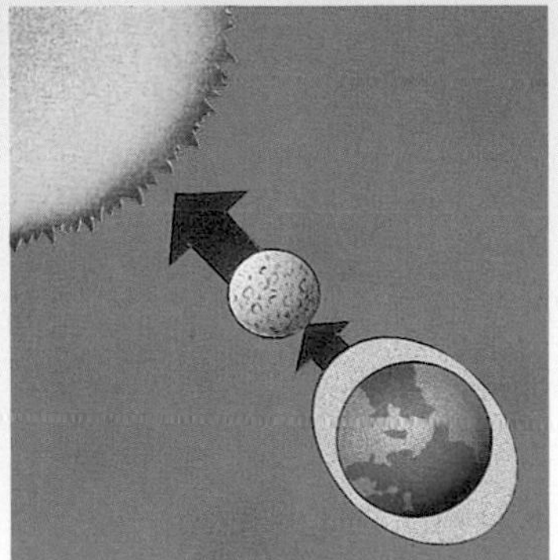

High tide

Low tide

▲ The pull of the Moon's gravity tugs at the Earth's oceans, making them rise and fall as the Moon circles the Earth. At high tide, the sea rises and at low tide it falls.

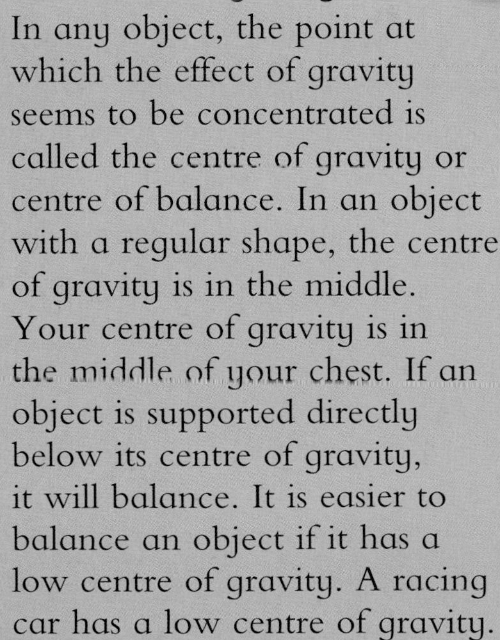

The centre of gravity

In any object, the point at which the effect of gravity seems to be concentrated is called the centre of gravity or centre of balance. In an object with a regular shape, the centre of gravity is in the middle. Your centre of gravity is in the middle of your chest. If an object is supported directly below its centre of gravity, it will balance. It is easier to balance an object if it has a low centre of gravity. A racing car has a low centre of gravity.

Light and colour

Light is a form of energy that travels faster than anything else. The Sun produces most of the natural light on Earth as a result of nuclear reactions. A few animals, such as fireflies and deep-sea fish, produce natural light using chemical reactions in their bodies. People produce artificial light in electric light bulbs.

Primary colours
Red, green and blue are the primary colours of light. You can mix them together to make almost any other colour. If red, green and blue lights are mixed, we see them as white (ordinary) light.

Rainbow colours in a drop of water

► Sunlight and electric light appear white but are made up of all the colours of the rainbow. The spray of water from a hose makes the colours spread out so you can see each one.

Rainbow route
An African legend tells how all the creatures on Earth were stolen from the sky god and creator Amma by the Dogon. A male and female of each animal in heaven and a sample of every plant were placed in a giant pyramid, which slid down to Earth on a rainbow.

The Sun at sunset

◀ The Sun makes its own light, and this takes only eight minutes to reach the Earth. The Moon cannot make its own light. It can only shine when it reflects light from the Sun down onto the Earth.

Candle

The Moon at night

▶ Burning a candle uses up the stored energy in the wax, which is a type of fuel. In a light bulb, electrical energy makes a wire so hot that it glows with a bright light.

Electric light bulb

▶ Light travels in straight lines and cannot bend around objects. If something, such as a large rock, blocks the light, a shadow forms behind it. It is much cooler in the shadows.

▲ Travellers in a desert sometimes think they see a pool of water. This is a mirage. What they see is really a reflection of the sky.

CREATIVE CORNER

Make a rainbow disc

On a circle of white card, colour six equal sections in order: red, orange, yellow, green, blue, purple. Push a small, sharp pencil through the middle of the card. Spin the disc fast. It will look white.

INTERNET LINKS: www.physics4kids.com/files/light_intro.html

Sound

Sound is a form of energy made by something moving rapidly back and forth (vibrating). It passes on the vibrations in the form of a travelling wave. Sound waves travel through solids, liquids and gases, but they cannot travel through space because there are no particles to vibrate.

Making sounds louder
Sound waves spread out like ripples from a stone thrown into a pond. Using a megaphone will make sounds louder because the sound is trapped inside the cone, instead of spreading out into the air.

◄ Animals cannot see sounds. Instead, they can pick up the vibrations through their ears.

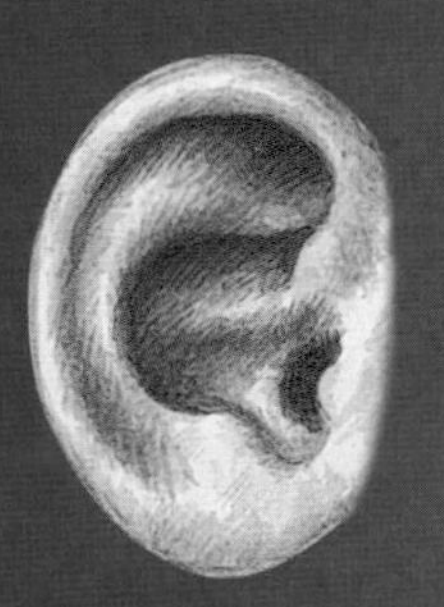

Humans have external ears

Bats have large external ears

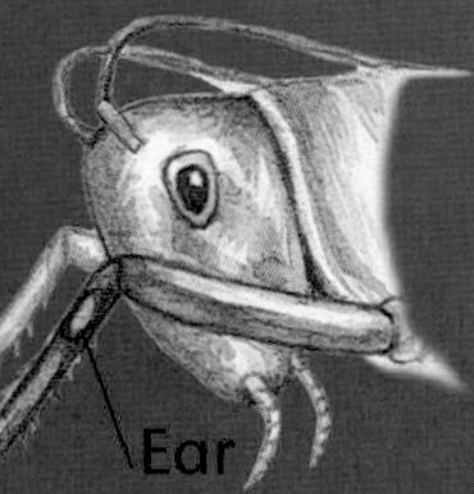

Crickets have their ears on their knees

Frogs have an eardrum on the side of the head

► Musical instruments make sounds by causing something to vibrate. This can be the strings in a violin, or the air in the pipe of a recorder or a trumpet. High notes come from rapid vibrations and low notes come from slower vibrations.

► Supersonic aircraft fly faster than the speed of sound. As the aircraft overtakes its own sound, it breaks through the sound barrier and makes a loud bang called a sonic boom.

▲ Sound waves bouncing back from surfaces are called echoes. They can be used to find the position of objects by timing how long the echo takes to return.

► Microphones can be used to record the sounds of a journalist's voice. They turn sound waves into electrical signals.

CREATIVE CORNER

Bottle music

Collect several small bottles, the same size and shape. Place them in a line and fill each bottle with a different amount of water. Blow gently across the tops of the bottles and compare the different notes they give out. Which bottles make high notes and which make low notes?

Changing our lives

Science helps us to understand how our lives are changing the future of the planet. We are polluting the air, land and water with our waste materials. Science can help us to care for our world and make it a better place to live in the future.

▼ Most forms of transport have a bad effect on the environment. Building planes, cars, ships and trains uses up energy and raw materials. They also use up energy in the form of fuel, and pollute the air with fumes.

Global warming
The world is getting warmer at a faster rate than it would do naturally because of polluting gases. These gases trap some of the heat given off by the Earth so it cannot escape into space.

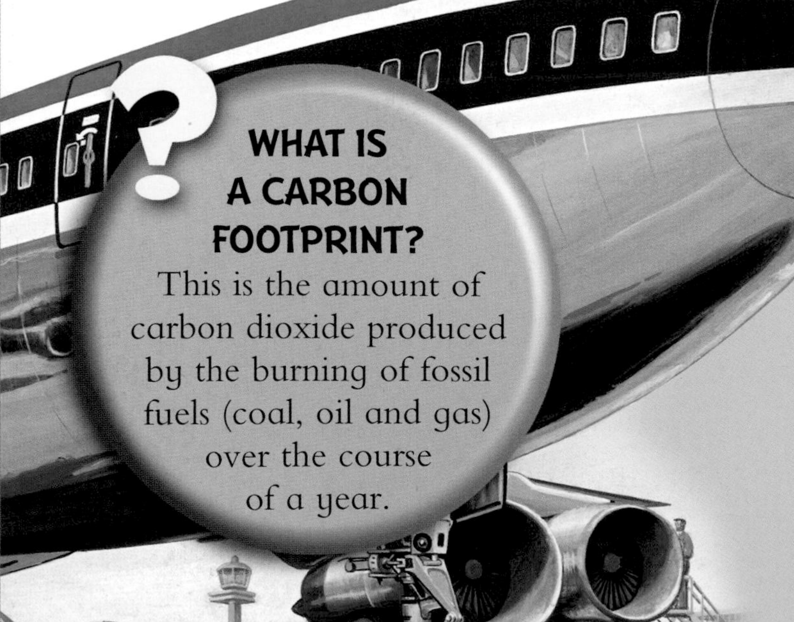

WHAT IS A CARBON FOOTPRINT?
This is the amount of carbon dioxide produced by the burning of fossil fuels (coal, oil and gas) over the course of a year.

► From paper and plastic to bottles and cans, all sorts of materials can be recycled. This saves using new raw materials, cuts down on the energy used and reduces pollution.

▲ Planting trees helps to soak up a lot of carbon dioxide, because all plants use carbon dioxide to make their own food.

▲ Biosphere 2 is an enormous greenhouse in Arizona, USA. It was built to test ways of managing ecosystems on Earth.

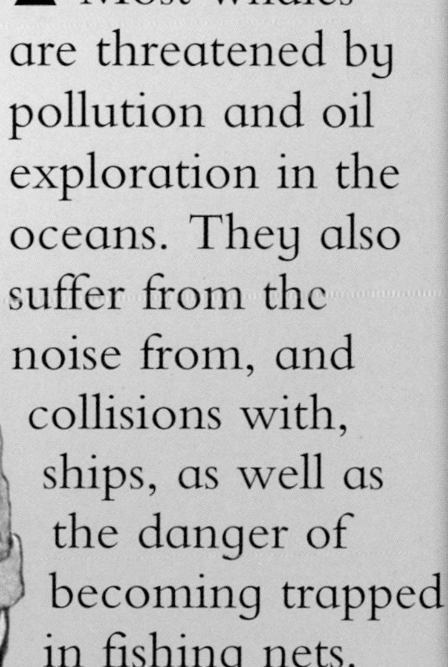

▲ Most whales are threatened by pollution and oil exploration in the oceans. They also suffer from the noise from, and collisions with, ships, as well as the danger of becoming trapped in fishing nets.

CREATIVE CORNER

Collage of recycled material

Collect small pieces of different kinds of materials that would be thrown away, such as shiny paper, plastic containers, wooden strips or sticks.

Use the recycled materials to make a collage showing a city of the future growing out of a rubbish tip.

Now you know!

▲ Natural materials, such as clay or wood, come from plants or animals, or are found in the ground.

▲ Baking a cake is a type of chemical reaction. As the cake cooks, the ingredients break apart and change into new substances.

▲ The most common states of matter are solids, liquids and gases. Water can be a liquid, a solid (ice) or a gas (water vapour).

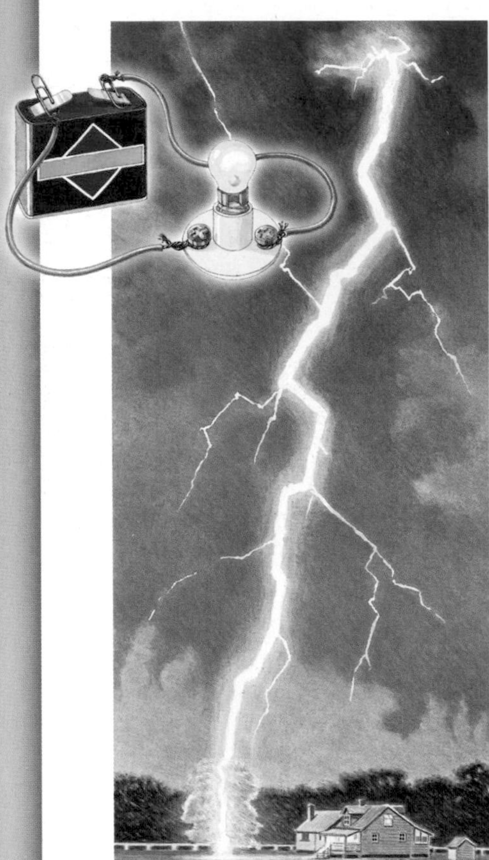

▲ Current electricity flows along wires in a path called a circuit. Static electricity is produced by rubbing things together.

▲ When one thing moves over another, a force called friction tries to stop the movement.

▲ Drops of water make the colours in light spread out so that you can see each colour by itself.

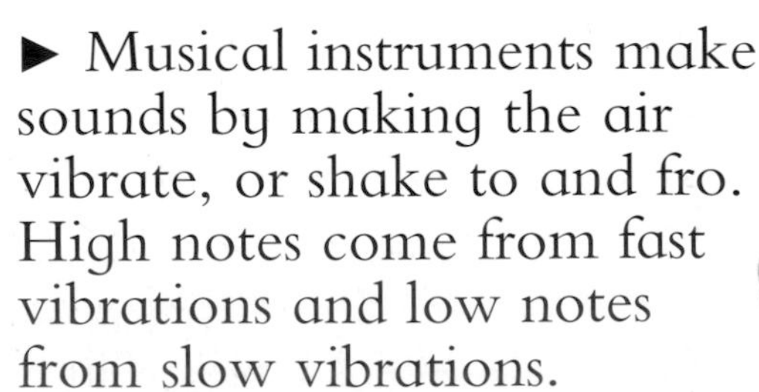

► Musical instruments make sounds by making the air vibrate, or shake to and fro. High notes come from fast vibrations and low notes from slow vibrations.

Space

How big is our Universe? How long has space been there? People have wondered about questions like these for at least as long as we have historical records. Today, it seems as though we are just beginning to find out just how enormous, and how complicated, space really is.

Our Universe

The Universe means everything that exists. It includes Earth and all the other planets, hundreds of billions of stars, and all of space. It is bigger than we can possibly imagine. People have studied the Universe since ancient times, and slowly we are beginning to understand how it works.

◀ The Saturn V rocket powered the Apollo 11 mission in 1969. This was the first mission to land astronauts on the Moon.

5. About a billion years later, galaxies form

4. 300,000 years later, the Universe fills with light

Vishnu and the Universe

In the Hindu religion, Vishnu is the god who looks after the Universe. When it is at peace, he sleeps on the snake-like coils of another divine being, Sesha. When there is disorder, Vishnu battles it himself, or sends a helper to restore peace.

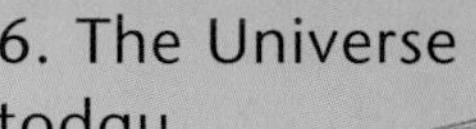

WHAT IS GRAVITY?

Gravity is the force that keeps everything, including people, on the surface of the Earth. It also holds whole of the Universe together.

▲ In 1929, astronomer Edwin Hubble proved that the Universe is expanding, which helped to confirm the Big Bang theory. The Hubble space telescope is named after him.

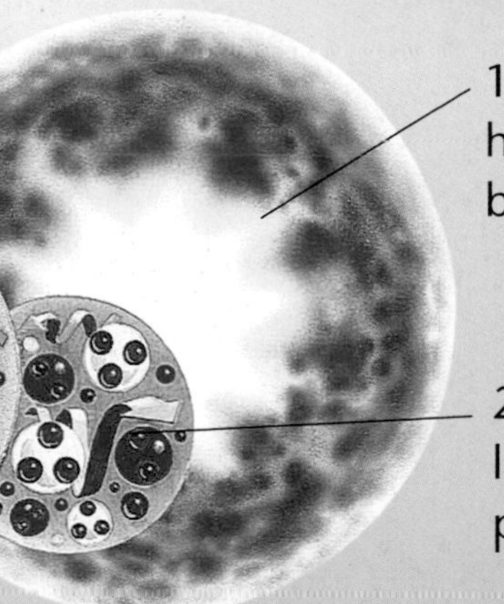

▲ Scientists believe the Universe was formed in a huge explosion, known as the 'Big Bang'.

CREATIVE CORNER

Make a model rocket

Cut slits in the top of a cardboard tube and overlap the tabs to make a narrow neck. Add triangular fins to the bottom. Cut a slit from the edge to the centre of a circle of card to form the nose cone and add it to the top of your rocket.

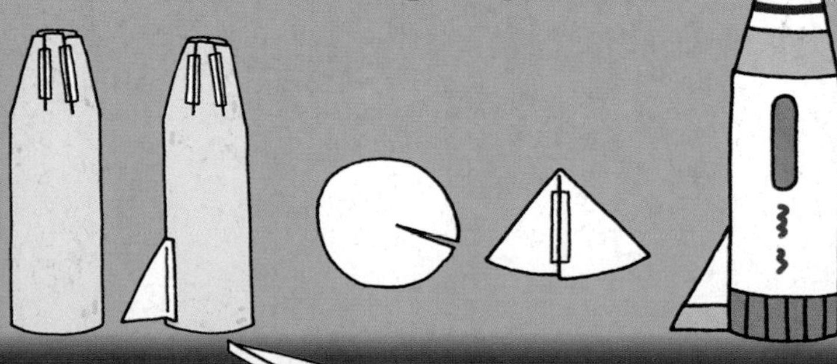

INTERNET LINKS: www.kidsastronomy.com/deep_space.htm • http://science.hq.nasa.gov/kids/universe.html

The Sun

The Sun is a star, and the centre of our Solar System. It is an enormous ball of burning gases, millions of times bigger than Earth. The Sun sends out heat and light. Without this, it would not be possible for plants and animals to live on Earth.

VOCABULARY

dawn
The first appearance of daylight at the beginning of the day.

star
A brightly shining object that can be seen in the sky.

▶ The middle, or core, of the Sun, is its hottest part. Hot gases bubble up from there to the surface. There, they form a halo of gases called a corona. There are dark patches on the surface, which are cooler. They are called sunspots.

Sunspot

▲ Cocks will often crow at dawn when, as we say, 'the Sun rises'. But the Sun does not really rise at all. In fact, day begins when the part of the Earth you are in spins to face the Sun.

How Kuat the Sun god brought daylight
In Brazil, there is a story about the Mamaiurans, Amazon Indians, who were forced to live in darkness because the wings of the birds blocked the sky. Kuat kidnapped the vulture king and forced him to agree to share daylight. This is why there is day and night.

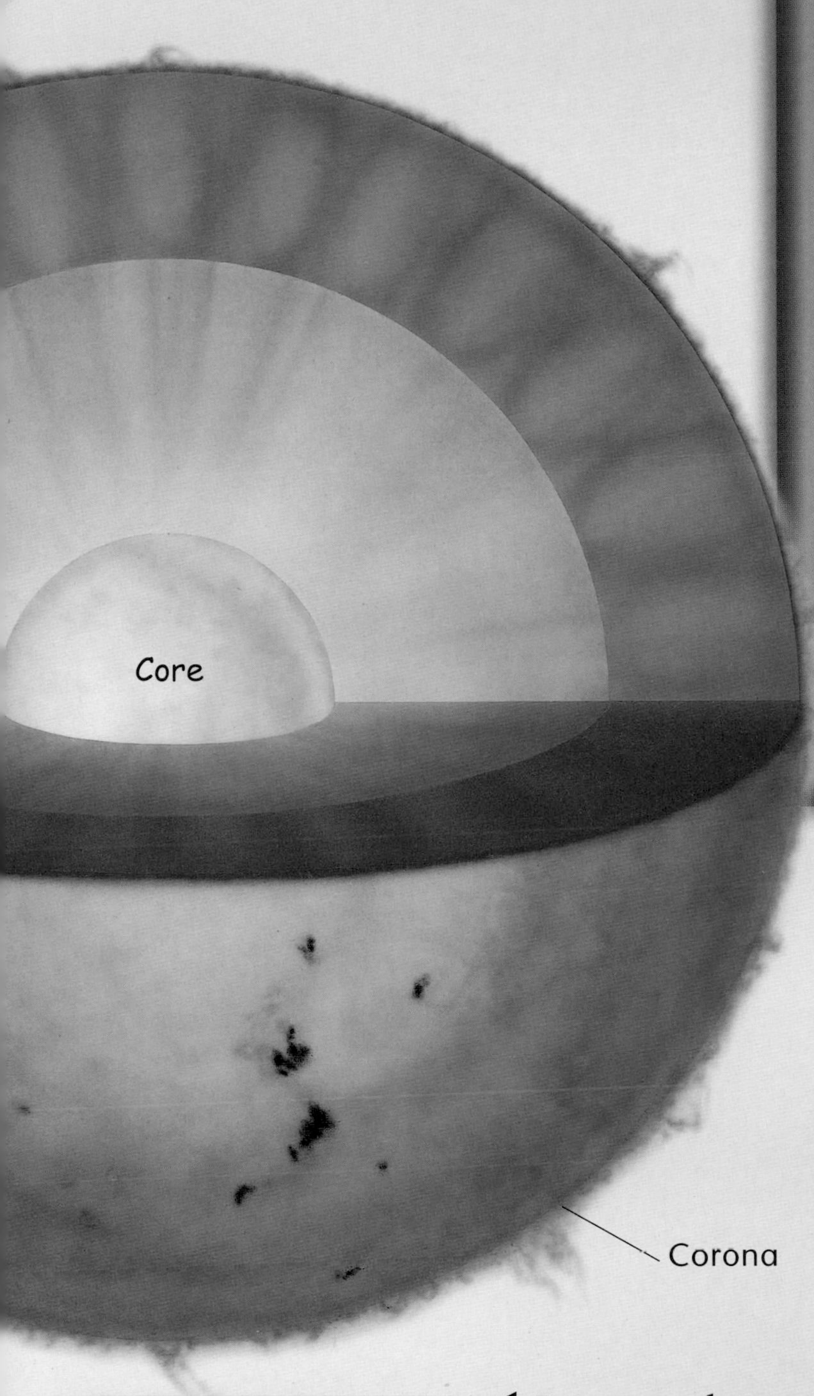

Solar eclipse
When the Moon passes between the Earth and the Sun, it causes a solar eclipse. During a total solar eclipse, the Moon's shadow covers the whole of the face of the Sun for a few minutes. The corona of the Sun, which we cannot normally see, becomes visible.

▼ Sometimes there are violent explosions on the Sun, and streams of electrically charged particles shoot up from the surface. These are called solar flares. Most of them happen around sunspots.

◀ In some places, the Sun may be seen for 24 hours a day. In the very north of Norway, the Sun does not set for 76 days from May to July.

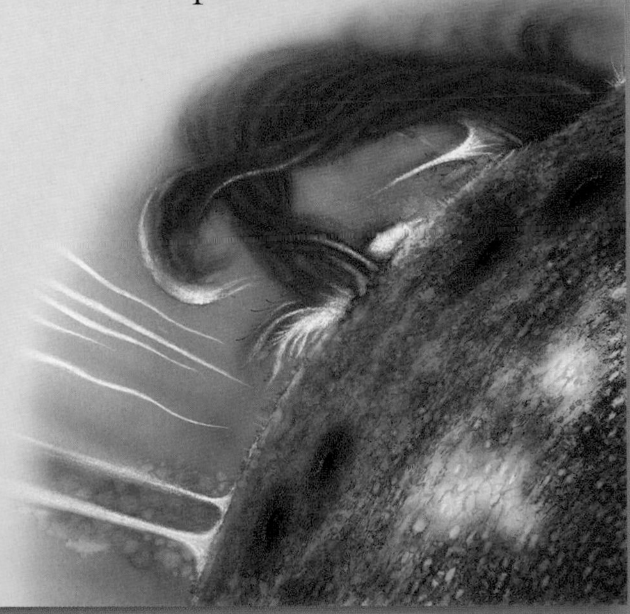

The Solar System

When we refer to the Solar System, we mean the Sun and everything that orbits, or circles, it. This includes the planets, their moons, comets, meteors and asteroids. All of these are held close to the Sun by its enormously strong gravity.

Neptune

► Stars and planets are formed from gas and dust. Our Solar System consists of our Sun, which is a star, and the planets that orbit it. The Sun formed and began to shine about five billion years ago. Then, over about half a billion years, the planets formed around it.

Uranus

Ancient gods

Apart from Earth, the planets in the Solar System are named after ancient gods. Jupiter was the father of the Roman gods. Other planets named after Roman gods are Mars, the god of war; Mercury, the messenger of the gods; Venus, goddess of love; Saturn, the god of the harvest; and Neptune, the god of the sea. Uranus was the ancient Greek god of the sky.

Saturn

Copernicus
Nicolaus Copernicus was the first person to suggest, in 1543, that Earth and the other planets revolved around the Sun. Before he made this claim, people believed that Earth was at the centre of the Universe.

CREATIVE CORNER

Play a memory game

Draw a picture of each of the eight planets in the Solar System on two sets of cards, and label them. Shuffle and lay the cards face down on a table. Take turns to turn over two cards. If they match, keep the pair and have another turn. The person with most pairs wins the game.

Galaxies

A galaxy is a cluster, or island, of stars in space. Our Sun is one of hundreds of billions of stars in our particular galaxy, which is the Milky Way. All the stars that we can see in the sky belong to the Milky Way. Our galaxy is only one of billions of galaxies that make up the Universe.

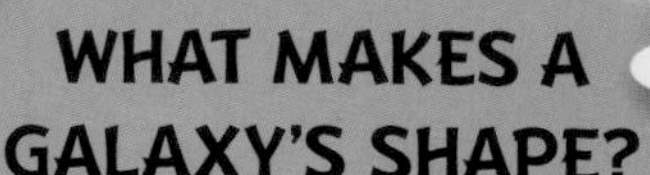

WHAT MAKES A GALAXY'S SHAPE?

All galaxies are held together by gravity, but scientists do not yet know what makes them a particular shape.

◀ There is a lot of gas and dust between the planets. We only notice this when sunlight reflects off the gas and dust. This makes them glow in the sky.

Yllapa and the Milky Way

The ancient South American people, the Incas, believed in a thunder god called Yllapa. He was said to gather water from the Milky Way and store it in a jug. When it rained, people said that Yllapa had broken the jug with a stone shot from his sling.

▶ The Milky Way is a spiral galaxy. Its central area contains many old stars, which give it a yellow-red glow. The younger stars in the spiral arms of the galaxy burn brighter, and they have a blue-white light.

Types of galaxies

▶ Elliptical galaxies are roughly egg-shaped. Some of the largest galaxies are ellipticals.

Elliptical galaxy

▶ Spiral galaxies have a central core, and curved 'arms'. The stars in the arms orbit the galactic centre.

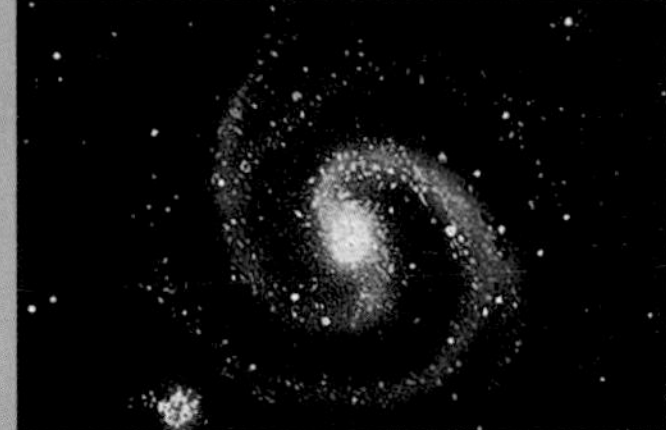
Spiral galaxy

▶ Galaxies that cannot be described as either of the above types are called irregular.

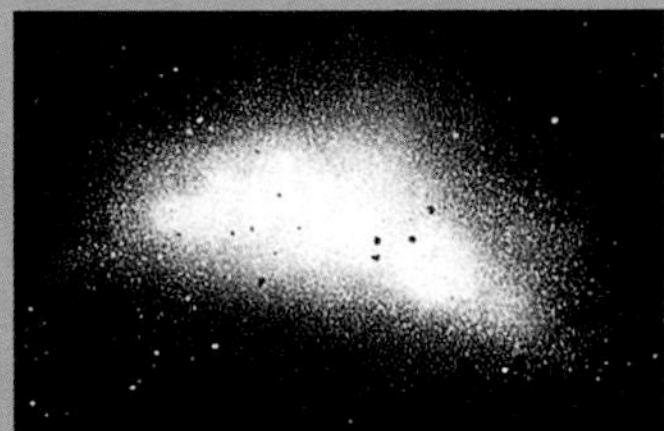
Irregular galaxy

CREATIVE CORNER

Make a galaxy greetings card

Fold a piece of card or thick paper in half. Paint the front dark blue or black, for the night sky. Using clear glue, draw some curvy, swirly shapes. Sprinkle glitter or salt over it. Then tip off the excess to see your own galaxy!

Rocky planets

Of the eight planets that orbit the Sun, four are called 'rocky planets'. These are the four planets closest to the Sun: Mercury, Venus, Earth and Mars. The four rocky planets are much smaller than the four 'gas giants' furthest from the Sun.

HOW DID THEY FORM?
The rocky planets began as dust and gas. Over time, they grew, gathering dust and gas, until, finally, they were planets.

▶ Venus is almost the same size as Earth, but closer to the Sun. It is covered in thick, poisonous clouds, and its surface is hot, at about 475°C.

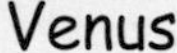

Venus

Charon
Charon, the name of Pluto's neighbour, was the ferryman of the dead in ancient Greek legend. Charon had close links to Hades, the god of the underworld, who was renamed Pluto by the Romans.

▼ Mercury is the planet closest to the Sun. It has no protective atmosphere. This means that the surface facing the Sun is extremely hot, while the surface facing away from the Sun is extremely cold.

▼ Earth is the only planet known to support life. It is not too hot or too cold. It also has water and oxygen, both of which are needed for life.

Pluto and Charon
Until recently, Pluto (below, bottom) was believed to be a planet. But scientists have recently decided that it does not qualify, and it is no longer counted among the planets in the Solar System. Pluto is now called a dwarf planet along with its neighbour, Charon (at left, centre).

Earth

Mars

◀ Mars has similar features to those on Earth, such as valleys, mountains and polar ice caps. It is possible that, once, Mars was also home to a form of life.

VOCABULARY
atmosphere
A layer of gases around a planet. Earth's atmosphere provides the air that we breathe.
polar
At the far north or south of a planet.

Gas giants

The four planets furthest from the Sun – Jupiter, Saturn, Uranus and Neptune – are known as gas giants. They have only a small rocky core, which is surrounded by gas and liquid. All four have rings and moons, and impressive storms can happen in their atmospheres.

▲ William Herschel discovered Uranus in 1781. It was the first planet to be identified using a telescope.

◀ Saturn is almost as big as Jupiter, and it has the most moons. Scientists have named 35 of them.

Viking Valhalla

Early peoples often believed that the gods lived in the sky. The Vikings thought the souls of warriors who fought bravely and died in battle would go to Valhalla. This was a great hall in the sky where they would feast and be happy forever.

▶ Jupiter is the biggest planet of all, and the fastest spinning. It has 16 moons, and swirling gas clouds cover its surface.

▶ Uranus has 21 moons and faint rings. Its blue-green colour is probably caused by methane gas in its atmosphere.

◀ Neptune, the planet furthest from the Sun, is a very cold, dark planet. It has three rings and eight moons, and the stormiest weather of all the planets in the Solar System.

CREATIVE CORNER

Make a mobile of Saturn and its rings

Make two half-planets out of papier mâché. When dry, trim the edges so that the pieces fit together, and then paint yellow. Take a large paper plate and paint it with dark and light rings. Thread a knotted piece of string through the centre of all three pieces to hang up your mobile!

Earth and Moon

Our planet, Earth, is the only planet on which we know there is life. From space, a lot of the Earth looks blue. This is because three-quarters of its surface is covered by water. This water, the air in the atmosphere and the temperature are what allow life on Earth to exist.

► Most astronomers believe that the Moon and the Earth formed about 4.5 billion years ago, from a cloud of dust and gas.

VOCABULARY

astronomer
A scientist who studies the Universe and everything in it.

gas
A shapeless substance, such as air, that is not solid or liquid.

Shape-changing Moon
Earth has only one moon. At night, it often seems to glow with its own light. In fact, this light is reflected sunlight. As the Moon orbits the Earth, we see different shapes, or phases of the Moon. This depends on how much of the sunlit side of the Moon we can see from the Earth.

Walking on the Moon

Apollo 14 was the eighth manned Apollo mission, and the third to land on the Moon. Two crew members walked on the surface, and one even hit a golf ball. This mission brought back over 42kg of samples from the surface.

Low tide

High tide

▲ Tides are caused by the Moon's gravity as it orbits Earth. It pulls the water towards it, causing high tides. The Moon also pulls Earth towards it, making the water rise on the other side of Earth and causing low tides.

CREATIVE CORNER

Keep a Moon diary

Take a sheet of paper and divide it into columns. Label each column with the day of the week. Every evening for a month, draw the shape you see that day in the box in its column. You will soon see a pattern in the shapes.

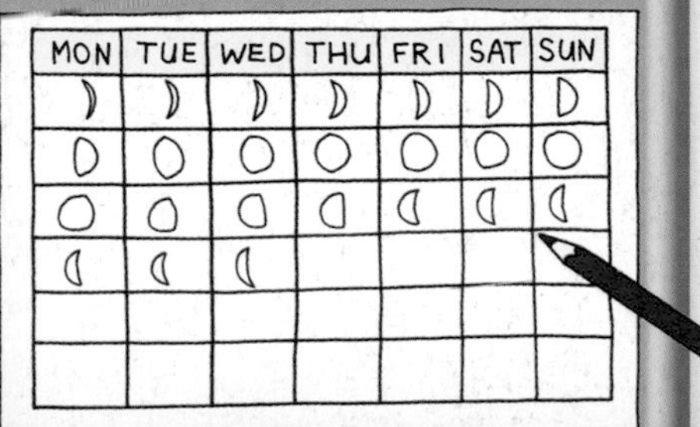

INTERNET LINKS: http://aldertrootes.wcpss.net/moonwebquest.html • http://science.hq.nasa.gov/kids/earth.html

Asteroids and comets

Asteroids and comets are small, rocky bodies that orbit the Sun. However, their gravity is not strong enough to pull them into a spherical shape like the planets. Meteors are bits of rock, up to about the size of a cricket ball, that have broken off comets or asteroids. We see them in the sky as 'shooting stars'.

VOCABULARY

crater
A hollow made in a planet. Craters can be caused by the impact of rocks, such as meteorites.

spherical
Round, like a ball or a planet.

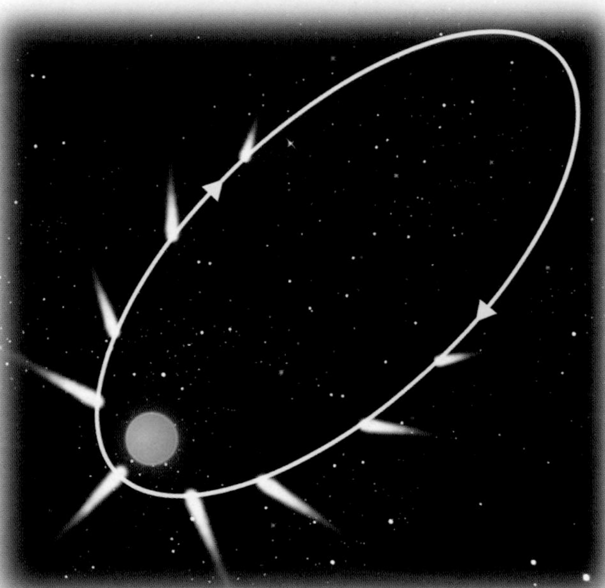

◀ Comets have long, oval-shaped orbits. They are 'active' and glowing when they are close to the Sun. This is when we can see them, often for several days at a time.

Pahokatawa
A native American people, the Pawnee, had a story about a man named Pahokatawa, who was killed and eaten by wild animals. He was brought back to life by the gods and returned to Earth as a meteor.

▲ Most asteroids are found between Mars and Jupiter, in an area called the Asteroid Belt.

▼ Comets have two tails. The gas tail points away from the Sun and looks bluish. The dust tail is often curved, and glows white.

Meteorite

When a meteor falls to Earth, it is called a meteorite. About 500 meteorites reach Earth each year. We hardly notice most of them but, sometimes, a large meteorite can cause a lot of damage. This crater, in Arizona, USA, was caused by a meteorite.

CAN YOU FIND?

1. a comet
2. an asteroid
3. a crater
4. two astronomers
5. the Moon

INTERNET LINKS: http://library.thinkquest.org/3645/comets.html • www.kidsastronomy.com/asteroid.htm

1. A star forms inside a nebula

2. Gas and dust condense

Life of a star

Stars are formed out of dust and gas, and grow larger as they grow older. They burn brightly for a while, but then begin to run out of gases to burn. Gradually, they collapse and die. When a star dies, it creates dust and gas that may become part of another star.

Iroquois stars

An ancient story from an Iroquois tribe of North America tells of people who behaved so badly that the Sun and Moon left. Some children floated up to the sky with fires and became stars. The Sun and Moon were so pleased that they returned.

▲ When they die, really massive stars collapse into black holes. The gravity of a black hole is so strong that it sucks in everything near it, including light.

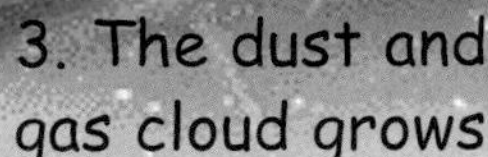

3. The dust and gas cloud grows

4. Gases fuse and release heat and light

5. A new star begins to shine

▲ A star forms in a nebula, where dust and gas condense (squash together) and attract more dust and gas. As the cloud grows, hydrogen gas atoms fuse (join together) to form helium. This releases heat and light, and the star begins to shine.

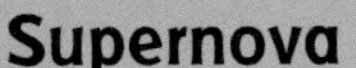

Supernova

A supernova happens just before a neutron star or a black hole forms. When a dying star explodes, it burns brightly for a few weeks or months. During this time, it makes as much energy as our Sun would in 10 billion years!

► The Horsehead Nebula is found in the constellation, or group of stars, known as Orion. Dark clouds like this one are the parts of nebulae in which new stars form.

Looking into space

People have been fascinated by the stars since ancient times. Early civilizations, including the Sumerians, Babylonians and Egyptians, spent a lot of time studying the sky and how it changed over time. The ancient Greeks learned a lot from earlier societies, and made huge advances in astronomy – the study of the Universe.

▲ Early people did not know why the stars seemed to move, but they observed their patterns. They used the stars for directions when exploring new lands.

▼ Observatories, such as this one, house huge telescopes. As the Sun sets, the dome slides open and the telescope can be directed at an area of the sky to be studied.

WHY ARE HILLS GOOD FOR STARS?
Observatories are often built on hills, because this gives astronomers the best chance for a clear view of the sky and the stars.

Early astronomers

In the 9th century CE, a new school of astronomy was founded in Arabia, and study continued there until the middle of the 15th century. Arab astronomers often drew constellations in human form, such as this one, called Cepheus.

▲ The Hubble Space Telescope has been orbiting the Earth since 1990. Because it is outside our atmosphere, it sends back clearer pictures than we get from any telescope on Earth.

▼ If you want to see more in space, a simple telescope is useful. On a clear night, you will see a lot of stars and constellations.

CREATIVE CORNER

Make your own constellation

Most constellations are made of bright stars that you can see with the naked eye. This one, in the northern hemisphere, is called the Plough. Spot a simple shape in the night sky for yourself, draw it on a piece of paper and give it a name. Now you have your own constellation!

INTERNET LINKS: www.kidsastronomy.com/astroskymap/index.htm • http://www.space.kids.us/hubbletelescope.html

Constellations

There are so many stars in the sky on a clear night that it can be difficult to imagine how people remember them. If you look closely, you will see patterns in the brighter stars. People drew shapes around the patterns and gave them names – these are the constellations.

HOW MANY HAVE WE FOUND?
There are 88 official constellations. And newly discovered stars are linked to the constellation closest to them.

Northern hemisphere

► Which stars you see depends on where you are in the world and the time of year. In the northern hemisphere each season, different constellations can be seen from those seen in the southern hemisphere.

Perseus, the hero
The constellation of Perseus was named after a man who found out that his mother was being treated badly by the king. Perseus held up the head of the snake-haired monster, Medusa, and the king turned to stone.

► The Lynx constellation is so-called because you need the eyes of a lynx (a cat) to see its faint shape.

Pegasus

Scorpio

Great Bear

▲ Most constellations are named after figures from myth and legend, including those above. But many recently named constellations, such as the Lynx, are not.

Southern hemisphere

Ptolemy and the stars
In the 2nd century CE, the Roman astronomer Ptolemy grouped over 1,000 stars into 48 constellations. Although he did not include the stars of the southern hemisphere, his star patterns still form the basis for constellations today.

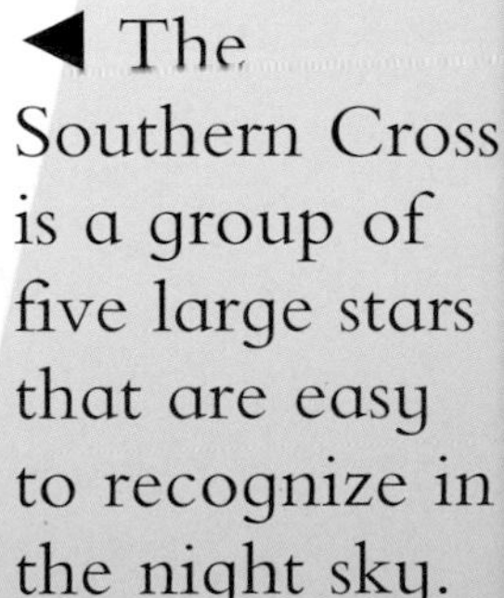

◀ The Southern Cross is a group of five large stars that are easy to recognize in the night sky.

CREATIVE CORNER

The Great Bear game

Copy the stars and lines shown here onto paper. With a counter each and a dice, race a friend from the bear's nose to its tail. Visit all four feet first. To win, throw the exact number to land on the tail without visiting any dot more than once.

INTERNET LINKS: www.kidsastronomy.com/astroskymap/constellation_hunt.htm

Space travel

The first human-made object to fly into space was a German rocket in 1942. Since then, people have sent many craft, both manned (with a human crew) and unmanned, into space on various missions. These missions have taught us much about space, and an enormous amount about our Earth and the Moon.

Luna space probes
In 1959, Russia sent three probes to investigate Earth's Moon. Luna 1 discovered solar wind, Luna 2 was the first craft to land on the Moon, and Luna 3 brought back the first images of the far side of the Moon.

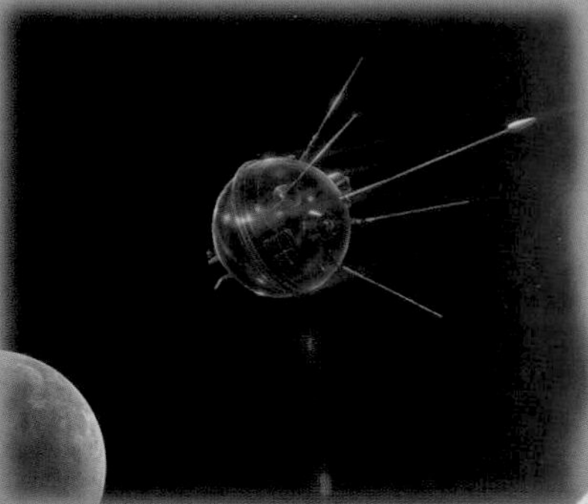

◀ For every mission into space, there is a large and experienced ground crew. They monitor equipment and communicate with the computers and people on board.

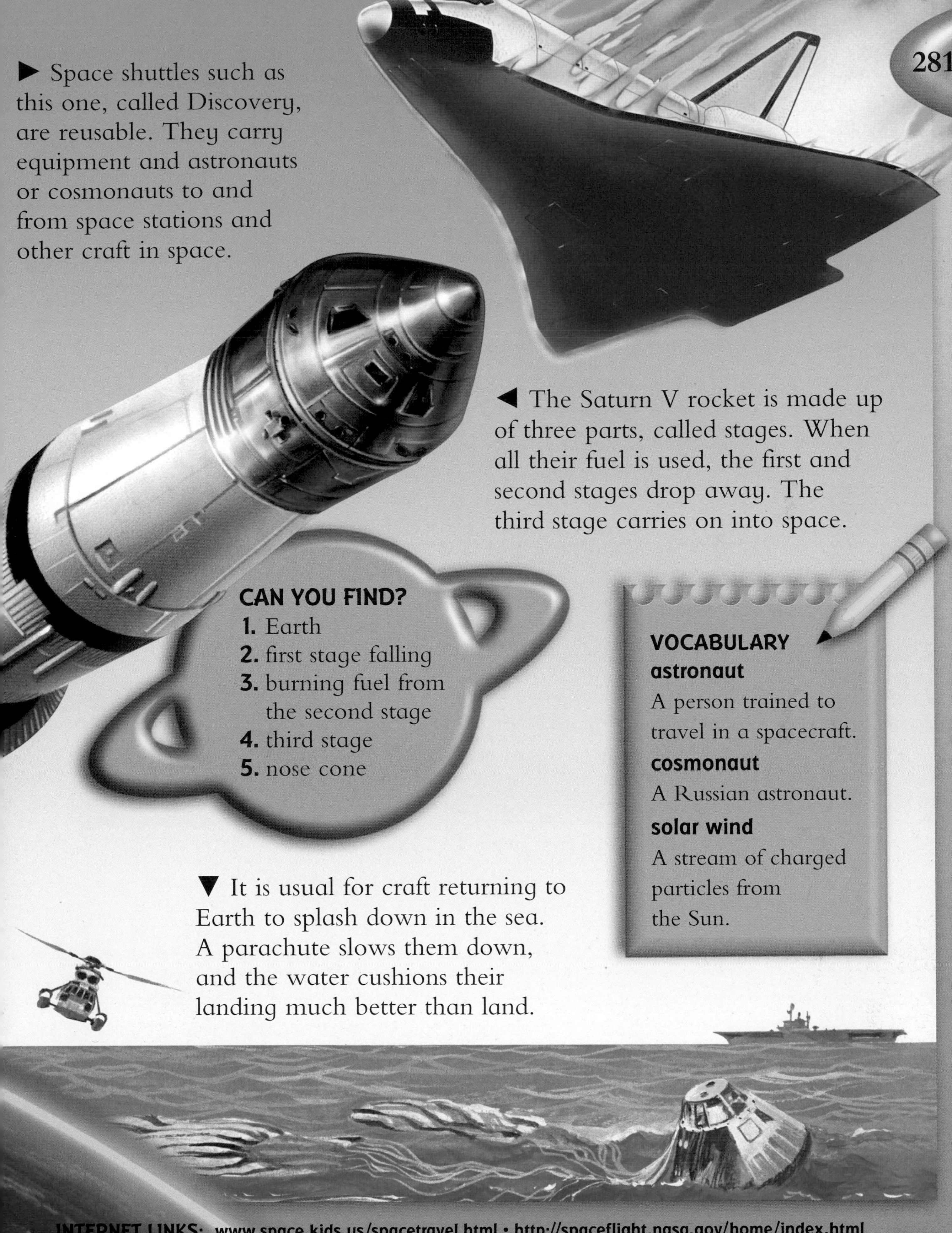

► Space shuttles such as this one, called Discovery, are reusable. They carry equipment and astronauts or cosmonauts to and from space stations and other craft in space.

◄ The Saturn V rocket is made up of three parts, called stages. When all their fuel is used, the first and second stages drop away. The third stage carries on into space.

CAN YOU FIND?

1. Earth
2. first stage falling
3. burning fuel from the second stage
4. third stage
5. nose cone

VOCABULARY

astronaut
A person trained to travel in a spacecraft.

cosmonaut
A Russian astronaut.

solar wind
A stream of charged particles from the Sun.

▼ It is usual for craft returning to Earth to splash down in the sea. A parachute slows them down, and the water cushions their landing much better than land.

INTERNET LINKS: www.space.kids.us/spacetravel.html • http://spaceflight.nasa.gov/home/index.html

Astronauts

It was not until the 1960s that the technology became available to allow people to travel into space. At that time, nobody knew what space travel does to a human body. Today, astronauts know what training they need to survive space.

Repairing the craft
Astronauts sometimes need to go outside a spacecraft to repair part of it. To do this safely, they wear special suits and breathing equipment, and remain securely attached to the craft at all times.

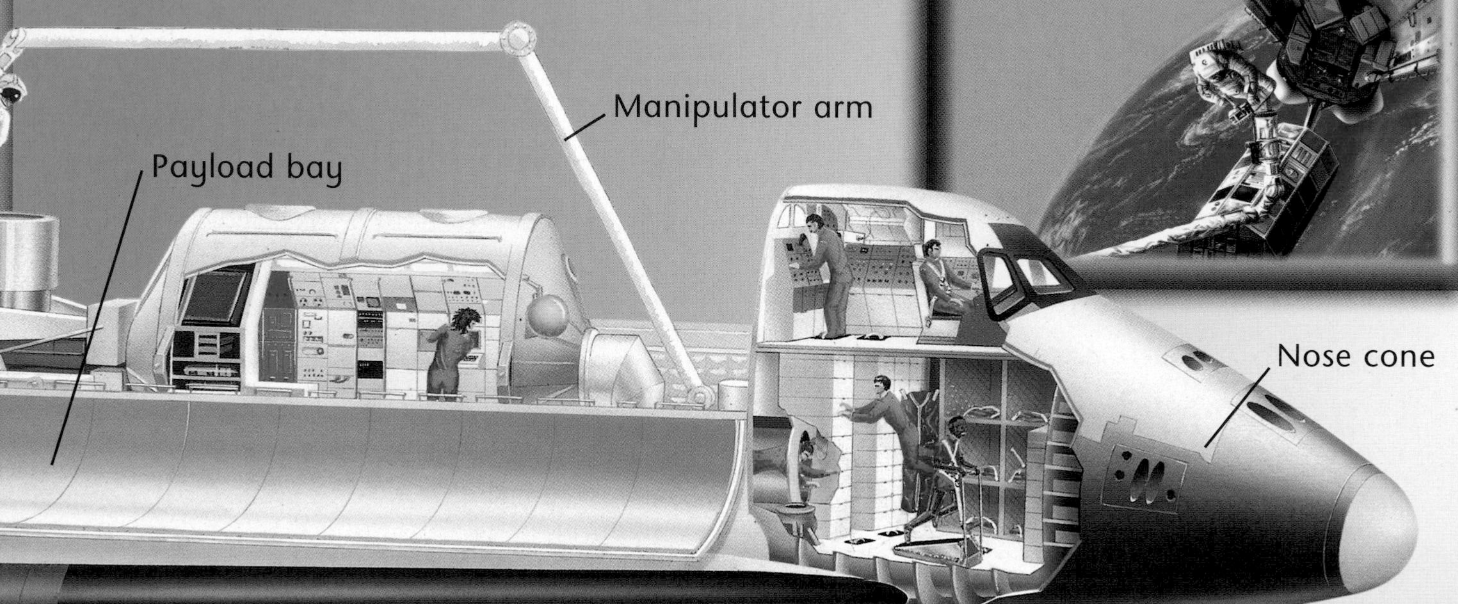

Yuri Gagarin
The first person to go into orbit around the Earth was Russian cosmonaut Yuri Gagarin on 12 April 1961. He made one orbit of the Earth in a spacecraft called Vostok 1 before returning to land. The flight lasted for one hour and 48 minutes.

▲ The flight deck and the crew's living space are in the nose cone of a space shuttle. The equipment and other cargo is carried in the payload bay. A manipulator arm loads and unloads the cargo.

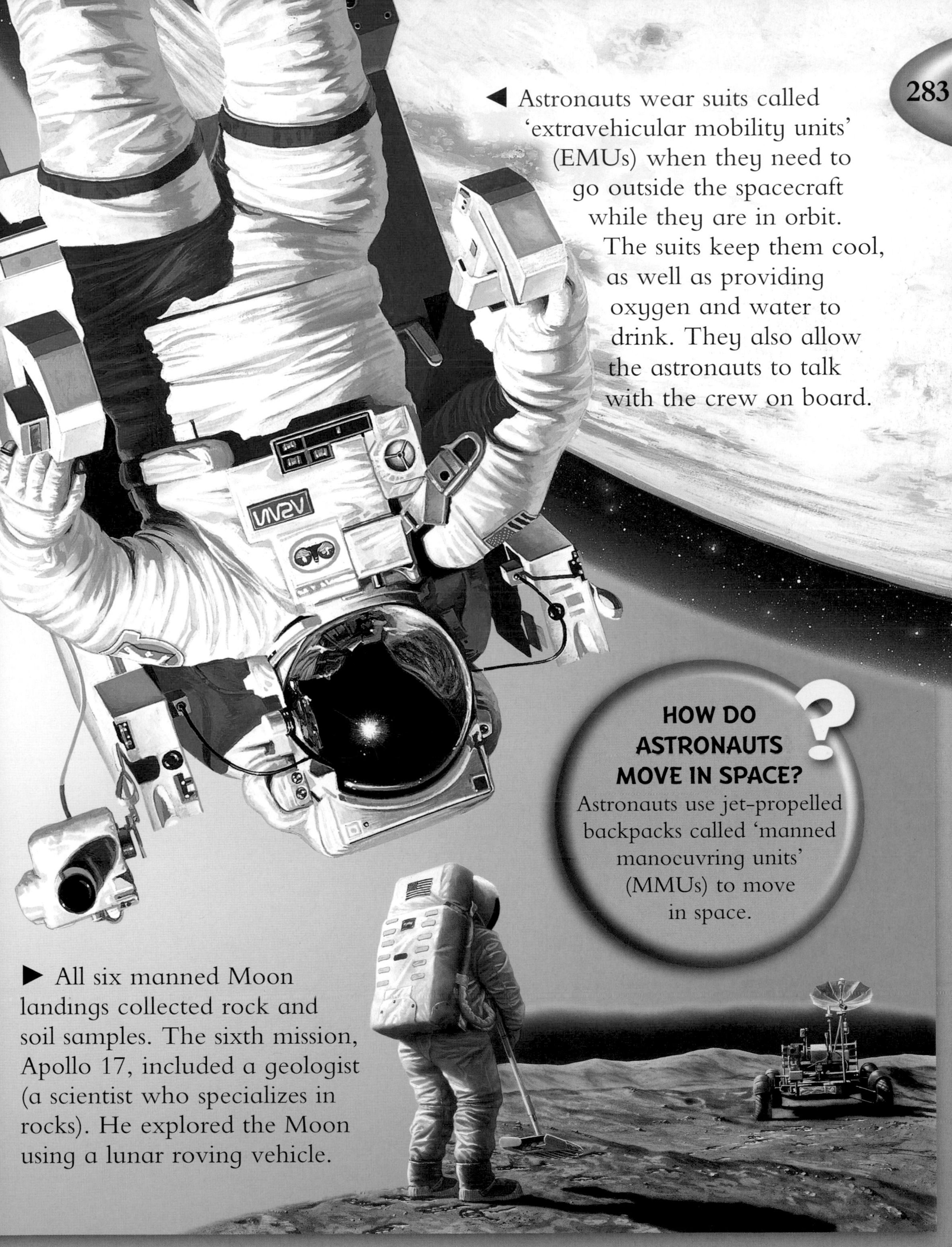

◀ Astronauts wear suits called 'extravehicular mobility units' (EMUs) when they need to go outside the spacecraft while they are in orbit. The suits keep them cool, as well as providing oxygen and water to drink. They also allow the astronauts to talk with the crew on board.

HOW DO ASTRONAUTS MOVE IN SPACE?

Astronauts use jet-propelled backpacks called 'manned manoeuvring units' (MMUs) to move in space.

▶ All six manned Moon landings collected rock and soil samples. The sixth mission, Apollo 17, included a geologist (a scientist who specializes in rocks). He explored the Moon using a lunar roving vehicle.

Space stations

Space stations are places where people can live and work in space. They are artificial satellites that orbit the Earth. Space station crews may live on a station for weeks or months at a time. Their work includes carrying out scientific experiments and studying the Universe from space.

VOCABULARY

dock
A platform at which a vehicle can unload.

satellite
An object that orbits a planet or star.

solar panels
Panels that take in energy from the Sun.

▼ Several countries are working together to build an International Space Station. Crews arrive on a space shuttle with supplies to build the space station.

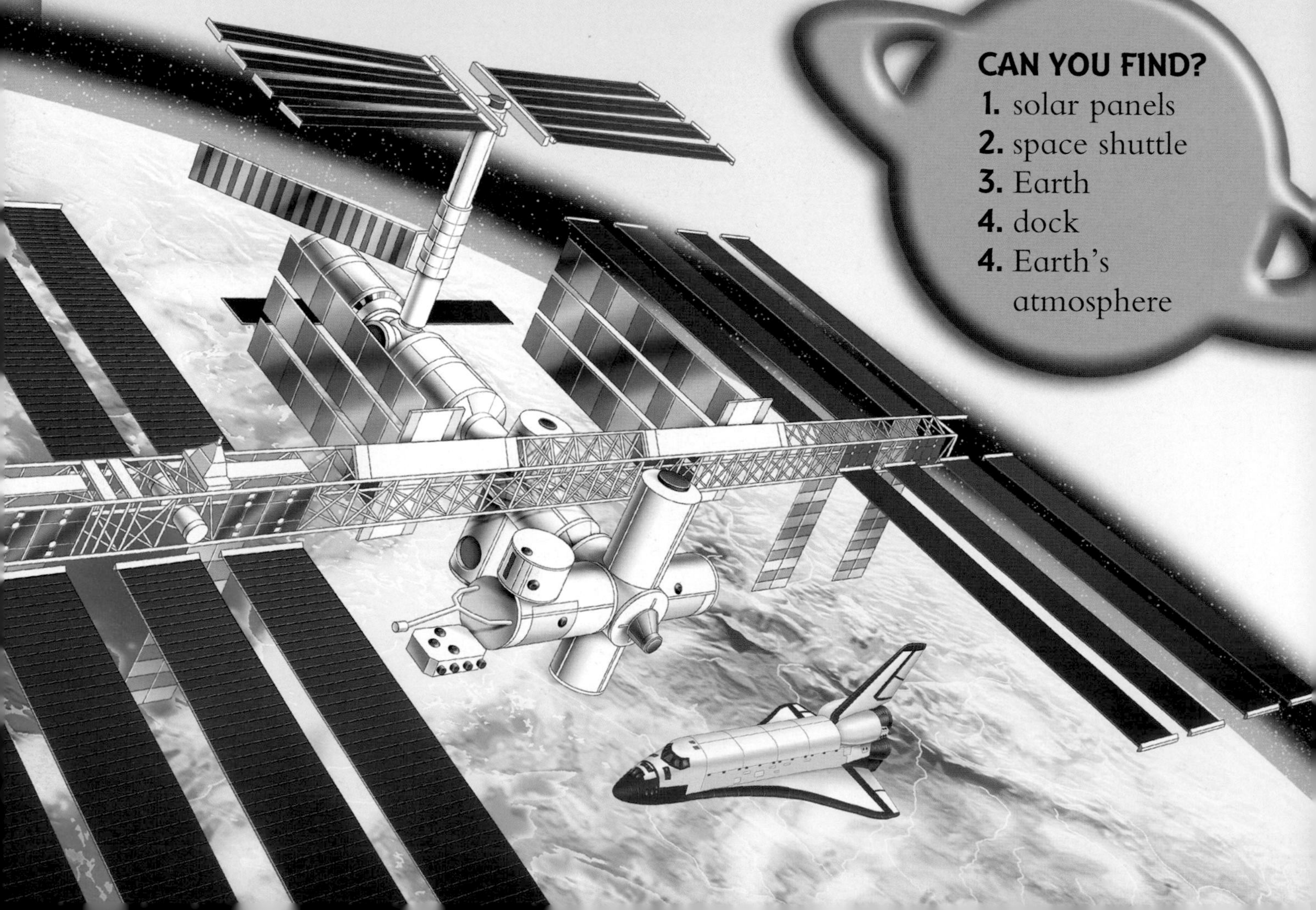

CAN YOU FIND?

1. solar panels
2. space shuttle
3. Earth
4. dock
4. Earth's atmosphere

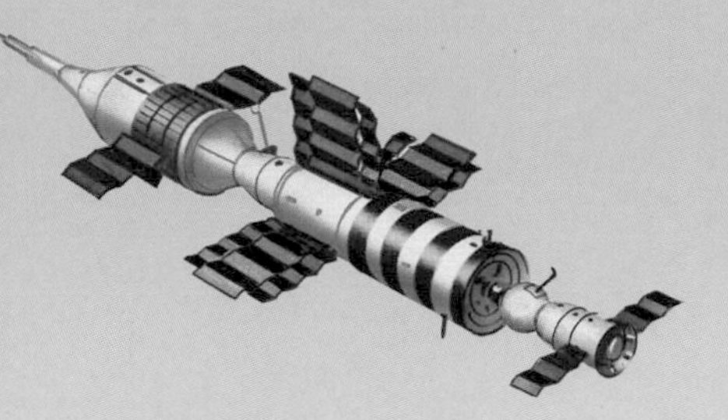
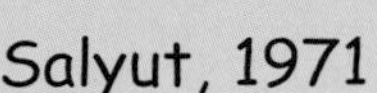

Salyut, 1971

Skylab, 1973

Mir, 1986

▲ The USSR launched the first space station, Salyut 1, in 1971. Since then, space stations have grown in size and improved in technology. The International Space Station will be over 1 kilometre wide when built.

▲ Some people thought that space stations could be built to look round like a planet. They would then spin and have their own gravity.

▲ Scientists are hoping to build a base on the Moon. From there, they could launch manned craft further into space – to Mars and perhaps more distant planets.

CREATIVE CORNER

Make a model space station

Why not design your own station, using boxes, cardboard tubes and other empty or unwanted household objects? Remember to include living quarters, docking ports and solar panels!

Satellites and probes

The first artificial satellite to be launched was Sputnik 1, in 1957. It was small and sent a signal back to Earth for only three weeks. Today, thousands of satellites orbit the Earth, including those that we use for television and telephone signals. Each has a different orbit, so that they do not crash into each other.

Visiting Venus

In 1962, Venus was the first planet to be reached by a space probe. In 1982, the Venera 13 probe sent the first colour images from the planet. The Magellan probe mapped Venus from 1990 to 1994.

Venera 13

▲ Robotic rovers are exploring Mars. They carry equipment, such as cameras and magnets, to collect magnetic dust particles. Their aim is to find evidence of water and a possibility of life on Mars.

► As well as sending pictures and information about other planets, satellites can give us information about Earth as it is seen from space.

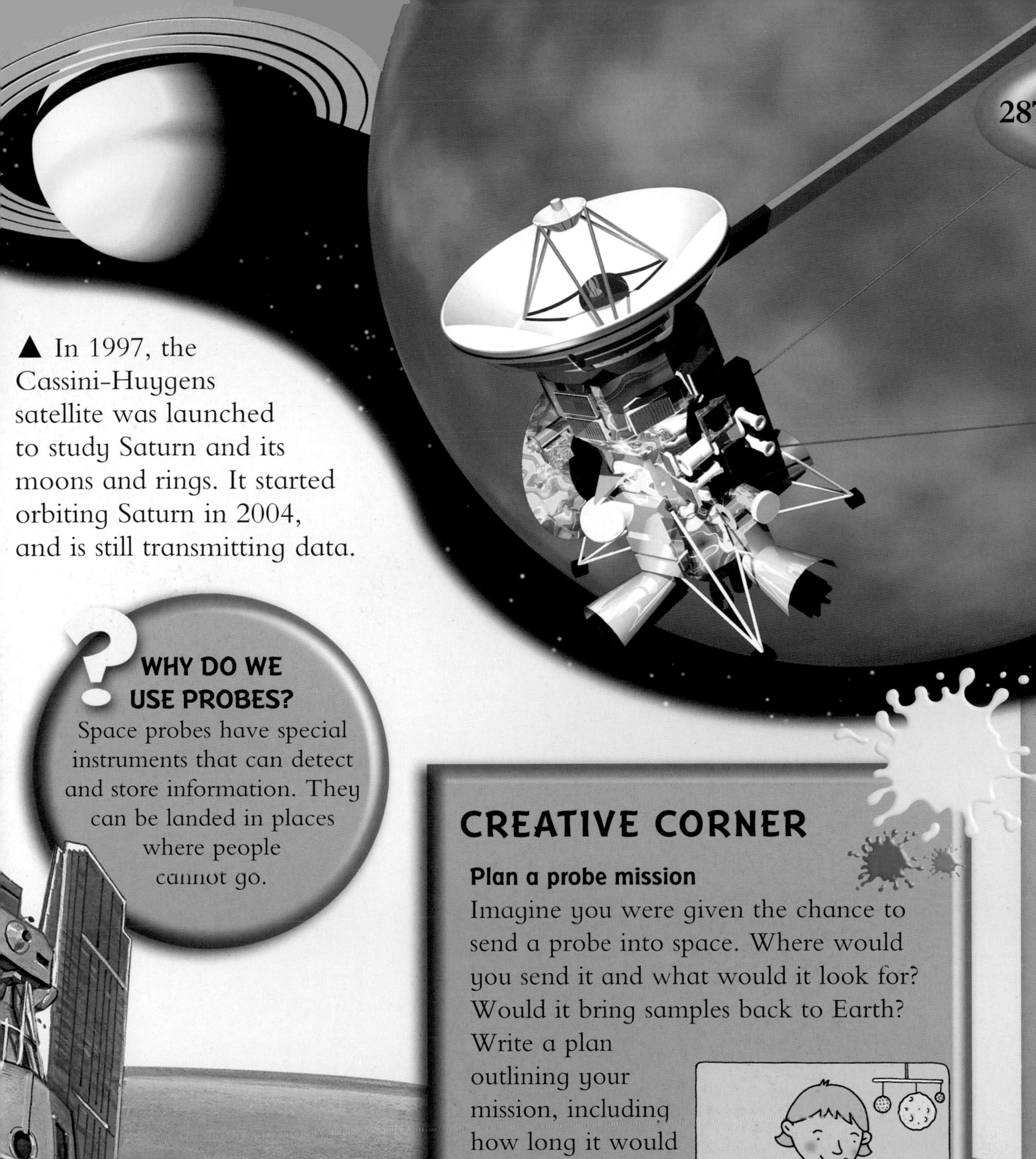

▲ In 1997, the Cassini-Huygens satellite was launched to study Saturn and its moons and rings. It started orbiting Saturn in 2004, and is still transmitting data.

WHY DO WE USE PROBES?

Space probes have special instruments that can detect and store information. They can be landed in places where people cannot go.

CREATIVE CORNER

Plan a probe mission

Imagine you were given the chance to send a probe into space. Where would you send it and what would it look for? Would it bring samples back to Earth? Write a plan outlining your mission, including how long it would take, the sort of equipment it would need, and what you want it to do.

INTERNET LINKS: http://spaceplace.nasa.gov/en/kids/goes/goes_poes_orbits.shtml

Now you know!

▲ The Big Bang, which most scientists believe formed our Universe, happened about 14 billion years ago.

▲ Everything that orbits the Sun is part of our Solar System. There may be many other solar systems in the Universe.

▲ Earth is the third planet from the Sun. It is further from it than Mercury and Venus, but closer than Mars.

▲ Not all planets are as solid as Earth. In our Solar System, the four planets furthest from the Sun are known as 'gas giants'.

▲ Comets are small chunks of rock that orbit the Sun.

▲ To people on Earth, the Moon seems to give off its own light. But really, it only reflects the light of the Sun.

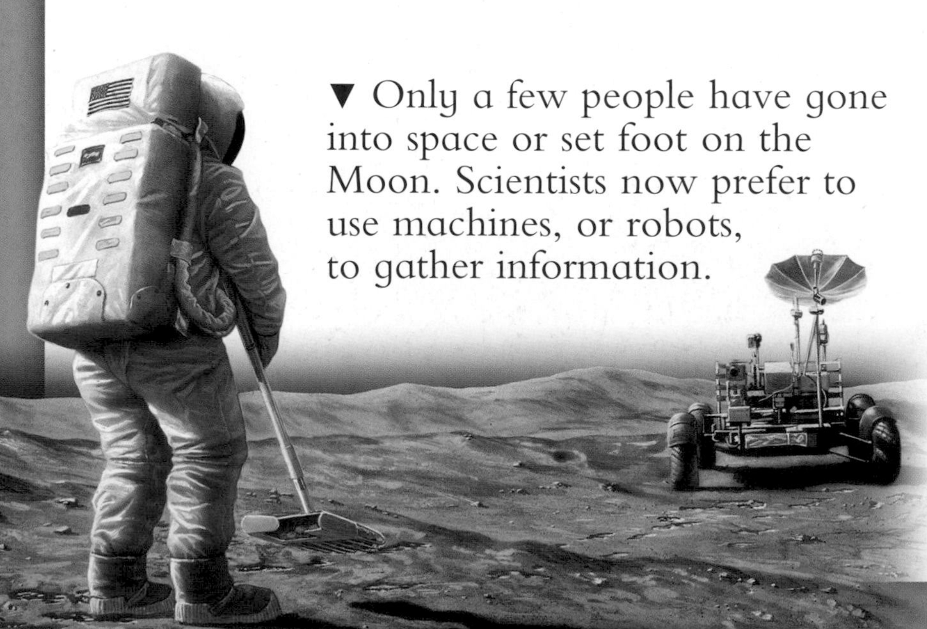

▼ Only a few people have gone into space or set foot on the Moon. Scientists now prefer to use machines, or robots, to gather information.

▲ Today, there are many artificial satellites in space. They send back information to Earth about the planets and stars around us.

Machines

Centuries ago, people were using simple machines on which many of our modern machines are based. Today, machines help us in all sorts of ways, and some of the jobs they do would be impossible for people to do alone.

What is a machine?

A machine is something that can help us to do a job. There are simple machines, such as levers, pulleys, gears and screws. They help us to lift heavy weights, alter the direction of a force, or change the force and speed of an object to make it more efficient.

Barcode reading
Barcodes are found on most things we buy today. They contain information, such as prices. The machine that reads them, a reader, decodes the information.

► Most people who have a bank account get money out of an automatic teller, or cashpoint machine. These are usually set in the wall of a building.

Mechanical robots
Robots are machines created to do the sort of work people either cannot, or do not want, to do. They are often designed to look like us, although in most cases this is not necessary for the work that they do.

► We use all sorts of machines for getting from one place to another. In general, over land, sea and air, our means of transport are getting faster.

Jet bike

Submersible

▲ Today, we can travel fast on the ocean's surface on machines, such as the jet bike. We are also able to speed through the depths of the ocean in submersibles.

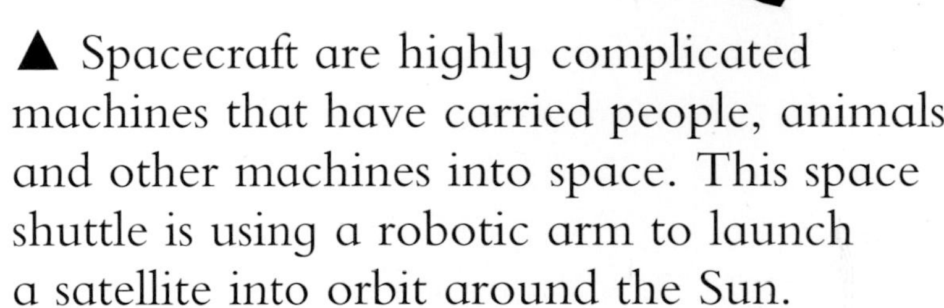

▲ Spacecraft are highly complicated machines that have carried people, animals and other machines into space. This space shuttle is using a robotic arm to launch a satellite into orbit around the Sun.

▼ The Sojourner Rover is a special robot built to collect and send back information to Earth from the surface of Mars, where it landed in 1997.

Simple machines

The wheel may be a simple machine, but it is extremely useful to people. Its most obvious use is for transporting people and objects around on land, and we use wheels all the time for this. But we also use wheels as part of other machines, such as pulleys and gears. Without wheels, life would be very different!

Wheels through time
The earliest wheels were made of solid wood, and were very heavy. Wheels with spokes, such as modern bicycle wheels, were being used in about 1500BCE and they did not change much from then until air-filled tyres were invented, in the early 19th century.

► This hammer works as a lever. We push on the handle and the curve of the hammer changes the direction of the force so that it pulls out the nail.

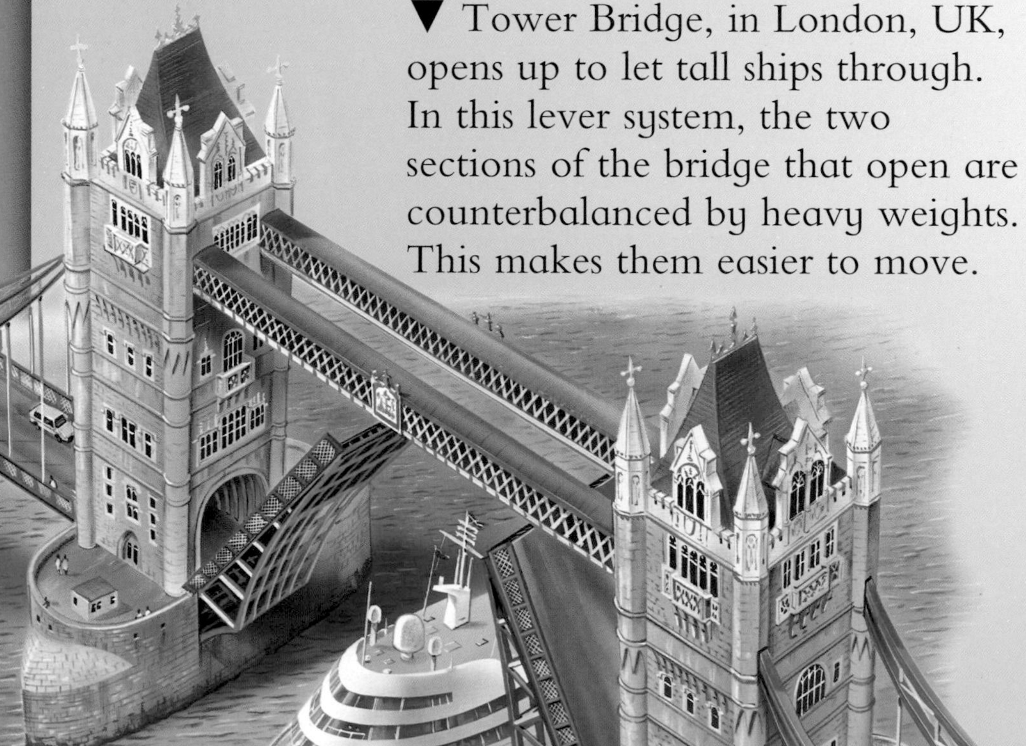

▼ Tower Bridge, in London, UK, opens up to let tall ships through. In this lever system, the two sections of the bridge that open are counterbalanced by heavy weights. This makes them easier to move.

▲ A baseball bat extends the length of our swing, so we can hit the ball further. This is also a kind of lever.

► Cranes are giant levers that can lift heavy weights. We use them to erect tall buildings. You will see cranes at work on building sites like this one lifting heavy steel frames into position.

▲ For centuries, people have used animals, such as horses, to pull carriages and carts along on wheels.

◄ Water wheels are powered by the flow of the water in a river. Windmills work in the same way, but get their energy from the wind.

VOCABULARY

gear
A disc or wheel that is cut with regular tooth shapes. These engage with teeth in another piece of machinery to make something work.

crane
A machine for lifting and moving heavy weights through the air.

► The simplest type of pulley is a single wheel with a groove in its rim. A rope can be pulled down in order to lift something up at the other end.

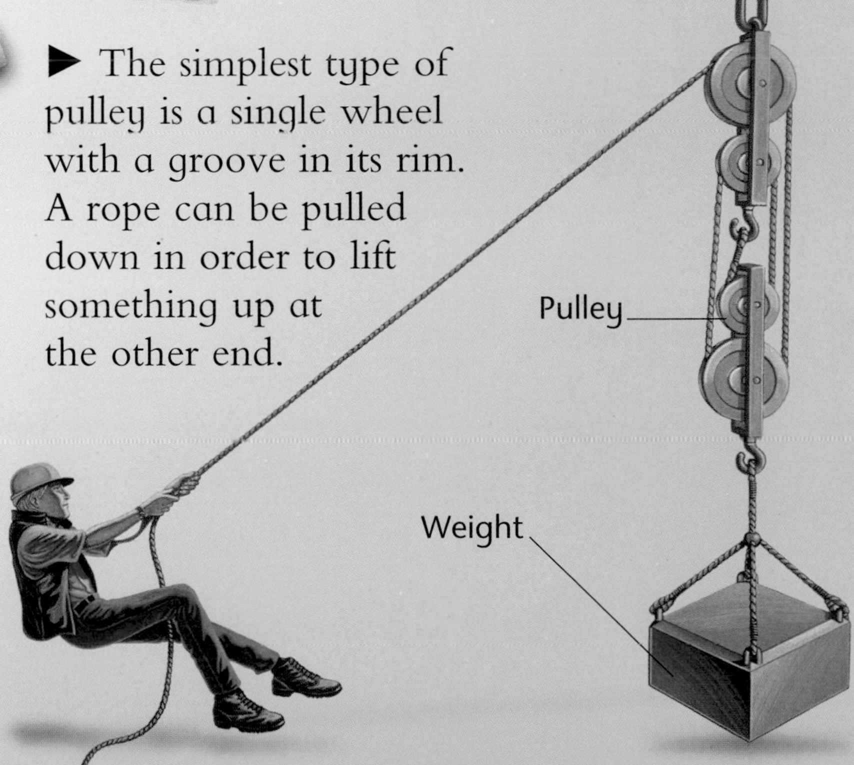

INTERNET LINKS: www.brainpop.com/technology/simplemachines/pulley/

Bikes and motorbikes

Bicycles were invented just over two centuries ago. They are a cheap and convenient way of getting around faster than people can walk, and they cause very little harm to the environment. Motorbikes are faster than bicycles but, because they use a motor, they are not as kind to the environment.

On one wheel
Unicycles are like bicycles, but with one wheel instead of two. They are more difficult to ride, and are popular in circuses. Clowns often teeter around the ring on them to make people laugh.

▼ When motorcyclists take a corner, they need to lean into the bend – or the bike would slip out from under them! These racers have protective pads for their elbows and knees.

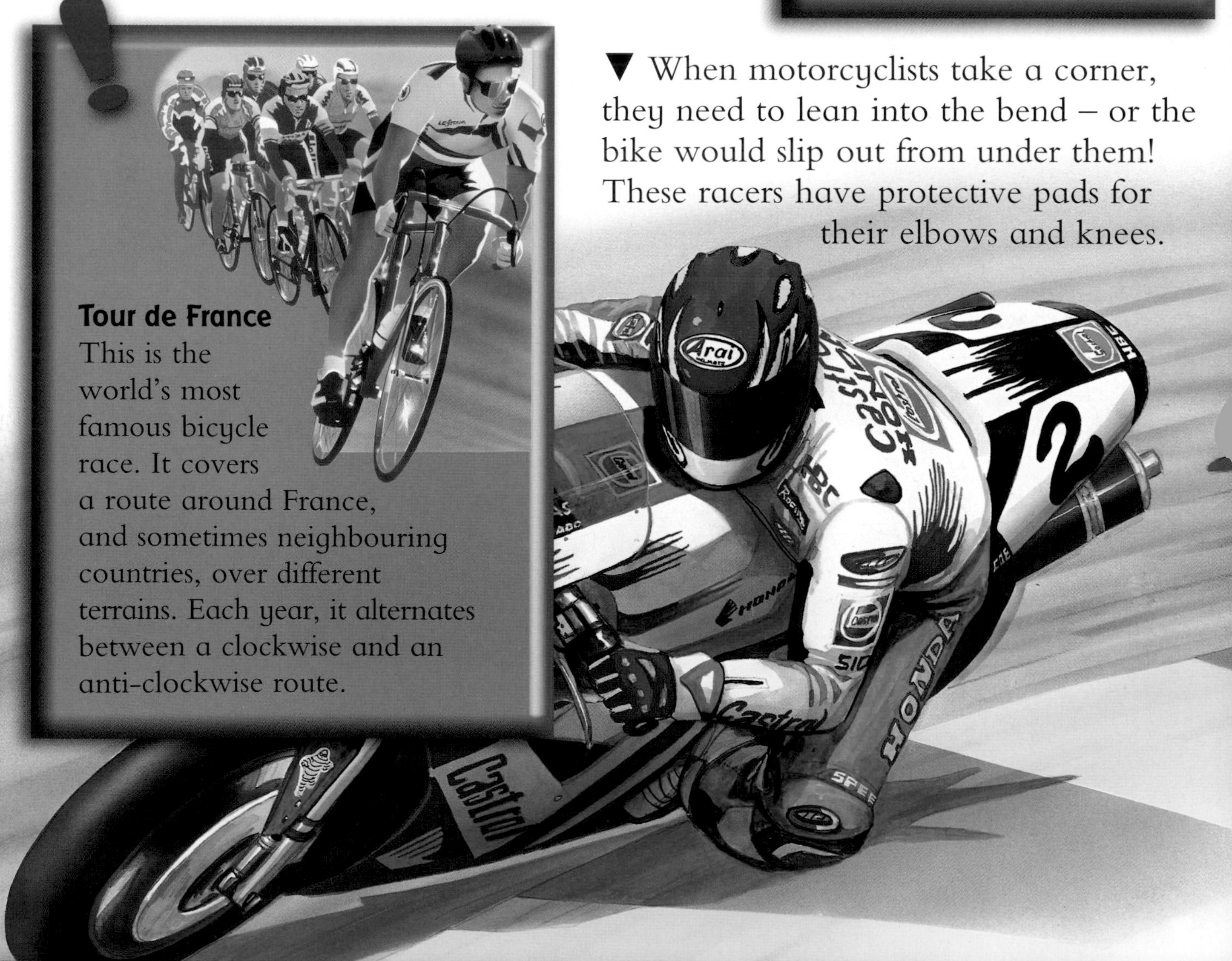

Tour de France
This is the world's most famous bicycle race. It covers a route around France, and sometimes neighbouring countries, over different terrains. Each year, it alternates between a clockwise and an anti-clockwise route.

▲ Mountain bikes have lots of gears to help climb hills, and tyres that grip well. But if the going gets tough, sometimes walking is the only way to go forwards!

► Speed cycling is an Olympic sport. The riders compete in a stadium shaped like a bowl, with steep sides that help them to go faster.

HOW FAST CAN THEY GO?
The fastest motorcycles can reach speeds of over 560 kilometres per hour – and they keep making them faster!

► There are stunt motorcyclists who can perform amazing tricks. They often jump over rows of buses or trucks.

► Designs where the rider lies back in his seat (like this tricycle) can go faster than many upright bicycles or tricycles. Their streamlined shape helps them travel more easily through the air.

INTERNET LINKS: www.pedalinghistory.com/PHhistory.html • www.factmonster.com/ipka/A0933211.html

Cars, buses and trucks

Most cars are designed to carry a small number of people on trips to school or work, on holidays and for shopping. Buses carry many more people. They are more economical than cars, and most are better for the environment. Trucks are mostly used to carry heavy materials, rather than people.

Taller than a man
Some of the biggest tyres in the world are made for dumper trucks. They carry heavy loads around building sites, and the tyres help cushion the weight.

► Our towns and cities are packed with cars and other vehicles. Many countries have had to build more and wider roads to prevent traffic building up.

▲ Cars travel from factories where they are made to the showroom to be sold. They are carried on car transporters.

Beetle story
The Volkswagen Beetle is probably the most easily recognized car in the world. It was designed and built in the 20th century as a car for ordinary people. Its name comes from people thinking that it looked like a beetle.

▲ Trucks of all kinds move products all distances. Some, like this one, can tip their containers up to deliver goods.

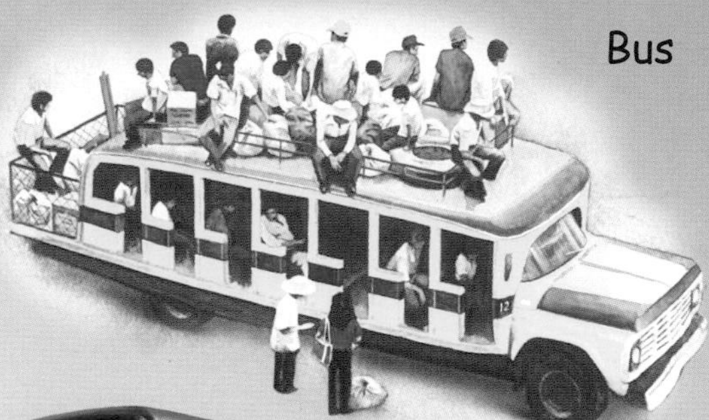

Bus

Tram

▲ Trams, like buses, are a kind of public transport. They run on rails in the ground, but they get electric power from cables above them.

Coach

▲ People travel on all kinds of vehicles. The bus (top) is in Ecuador. The US coach (above) is more comfortable.

CAN YOU FIND?

1. ambulance
2. firefighters
3. stretcher
4. lifting platform
5. hosepipe

▼ Fire engines are fitted with all kinds of emergency equipment. The long, crane-like arm can move the firefighters close to the centre of the fire to put it out quickly.

INTERNET LINKS: www.dos.state.ny.us/kidsroom/firesafe/trucks.html • www.factmonster.com/ce6/sci/A0809578.html

Building machines

All sorts of machines are used on building sites, including diggers, dumpers, bulldozers, rollers and pavers. Each of them has a special job to do. All of these machines are designed to work hard and keep the people who operate them safe.

Preparing the site
Bulldozers clear the ground so that it is flat enough to build on. A sharp blade at the front of the bucket cuts through whatever is in the way. The bulldozer is rather like a giant lawnmower!

▼ Today we dig, or bore, tunnels with huge digging machines. A large, round cutting head at the front cuts into the rock or soil, and behind it the tunnel is lined with material, such as concrete.

▲ On a busy building site, there are many different jobs. Surveyors measure the site and engineers check it is safe. Demolition cranes knock down old buildings.

◀ Hammer drills like this break up the ground quickly, but they are very noisy. Workers on the site need to wear ear protectors to save their hearing.

◀ Bridges help us cross obstacles, such as rivers. They are usually built of heavy materials, such as concrete and steel, lifted into place by cranes and other machines.

▶ In road-building, dumper trucks move materials from one place to another. Graders make the ground smooth.

Grader

Roller

Paver

◀ Paver machines lay the surface of the road, while heavy rollers follow on behind them, flattening and levelling the surface.

▲ Giant bulldozers can cut through and clear large amounts of rubble and waste very quickly.

CREATIVE CORNER

Building words game

Play against a friend. Think of a word or phrase about building vehicles, such as 'caterpillar tracks'. Write down any other words you can make out of the letters in five minutes. Score one point for each correctly spelled word.

INTERNET LINKS: www.kenkenkikki.jp/e_index2.html • www.factmonster.com/ce6/sci/A0849518.html

Trains

Trains run on rails, carrying people and goods on short or long overland journeys. They are a cheaper form of transport than cars, and kinder to the environment. Many people use trains to commute, or travel, into work in cities and towns and most large cities have at least one major railway station.

▲ Most trains run on tracks with two rails, for stability. But monorails (above) have only one rail.

◀ Australia's Katoomba Scenic Railway was built in the 19th century for use in mining. Since the 1930s it has been used for tourists.

▶ Trains, like cars, need signals so that the driver knows when it is safe to move on. A red light means 'stop', and a green light means 'go'.

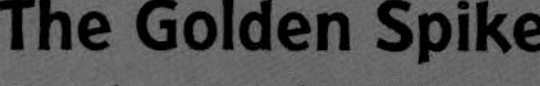

The Golden Spike

In the 19th century, two railroads were joined to make the first railroad to cross the USA from one coast to another. The last spike to be driven in was a golden one to mark the ceremony.

▶ Goods trains often use the same tracks as passenger trains, but may travel at night, when the tracks would otherwise be quiet, or even empty. These trains are an efficient way of transporting goods.

▼ In a large, modern city, railway stations often link overground and underground railway lines. They also link to flight terminals, and give access to public and private road transport. They may be built on several different levels, connected by stairs, escalators and lifts.

CAN YOU FIND?

1. undergound train
2. escalator
3. tram
4. monorail
5. overground train
6. ticket office

▲ Some steam engines, such as this one in the Rocky mountains, Colorado, USA, are still used today and are popular with tourists.

9027

9026

INTERNET LINKS: www.trakkies.co.uk • www.collectionscanada.ca/trains/kids/index-e.html

Ships and boats

Our ancestors would have used small boats for fishing and sailing on rivers and streams. As they found ways of making bigger and better boats, they used them for travelling further, and finding new places to live. Today's ships are packed with technology and safety devices.

Paddle steamers

This type of boat was one of the earliest mechanically powered boats and they are still popular today. A steam engine drives the large wheel, or paddle, on the stern. This pushes the boat forwards.

◀ Inflatable boats, like this rubber raft, are light and easy to transport. They are often used on rivers and lakes.

▶ Ocean liners are popular for travelling long distances, and the cruise industry is growing. These large ships carry thousands of passengers and crew. There is on-board entertainment for the passengers.

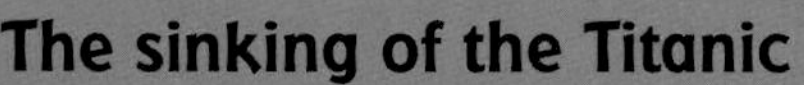

The sinking of the Titanic

The Titanic was a huge passenger and mail ship. It was said to be practically unsinkable. But on its maiden (first) voyage, from Southampton, England, to New York in 1912, it hit an iceberg and split in two.

▲ Hovercraft travel on a cushion of air, which is produced by a large fan. This makes the hovercraft float above both land and water.

VOCABULARY

hull
The hollow, main body of a boat or ship. It floats partly underwater.

stern
The rear section of a ship or boat.

▲ Powerboats are small, fast boats, with powerful engines. People use them for racing or just for the thrill of travelling fast over the water.

▼ No matter how safe boats become, the sea is always unpredictable, and therefore dangerous. Lifeboats are at the ready at all times to rescue people who are in trouble.

► Catamarans are boats that have two hulls. They can be powered either by sails or engines. Catamarans are generally faster and more stable than single-hulled boats.

Aircraft

Aeroplanes travel faster than ships, cars or trains. This is partly because they can simply fly over obstacles, rather than having to go around them. Also, air slows objects down less than water or land. Nevertheless, to get off the ground at all, aircraft need powerful engines and specially designed wings to provide lift.

First flight
The first time an aeroplane flew with a pilot on board was in 1903. Orville Wright flew the 'Flyer', an aeroplane he and his brother Wilbur had designed. It flew for 37 metres and was in the air for only 12 seconds before it landed again.

▼ Modern airports have planes taking off and landing all the time. Some large airports have more than 1,000 planes landing every day! Buses and trucks carry people, luggage and other goods around the site.

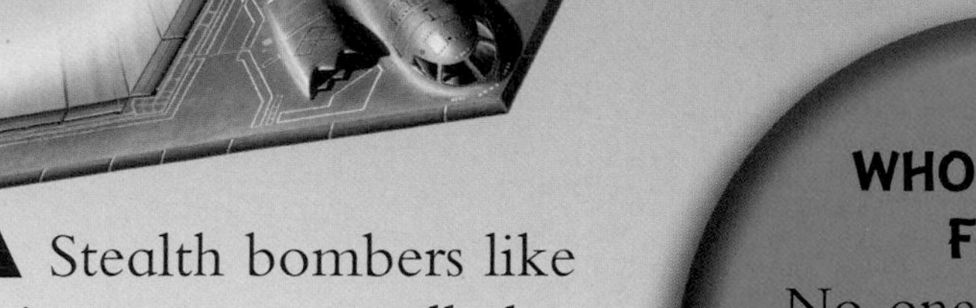

▲ Stealth bombers like this one are so-called because they absorb and reflect radar. This makes them difficult to detect.

WHO INVENTED FLYING?
No-one really knows. However, there are many ancient stories about people using kites or wings.

▲ Airships contain a gas, such as helium, that is lighter than air. But they also have engines to power them.

▲ Jump jets are designed to be able to take off and land on very short runways. They are able to take off from the deck of a ship.

▲ Gliders have no engines. The pilots have to find pockets of warm, rising air, called thermals, to stay up in the air.

▲ Helicopters take off vertically. They are used where other aircraft cannot land or take off.

▲ Small planes are often used when a few people need to travel quickly over long distances. They are often used to reach remote places.

CREATIVE CORNER

Make a glider

1. Take a piece of A4 paper. Fold one end back so that it is roughly square. **2.** Now fold in the corners as shown. **3.** Crease along the centre line and then fold the wings out again. **4.** Now you are ready to launch your glider!

1.
2.
3.
4.

Machines at work

Machines are useful in all kinds of work situations, from factories to farms, and offices to building sites. We use machines for nearly every task that we carry out. They do both light and heavy work, and we are inventing new machines to help us do our jobs all the time.

VOCABULARY

microphone
An electronic instrument that is used to pick up sound waves to be broadcast.

factory
A building, or group of buildings, in which objects are produced in large numbers.

▲ Using a milking machine to milk cows is quick and easy. It saves time compared with doing it by hand, as people used to do.

Robot paint sprayer
In car factories, the body of the car is spray-painted by machine. Today, the machine is often a robot and works automatically. The machine is carefully controlled to spray an even layer of paint on each part of the car.

▲ Snow blowers remove snow from roads or other places where it is not wanted. These road machines are powered by electricity or an engine. They blow the snow out of the way, or into a truck that carries it away.

▶ Most offices use computers, photocopiers, telephones and printers. Computers help us to communicate, calculate numbers, plan our work and design all sorts of things, from the pages of a book to a towering office block.

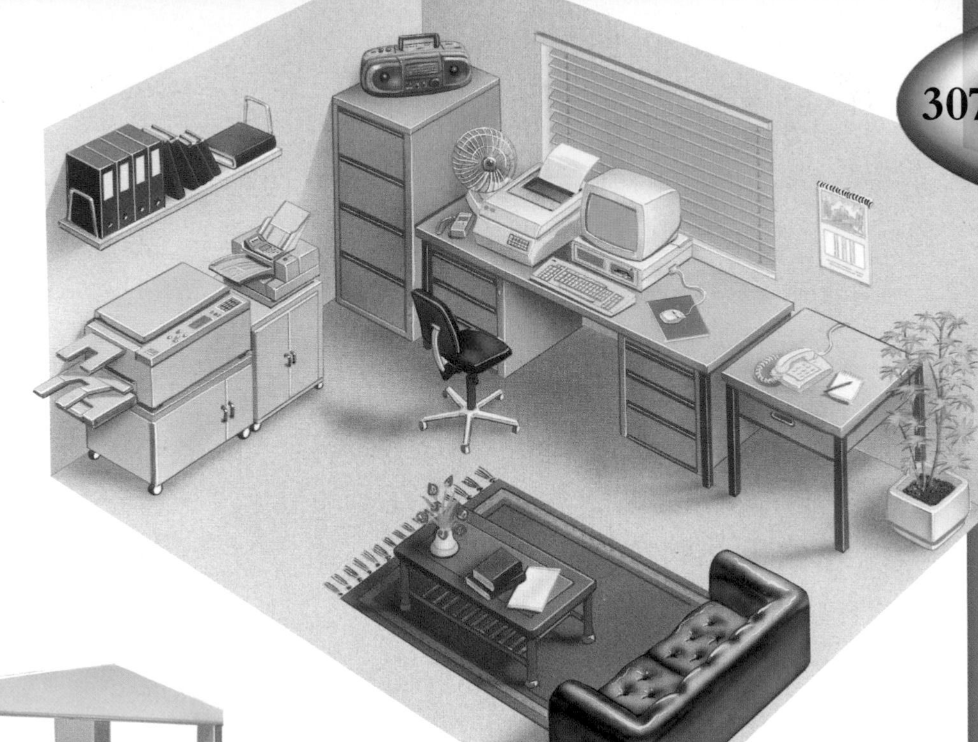

◀ Paper is made on huge pieces of machinery. Many are the length of two football pitches. They can produce giant rolls of paper, like those shown here, at up to 2,000 metres a minute.

▲ TV studios use many kinds of machinery. They have cameras, microphones, lighting, and sometimes autocues from which the presenter reads the script.

CREATIVE CORNER

Make a cotton reel motor

Thread an elastic band through a cotton reel. Loop one end around an eraser and the other around a pencil. Wind up the elastic band by turning the pencil. Add a blob of modelling clay or tape a coin to the pencil, place the reel on the floor and watch it go!

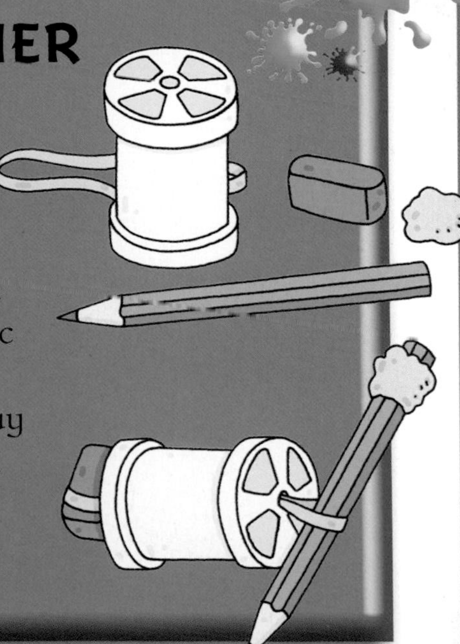

Machines in the home

Even in our homes, we use many machines to help us with all kinds of tasks. A modern home often includes machines that cook, wash and clean for us. Other machines heat or cool the air so that we are comfortable. Still more keep us entertained.

Robot helper
Designers are working hard to produce small, efficient robots that can perform tasks around the home. They could clean and operate the other machines.

CAN YOU FIND?

1. washing machine
2. toaster
3. food mixer
4. microwave oven
5. refrigerator

▼ Today's kitchens are full of machinery. Most of them run on electricity or gas. Microwave ovens are a good, energy-saving alternative for cooking.

▼ A modern bedroom uses a lot of electricity. Televisions and computers, lighting, and radios or CD players all run on it. They do this from the mains (through a power point in the wall) or batteries.

▲ Sewing machines allow us to make and mend clothes much more quickly than we can by hand.

► Vacuum cleaners make it much easier to keep our floors clean. But nobody has yet invented a machine that can tidy up for us!

▲ Many of us own special machines that are designed for personal use. These include music players, cameras and game machines.

CREATIVE CORNER

Make a poster

Collect pictures of machines you find in the home and sort into groups to put on a poster – for example, some that help you prepare food. Stick on a piece of paper and label each group.

Hospitals and health

Modern hospitals use a vast range of machines. Some help medical staff find out what is wrong with a patient by testing them for different diseases and symptoms. Others are used to treat illnesses. The staff have to be trained to use the machines correctly, and understand all the information that they provide.

▲ Sometimes surgeons need to operate to make someone well. This is done in an operating theatre while the patient is asleep.

WHAT IS BLOOD PRESSURE?
It is the amount of pressure of the blood on the walls of the arteries. Either too much or too little is bad for your health.

▲ Blood pressure can be measured accurately on a machine. It tells us if our blood pressure is too high or low.

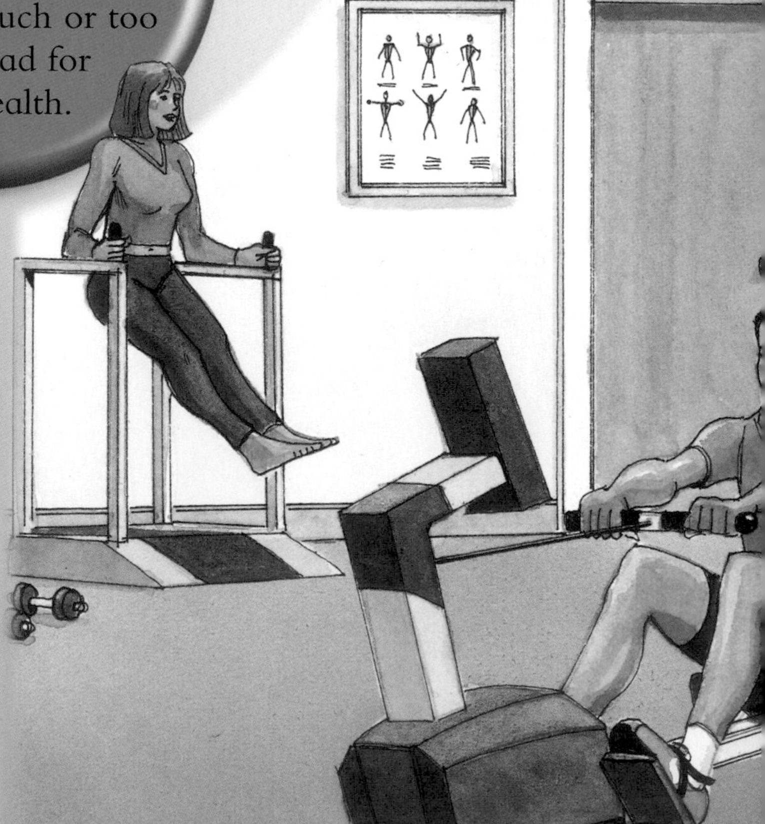

► Hospitals often have an area with special fitness machines, which patients can use to get fit after illness. Different machines are designed to allow them to exercise different parts of their bodies.

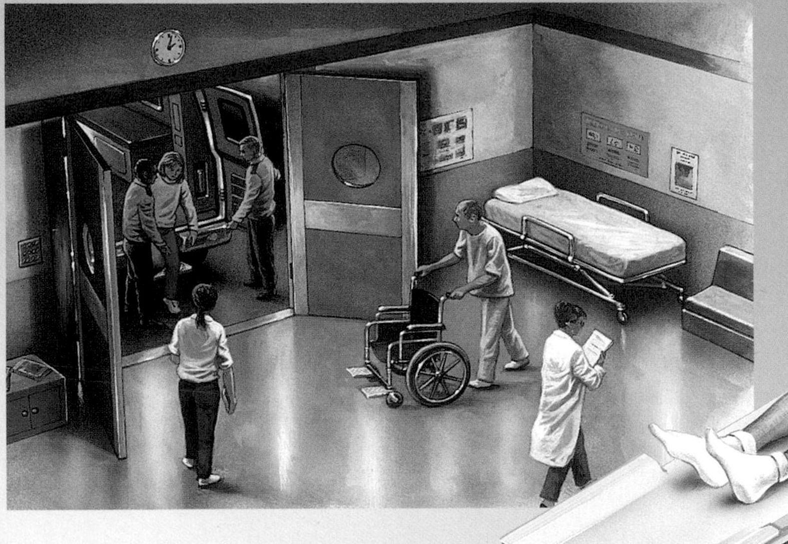

▲ People who have an injury or suddenly become ill may be taken to an accident and emergency department. They may travel in an ambulance full of special machinery to keep them as well as possible until they arrive.

▲Special scanners use X-rays to look at what is going on inside a patient's body. Doctors use the resulting scans to decide on the best treatment.

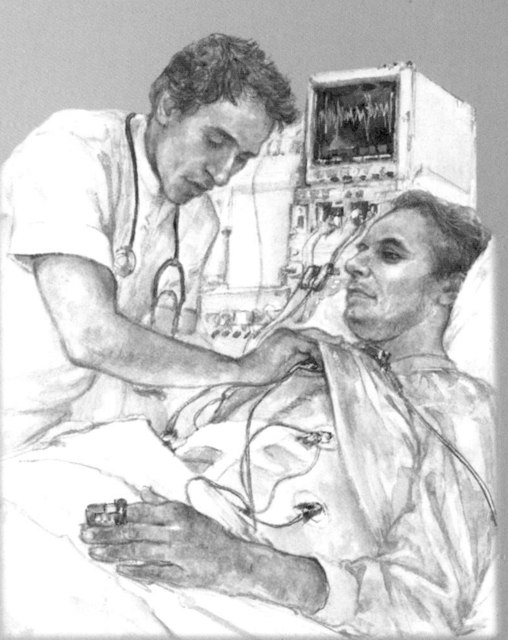

▲ This patient's heart is being monitored. The steady heartbeats are displayed on the monitor next to his bed.

INTERNET LINKS: **www.knowitall.org/kidswork/hospital/history/modern/index.html**

Now you know!

▲ Robots are often designed to look like us, although in most cases this is not necessary for work.

▲ Trams run on rails in the ground, but they get their electric power from cables above them.

► Catamarans are boats with two hulls.

► Stunt motorcyclists perform amazing tricks, such as jumping over buses and trucks.

▲ Paper-making machines produce giant rolls of paper at up to 2,000 metres per minute.

▲ Australia's Katoomba Scenic Railway was originally built in the 19th century for use in mining.

▲ Trains and tracks that run on one rail are called monorails.

▲ Hospitals often have a fitness area for patients to use to get fit after an illness.

Index

A

B

C

D

E

F

G

H

N

O

P

Q

R

S

T

U

V

W

X

Y

Acknowledgements

The publisher would like to thank the following illustrators:

Jonathan Adams, Julian Baum, Mark Bergin, Robin Boutell, Peter Bull, Robin Carter, Kuo Kang Chen, Peter Dennis (Linda Rogers), Richard Draper, Angelina Elsebach, Dianne Fawcett, James Field (Simon Girling & Associates), Chris Forsey, Terry Gabbey (AFA Ltd), Ruby Green, Terry Hadler, Tim Hayward (Bernard Thornton Artists), Christian Hook, Richard Hook, Biz Hull, Ian Jackson (Wildlife Art), Michael Johnson, Deborah Kindred (Simon Girling), Stuart Lafford, Terence Lambert, Stephen Lings, Patricia Ludlow, Chris Lyon, Kevin Maddison, Maltings Partners, David McAllister, Steve Noon (Garden Studio), Nicki Palin, Eric Roe, Mike Rowe, Sebastien Quigley (Linden Artists), Bernard Robinson, Elizabeth Sawyer (SGA), Rob Shone, Guy Smith (Mainline Design), Roger Stewart, Gareth Williams, David Wright (Kathy Jakeman).

Creative Corner illustrations throughout: Jo Moore